Christianity
and
Nature-based Spirituality

*An Integral Approach to Christianity
and The Medicine Wheel*

Lillie Foley Rowden, D. Min.

Published by:
    2nd Tier Publishing
    501 Wimberley Oaks Dr
    Wimberley, TX 78676

ISBN 978-0-9894642-3-9

Cover and book design by Dan Gauthier

TO

Dr. William S. Taegel
Whose patience and caring
brought the gift of grace into my life.

Dr. Judith L. Yost
Whose loving laughter
and wisdom warms my heart.

and

Paula Kathleen Manuel, Charles David Rowden
and Mandy Rowden, Justin Trahan Manuel,
Charles David Rowden, Jr., Alexandria "Alex" Owens
and Jacob Daniel Oakley Brock
Beloved children and grandchildren,
may your future be blessed.

Table of Contents

CHAPTER ONE

An Introduction to One Soul's Quest

W hat so amazes me about my journey is that when I was forty-five years old, I became so distressed I felt somewhat suicidal. I simply wanted to "pack it in." Now that I have passed my seventy-fifth birthday, life has become so meaningful and filled with joy, creativity and an inner sense of awe and inquiry. This book is about my own personal journey toward spiritual wholeness, and the tools I found useful for myself and my work with others to find spiritual balance—a balance I hope for myself, others and the planet.

Over a period of approximately thirty years, I have been a member of a spiritual community called the Earthtribe. It was founded by Dr. William S. Taegel and Dr. Judith L. Yost as an expansion for spiritual growth of their psychotherapy practice in Houston, Texas. The Earthtribe meets on a monthly basis for the purpose of healing and prayer. It is comprised of Christians, Jews, Muslims, Sufis, Buddhists and some who are non-attached to a specific major religious group.

At the time I met this group of people, I was struggling through a depression surrounding the divorce from my husband of thirty-one years. I was nearly fifty years old and lost. I had completed a Master's in Psychology and was in the process of completing my practicum hours prior to the state board examinations and licensure as a psychotherapist.

Bear Heart in his book, *The Wind Is My Mother,* eloquently addresses where I was at this period of my life. We wonder about our purpose, our role in life, "because of it we can get glimpses of what it means to walk what we call the Spirit Road...universal love is gathered together. Universal love is gathered together on that one road."[1] It is not determined growth from a particular denominational, world religious perspective. "The caring and love that we generate from our hearts into the lives of others can carry us forward."[2] I was yet to evolve into the strength of this spiritual place. However, in the chapters to come, I will share many experiences I encountered within this group and along this path.

The beginning

One afternoon, waiting on a client's arrival, I noted a beautiful, iridescent, turquoise and blue beetle flying about the room. It landed on a small table beside a chair. Approaching closely to look at it, possibly catch it and place it back outside into its natural environment, I noticed some flyers. The small slips of paper were announcing that a shaman named Bear Heart would be coming to Houston and meeting with those that might be interested in his spiritual pathway. After mentioning the flyer to my supervising therapist, it was decided that I would attend. We met outside under the trees, and I listened carefully. In my bloodline there is Native American heritage on my father's side of the family, and I was very curious about the "good red road," the Native American spiritual pathway.

A few weeks later, I drove from Northeast Texas where I was working at Hope Center as a counselor/teacher and saw a double rainbow in the sky in front of my windshield. I decided it was a good omen for my first attendance at a sweatlodge (*inipi*) the following day. There was little awareness that my spiritual world was about to explode into a much larger framework. Or, as Bear Heart so succinctly stated, "In our struggles we may think we can't go any further, not realizing that it is merely a turning point in our life."[3]

This was more than a turning point for me. As I struggled with my depression, it literally was my salvation. I had no internal skills for coping with my emotional pain. Bear Heart speaks to my struggle, "Coping with suffering gives meaning to life—it is what gives us our strength."[4] I had yet to integrate this great teaching at an experiential level.

Driving to a location south of Houston, I nervously approached this new group. The prayer in the lodge was intense. I remember that I remained silent and just listened. The warmth of the lodge and the darkness of its "womb" were very comforting to me. I did not understand the order of the prayers or the use of the Pipe, but the symbolism resonated somewhere deep in my DNA.

There are four "rounds" of prayer in the sweatlodge, usually the first four cardinal directions. However, occasionally, we pray the last four directions. Within the sweatlodge herbs are used: sage for purification and sweet grass to bring in good spirits. Other herbs are used in the Earthtribe lodges, as well. The herbs honor the living plants of the earth. Water is poured on the heated rocks. As it turns into steam, it releases negative ions that are physically healing.

My traditional religious membership was and is in the Episcopal Church. For several years, I taught the intuitions and projections onto the Ultimate Reality, God, Sacred Mystery, Creator, the One—the One of many names, the Nameless of our spiritual lives—for the Episcopal Diocese of Texas in its spiritual direction school and led a spiritual direction group for clergy. The directions of the Medicine Wheel are aspects or projections onto Ultimate Reality. The Native American believes in Sacred Mystery, the One and Many. These directions or nature-based connections are sometimes misinterpreted as separate "gods," but that is not the case. Like many religions, the One is called by many names. My personal experiences with the Medicine Wheel, teaching in the diocesan school for spiritual directors, work with the clergy and other ministries led to my inner question of "How does my Christian based religion correlate with the *Medicine Wheel?*"

During the subsequent years, I have continued the practice of the Native American Medicine Wheel, as we practice it in the Earthtribe. This process in my life has expanded my awareness and spiritual life in many major ways. There is a greater scope and depth. It also on occasion caused conflict with my traditional church and within my family of origin. Some in my traditional church and my primary family were vocally looking askance at my spiritual choices and practices. It would take time and experience to resolve these issues, and the resolution would enrich my spiritual life and convictions exponentially.

Becoming a Pipe carrier in the Earthtribe

In teaching about the role of a Pipe carrier, Bear Heart enumerates certain traits that must be present before one is invited to "pick up a Pipe." He describes the life-time commitment, responsibility and discernment required in being and living a life dedicated to Spirit and all living beings. Some of the qualities Bear Heart designates as necessary to develop before such a commitment are "humility, courage, loyalty and compassion."[5] These are qualities I perceive evident in bridging my Christian and nature-based spirituality, and I explore these qualities throughout this book.

The Pipe represents mankind with the stem and the universe with the bowl. Bear Heart states, "One of the great teachings of the Pipe is to always keep our Pipe stem clean... Is it clear? Likewise is our life clear?"[6] Much of my Pipe training

4

was centered on clearing psychological and emotional baggage. Bear Heart's book has many teachings on living with respect, balance, wisdom and harmony.

Bear Heart speaks of the pathway of becoming a medicine man/woman, which is also true of becoming a Pipe carrier. If one becomes a medicine person, it is because one has been observed for a long period of time by a medicine man or woman, who has discerned that you would be acceptable to be taught. The medicine person then asks if you are willing to be taught. In the fall of 1999, I was asked by my Pipe trainer if I was willing to begin training and pick up a Pipe in the spring of 2000, when I was to quest. If so, I was to write my vows to the Pipe and Sacred Mystery. If one agrees (and I did), there will be many tests along the way to ascertain one's commitment, dedication and teachability. I have completed my eight years of required training, but continue on because I find it helpful and fulfilling. Therefore, my trainer still occasionally places a test in my path. I will later give an example of these types of Pipe training and tests in the story of "Liliput."

Pipe training is often difficult. When Boyd meets with Rolling Thunder and asks to work with him, Rolling Thunder says, "You can't just sit down and talk about the truth... You have to live it and be part of it and you *might* get to know it... It's slow and gradual and it don't come easy."[7]

A sense of the need for the expansion of ideas was a major part of my journey with my spiritual mentor/Pipe trainer. During my training, we worked with the inner voices of my personality and with altered states. Occasionally, these altered states still need to be processed with my Pipe trainer (for instance, vision quests and other phenomenon I encounter).

Rolling Thunder teaches Boyd about purification and patience and most importantly that "man's inner nature is identical with the nature of the universe, and thus man learns about his own nature from nature itself."[8] This truth can be witnessed in my vision quests and other nature-based events mentioned in my writing.

In the Kwehar-rehnuh Komatsi tradition, if one could hear these voices well enough to have a powerful, elaborate vision, they obtained *puha* (power that comes from increased awareness) and became a *puhakut* (shaman or medicine person). The *puhakut* was then a guide for others that entered a vision that connected with an animal spirit. In Pipe training, one is not qualified to walk with others in this manner until the eight formal years of training are complete.

Later in my training my Pipe trainer told me it was time to learn "tracking." At first I did not know what he meant. Later, when I was ready, strong and mature enough, we tracked down my disowned self, Liliput. I did not understand it then, but it became clear at a vision quest and in the processing year or so that followed the vision quest in 2006.

Things need to heat up for transformation to take place. Sometimes, I refer to this as heating up the bowl of the Pipe. Our traumas and deep emotional experiences open the door for healing and spiritual growth even though we fear to encounter these experiences. Our natural tendency in our minds is to try to escape or deny them because of the deep psychological and emotional pain.

In May 2000, I entered the traditional eight year training as a Pipe carrier. For fifteen years prior to accepting the responsibility of carrying the Pipe, I was in training as an elder (leader). In my traditional pathway of a Pipe carrier, it is a serious, sacred matter to "pick up the Pipe." It is a life-long, life-altering commitment to Spirit and others.

The Pipe is not in ceremony until the stem and bowl are connected. The stem of the Pipe I carry is made of juniper and is the length of my arm from elbow to wrist. The bowl is made of catlinite: a soft, red, easily carved stone used by Native Americans for Pipe bowls and other sacred objects. The shape of the bowl of the Pipe is similar to those used by the Lakota. There is an extended point to the turn of the bowl for resting it on the ground against the altar. If you turn it 180 degrees, it looks very much like a Tau cross. I treasure the shape of the bowl of the Pipe I carry because of my lineage. There are some conflicts among Native Americans about the role I fulfill.

Ed McGaa, Eagle Man, discusses the Pipe in his book *Mother Earth Spirituality*, as follows:

> Some Sioux have objected to "outsiders" using catlinite for their Pipes. Many do not object...and make the Pipe available. (They) believe the more the dominant society becomes acculturated from learning Indian spiritual concepts the sooner we will all progress toward a healthy Mother Earth spirituality.[9]

More importantly, as I pray, I treasure the Pipe (the most sacred object of the Plains Indians, used in all their ceremonies, and from which their religion flows) for these spiritual reasons expressed by Lame Deer:

> As we stand on Grandmother Earth, raising our Sacred Pipe in prayer, its stem forms a bridge from earth through our own bodies, to the sky, to Wakan Tanka... As the Pipe is filled with our sacred...tobacco, each tiny grain represents one of the living things on this earth. All of the Great Spirit's creations, the whole universe,... All of us is in that Pipe at the moment of prayer.[10]

With both the Pipe and the Eucharist, we seek connection to the Divine.

Questions began to arise

As I attended the sweatlodges and my traditional church, I continued to wonder how the Christian church fit into the Medicine Wheel's directional meanings. Or to say this another way, "How does man project his beliefs and hopes onto an Ultimate Reality from the perspective of beliefs, traditions and practices?" This led me to the purposes I wish to propose.

I propose to explore the relationship between the Native American Medicine Wheel and other indigenous practices, life events, my studies and experiences, the care of the Earth and religion. There are three proposals that I have pondered and wish to address:

- First, the integration of Christianity and Nature-based Spirituality impacts one's life path and spiritual belief system, yet transcends and includes both traditional belief systems.

- Second, this integration is relevant to a ministry for the spiritual, psychological, emotional, physical growth and healing of individuals and groups by utilizing my form of integrated Nature-based Spirituality, leadership skills and mentoring tools.

- Third, the expansion of ideas and beliefs address the practical and spiritual purposes of sustaining the earth in the current planetary crises.

Explorations

I will begin with the events in my life—physical, mental, emotional and spiritual—and relate and connect them to the energy and intention often referred to as prayer with the *Medicine Wheel*. Also, I will explore reciprocity for the gifts of the earth and sustainability. I will examine the use of the tools for trauma mentoring and knowledge gained from my education and the expansion of my life and purpose in the world, and demonstrate how those tools informed my prayer life on the Medicine

Wheel and would be useful in mentoring others. In conclusion, I will address how the Medicine Wheel correlates with my beliefs and brings me to a belief system that transcends and yet includes my traditional religious upbringing.

The religions on which I focus are Christianity and the primal religions of the Native American and Australian Aboriginal. My interest is in how their values and some of the practices appear to coincide and integrate, and coincidentally how they might differ, as my life unfolded over the past thirty years around the Medicine Wheel, as I practice it in the context of what I have learned in the Earthtribe. The wheel symbol is a common symbol in many cultures, including the Celtic race of which I have a strong heritage.

Beginning to look at how I personally integrated this pathway into my own traditional Christian background, and how the Medicine Wheel applied to my life experiences and meditational practices, I started out by reading *The Pipe and Christ: A Christian-Sioux Dialogue* by William Stolzman and *That They May Have Life: The Episcopal Church In South Dakota* by Virginia Driving Hawk Sneve. One of the beautiful passages from Sneve's book is the Decalogue from the 1929 Episcopal prayer book in Dakota and English:

> God spake these words, and said:
> I am the Lord thy God;
> Thou shalt have none other gods but me.
> *Lord have mercy upon us, and incline our hearts to keep this law.*

> Wakantanka wicoie kin dena eye,
> ca heya; Wakantanka nitawa, Itancan kin he Miye:
> Mitokan taku wakan tokeca duha kte sni.
> *Itancan, onsiundapi kta e, cante yusunyan miye*[11]

My reading then expanded into several classics on Native American spirituality. This with my ongoing work in the Episcopal church led to the next step in my questioning to wonder how traditional religion might fit into the structure and projections of the Medicine Wheel.

The *Medicine Wheel* is the term used for the directions of prayer. We use eight directions in the Earthtribe: East, South, West, North, Grandmother Earth, Grandfather Sky, all of our Relations (animate and inanimate—all things created) and Ancestors (personal or spiritual). It is somewhat like a gyroscope with an infinite "over there" for the Ancestors: a horizontal hoop that includes the cardinal directions and planetary relations and a vertical hoop that includes Grandmother Earth, Grandfather Sky and celestial or universal relations. The hoops are limitless through the direction of the Ancestors.

Notice that everything I mention is in circles: the lodge, the way we gather in the lodge, the *sipapu* (pit or navel of the earth), the Medicine Wheel. It will become evident that my life has revolved full circle. Black Elk speaks to the significance of the circle and the significance of the four cardinal directions, as he is translated by John Neihardt:

> (The) Power of the World always works in circles, and everything tries to be round... This knowledge came to us from the outer world with our religion... (Thus,) the life of a man is a circle from childhood to childhood...[12]

Applications

I will speak of major and minor events in the circle of my life, as I celebrate being seventy-five years old and have entered the fourth cycle or winter of my life's path. These events are points on the Medicine Wheel that revolve through my life's pathway.

As a psychotherapist, lay chaplain and Lay Eucharistic Minister in the Episcopal Church, my focus in later life has been on healing and ministry to others. I have also developed licensure and skills as an educator. To these experiences, I will connect Native American traditions, the indigenous practices of the Australian Aborigines, my research and studies, reciprocity for Grandmother Earth and concepts of traditional Christian religion that appear in my mind to relate to the events and the directions.

In my writing, I approach many topics we encounter throughout our lives: hope and healing, vulnerability and money, terrorism and good versus evil, war, illness and nature-based healing, finding the transcendent in our lives, relationship, sacred leadership and community, mysticism, birth, death and the soul, trauma wounds to the soul, planetary crises and the integration of Christianity and nature-based spirituality.

As we approach the directions of the *Medicine Wheel*, I have connected my three proposals through events in my life as they appear to me to correlate with the directions of the Medicine Wheel and my personal nature-based Christian approach to spirituality. I have also included mentoring tools and my personal experiences of nature-based spirituality. Then I have noted concepts of sacred leadership and its role in sustainability in our current planetary crises.

Let us turn now to the East, the first direction of intention on the Earthtribe Medicine Wheel, and moments in the journey of my life with Spirit, the one I call *"Sacred Mystery, All That Is."*

CHAPTER TWO

The Direction of the East: A Healing Prayer, A Cry for Hope

As we turn now to the East with the energy and intention of a prayer of petition, a prayer of hope, I first would like to describe the symbolism of the East and my first vision quest, which was early in the journey of my nature-based spirituality.

Symbolism of the East

The East is the first spiritual direction with which I begin my prayers, or intentions, on the Medicine Wheel, as is the custom with the Earthtribe. It is the direction of new beginnings, "first steps," new directions, light, illuminations, clarity, insight and seeing a bigger picture (a greater "awareness," if you will). This is the direction of knowledge and wisdom.[1] It is the direction of hope. In the process of illumination and awareness, choices are made for the journey.

Since it is also a human direction that includes words (prayer and intent), for me it fits the Toltec first agreement from Ruiz's *The Four Agreements* to "be impeccable with your word. Speak with integrity. Say only what you mean. Avoid using the word to speak against yourself or to gossip about others. Use the power of your word in the direction of love and truth."[2]

There are symbols for the direction of the East on the Medicine Wheel that we use in the Earthtribe. Its color is yellow. Its totem is the osprey that can see far, and its musical instrument is the bell with its clarity. The osprey appears to crash into the water, then rises beautifully. The trust in the East is the knowing of predictability.

The season of the East is springtime and fire is its element. Black Elk states that the fire that is used to heat the rocks (in the sweatlodge) represents "the great power of *Wakan Tanka* which gives life to all things; it is as a ray from the sun, for the sun is the *Wakan Tanka* in a certain aspect... The round fireplace (pit) at the center of the sweatlodge is the center of the universe in which dwells *Wakan Tanka* with His power which is fire."[3] The sun connects to the pita, where the rocks are heated, then connects from there to the central pit of the sweatlodge.

This leads me to share the importance of the sacred fire that originally was kept in a central tipi by a tribal member appointed to keep the fire going from one encampment to another in the nomadic Native American lifestyle:

> (This) keeper would carry the fire in a small log, and
> when camp was set up again, each lodge would
> start its fire from this central source. The fire was ex-
> tinguished and a new one started, always in a ritual
> manner, only after there had been some great cata-
> strophe, or when a complete purification was
> needed for the whole camp.[4]

In my way of thinking this also includes the inner fire of our passions and inner council, sometimes they need to be treated in the same manner. Two ways to address this purification or change would be in the form of a vision quest or sweatlodge ceremony.

New beginnings: Vision quest of 1985

Black Elk tells us, "Every dawn that comes is a holy event, and every day is holy, for the light comes from your Father Wakan Tanka; and also you must always remember that the two-leggeds and all the other peoples (species) that stand upon the earth are sacred and should be treated as such."[5]

In 1985, I decided to go on my first vision quest led by Bear Heart and Winged Medicine. Black Elk teaches, "When going out to lament it is necessary to choose a wise old medicine man, who is quiet and generous, to help,...offer the Pipe to the Six Powers and to the four-leggeds and the wings of the air; and he must go along to watch."[6]

It was fall, and I had separated from my husband only weeks before. We were invited to go find our vision quest site, where we would fast and pray. I came to a small grove of trees. While I was looking around to see if I felt comfortable in that spot, a blue and black butterfly flew in from the west and landed on a bush in the east. Then another yellow butterfly flew in from the east and landed on a bush to the west. A white butterfly flew from the south and landed on the bark of a tree to the north.

I waited, but no other butterflies appeared. I decided the direction of the south was open and walked that direction. In front of me was a circle of sage-like plants with a tree to the west. I knew that shade would be needed in the afternoons. I saw a bit of rabbit fur caught on the sagebrush and decided this circle was the right place for me.

Later that day, following a sweatlodge, I was led out by two supporters to this site. My ring of prayer ties was placed on the ground with my sleeping bag in the center. Four willow poles were set up in the cardinal directions, and a fifth pole set near the east pole to form what is called a door. When my supporters left, I fell asleep for a short period as a result of the heat from the sweatlodge.

Soon, I was startled awake by loud snorts. Two bulls were snorting at the flags (colored cotton bags filled with tobacco that hung from the poles). One was a large white Brahma, the other was dark, almost black. They walked away when I sat up. The prayer ties and flags form a boundary of safety surrounding the site of the quester.

Awake now, I filled an abalone shell with sage and lit it to pray. Sitting on the ground, I began to pray turning to face each direction beginning with the East. When I came to the direction of the North, the sage was smoking well. To my awe and astonishment, a monarch butterfly flew straight at me, eye level from across the field, entered the prayer smoke, rose up the smoke thermals, then flew back to the north. It had completed the cardinal directions of the Medicine Wheel begun by the butterflies, when I sought a site.

That night I was again startled awake by some small creature in the brush near my head and the tree. Standing, I walked to the eastern door of my vision circle. Bear Heart had told me to watch the skies. For some reason, I saw what appeared to be two moons rising. Puzzled by this, I stood there a good while, then went back to rest thinking that whatever the creature was that awakened me, it was smaller than I am.

I later woke again. Bear Heart was walking down the pathway by my site from west to east singing. Somehow, I sang with him in a language I actually do not know. He turned to the south and walked away. A little later, Winged Medicine came along the path from west to east and turned to the north where the encampment was located. Months later, I mentioned this incident and learned neither man had left the main encampment.

In the morning, when I awoke, I was so thirsty that I was gratefully licking the dew from the surface of my sleeping bag.

In a while, the birds began to fly into the field and sing. Two red-tailed hawks settled on trees to the northeast and other smaller birds circled around me and gathered in the small bushes and the tree by my site.

My supporters came to retrieve me, and I related these incidents to Bear Heart and Winged Medicine. I was given the nature name *Butterfly Woman* (a healer). Bear Heart told me that he was adopting me into the Muskogee tribe. He also told me I would "see clearly" and be a "gatherer of people." I do not know about the seeing clearly, but I have formed groups of people in the years since then.

My life's choice of purpose is to be a healer, and I hope the following incidents will offer some insight into my world. Bear Heart asks the quester to reflect on three questions: "Who am I? What have I become with the what that I am? Why am I here?"[7] These questions would unfold over the next twenty plus years.

Illuminations:
A healing prayer, a cry for hope

In the incidents I am about to share with you, once again I obtained a greater awareness of the connections with all living things, the power of prayer and a connection with the energy of the universe—scientifically this awareness can be called a connection with the eco-field. For the Native American, it would be a connection with the Sacred Web. If, and I believe it is true, our entire lives and experiences are a prayer (for good or ill), then this story is an unfolding prayer of connection with all living things, the implicate order and, most especially, a prayer of hope.

The incidents occurred in May of 2011, when I attended an intensive on "Earth Wisdom and the Primordial Mind" presented by Dr. William Taegel and Dr. Judith Yost. William Taegel defines primordial mind, as follows:

> We all have an indigenous mind. If you will follow your roots far enough back, you will find the indigenous self: perhaps, in Native America, or Europe, or the Middle East, or Africa. No inner council in this crucial time can be fully sacred without that indigenous self, child of the Primordial mind.[8]

As we go back into retrieving these parts of our selves/heritage, it can be defined or experienced in different ways. Personally, I can trace my heritage back to Celtic and Native American roots (both of these roots utilized a Medicine Wheel for a focus in prayer). My understanding is that I am a sixteenth Lakota Blackfoot, *Sihasapa,* from my father's maternal grandmother. My father's paternal grandmother came from County Kerry, Ireland as a bride and spoke only Gaelic.

Records are lost for my Native American ancestor with the exception that I know she was adopted by a minister and his family. At her wedding it is recorded that both of her fathers were present. This adoption was often done in regard to Native American children during those years. To my total surprise, I was to retrieve a part of the indigenous connection and a deeper connection to my primordial mind on my second day of the intensive.

As part of the illumination, an aspect of the East, an incident occurred during this class deeply related to the topic regarding eco-fields. A field was defined in class as "a region of non-material influence." An eco-field ("eco" coming from ecology and biology) is defined as "the space configuration meaning carrier (in which there is exchanged meaning) under the epistemological umbrella of a particular landscape."[9]

Robert Lawlor in his book, *Voices of the First Day*, speaks of the step from the primordial mind and the beginning of mankind's presence in the landscape as a Golden Age. (Beginnings are represented in the East on the Medicine Wheel.) As a perfect genesis, the Golden Age occurs at the beginning of time with the concept of revelation.

> Revelation can be defined as receiving inspiration or knowledge directly from a source that existed before this world. The belief in revelation presupposes that every form exists initially as an invisible potential within another... The patterns of manifestation of intellectual and material forms appear as a succession of metamorphoses, each a trope or symbol of its unseen predecessor.[10]

The Aboriginal cosmology understands the universe is manifesting in the eco-field as consciousness. This consciousness is external from the source. The source dreams the world of thoughts, forms and matter. The Australian Aboriginal initiatic culture is constructed entirely around the concept of revelation. They are "tuned" to hear the stage that came before physical life through their ceremonies, language, song and dance. Lawlor explains, "Maintaining this attunement allows the physical to resonate with the energy of the preceding state."[11]

Lame Deer defines the Native American conception of the eco-field, as follows: "I believe, with the Indians, that a landscape influences and forms the people living on it and that one cannot understand them and make friends with them without also understanding, and making friends with, the earth from which they came."[12] Rolling Thunder speaks something similar regarding the eco-field, "It includes a certain viewpoint (attitude) about the relationship between the sun, the earth (and all of nature), the healer and the...conscious presence of the Great Spirit. Absent from the real situation are skepticism and judgement."[13] Filing the information away, I did not know it would be so important later in a concrete experience of an eco-field.

Monday, the first day of class, we had an experiential learning period wherein we chose something in nature that connected us on a soul level. I felt called to a venerable old juniper. It was bent nearly to the ground, curving back up toward the sky. The top layer of the trunk had died in an old injury and had a large cavity. To me it spoke of the strength of aging and the healing of deep wounds. Thursday, I would be with this tree again with two male classmates for an exercise called a "birthing experience." I found it meaningful that the two men were drawn to the same tree I encountered on Monday. The tree spoke to me symbolically of the deep connection between birth and death.

On Tuesday, we had experiential learning in the afternoon that included a sweatlodge and a healing ceremony around a buffalo robe. Little did I know that this event would be so pivotal and powerful for me as an experience of the eco-field and hope.

For the sweatlodge event, I was outside taking care of the others in the lodge, and I did a little drumming. After the lodge, we went up on the hill to where a buffalo robe was laid out beneath a very large oak tree. A healer had placed objects between the tree and the buffalo robe forming what he termed an "energy line." The participants in the lodge talked about their experiences. Then our instructor invited the healer to describe his altar. When he had completed his talk, a classmate I will call Ann asked him if we could say prayers for someone not present, who was undergoing brain surgery for a tumor at that very moment. The healer said, "Yes, it could be done." Ann asked that I pray with her for our mutual friend. Ann and I lay face down on the buffalo robe with our heads in the South (the direction of compassion on the Medicine Wheel), our shoulders lightly touching.

As I lay down, jolts like fist blows of energy moved through my chakras from head to groin from the direction of the tree. Twice this occurred, until I had my face fully down on the deep brown fur of the buffalo robe. The jolts were as powerful as fire, or the bright rays of the dawning sun in the East.

James Gibson in his book, *A Reenchanted World*, speaks of this movement of energy and connection between living things that was my experience in the eco-field of the tree, the buffalo robe, the hospital, the people present including the healer and two other trees far across the country (One the healer stated was in Ireland.). The healer stated that these trees formed an energy triangle. I looked to Gibson to find words for this strong energy and vision connection through both the natural eco-field and the implicate order:

> Instead of portraying humans as the star species
> that progressed beyond all others, these thinkers
> (philosophers, cognitive scientists and scholars,
> such as David Abram) stress human development
> through our relationships with other species. In the
> culture of enchantment, consciousness and nature
> are one..."[14]

By far the most famous expression of this (new) consciousness was James Lovelock's "Gaia hypothesis"... Lovelock developed a model to describe the dynamics of planetary life that Gibson discusses, wherein Gibson explains that "All elements of life on the planet, as well as the rocks, the oceans and the atmosphere work together."[15]

The Australian Aborigines would not be stunned, as I was, by this strong voltage from the tree and the earth. They would receive it much as Robert Lawlor states:

Everything in the natural world is a symbolic foot-print of the metaphysical beings whose actions cre-ated our world. As a seed, the potency of an earthly location is wedded to its origin. The Aborigines called this potency the "Dreaming" of a place and the Dreaming constitutes the sacredness of the earth. Only in extraordinary states of consciousness can one be aware of, or attuned to, the inner dream-ing of the earth.[16]

The Australian Indigenous people believe the subtle mag-netic celestial or universal flow circulates as the blood of the gods in the veins of the earth. This concept underlies the study of ley lines, known in occult science as geomancy. John Mitchell is the most eloquent commentator on this topic.

A number of anthropologists and scientists have found that the Aborigines possess an acute sensitivity to magnetic and vital force flows emanating from the earth. The aborigines refer to these magnetic forces as songlines, fundamental to Aborigin-al initiatic knowledge and religion. The Aborigines map their world in songs, depicting mythic events at successive sites along a walking trail that winds through a region. The network of songlines are inherited by each tribe. Lawlor states:

(Living) systems are extraordinarily sensitive to magnetic fields. By extremely simple experiments it is shown that highly diverse plants and animals may have their orientation modified by artificial fields of the order of strength of the geo-magnetic field... The nature of the response properties suggest that the organism is normally integrated with its geo-magnetic environment to a striking degree.[17]

This connection to the eco-field, or geo-magnetic field, is evidently what occurred for me in the following prayer. I lay there on the buffalo robe and began to pray. "Be well, Paul. Be well, Paul." Over and over I continued this refrain. My mind filled with light. Then I saw a dark black mass with small nodes, but not tendrils. It occurred to me that I was seeing the tumor. I turned my head to the left to breathe, and my mind went dark. Simultaneously, Ann and I rose from the buffalo robe. Feeling a little stunned, I went around the circle of people and sat on the south side of the tree out of the eco-field I had encountered from the tree and around the altar and robe. I sat there in silence.

The vision of the light in my brain and the blackness and shape of the tumor could be scientifically explained, and Lawlor defines the patterns caused by neural firing in the brain in his book, *Voices of the First Day.*[18] The Native American shaman would call this vision of the tumor traveling to visit the circle of Paul's energy field, or connection with the Sacred Web; the Celt would say that I was *fey*. The Australian aboriginal would say that I had travelled the songlines. Modern science would determine that I had entered the eco-field.

Hope

Still reflecting on this phenomenon, I went the following day to join the class for an all day outing to Enchanted Rock. As I stepped out of my car that morning, Ann came to me and said, "I have been looking for you. The tumor in Paul's brain was not the virulent kind. It was contained like a cyst. The prognosis is good." I thought to myself, "That is what I saw." I was filled with hope for the survival of this dear friend of twenty years duration.

We packed our lunches, formed our caravan and drove to Enchanted Rock, where I once again encountered a snake. I had been surrounded by three rattle snakes the year before. This time, it was a water snake, maybe a water moccasin. It had a white head. It swam fluidly back and forth across the creek. It was so beautiful, and its motion was mesmerizing, a joy to watch. I in-

vited my instructor to come look at it with me. I was still thinking about Paul, feeling a sense of peace and just relaxed into the
beauty around me. Taegel eloquently describes the meditative
space I was enjoying when we relax, turn off our monkey minds,
breathe, open our chests, allow our shoulder blades to slide
down our backs, feel the breeze and the sun on our faces, listen
to the birds and place our bare feet upon the earth:

> Energy flows up through your bare feet, moving
> through your breath through tight spots in your
> body. The contractions slowly release... Your heart
> has room for the fire of the Untamed to radiate
> through your arms and out your fingers... You rest
> in the simple feeling of Being. You are who you
> were before there was a planet Earth. You float in
> your Original Self.[19]

Awareness

On Thursday morning, we had a processing group to talk about
our experiences. I described these two events to them. A classmate told us that she had put her foot on the buffalo robe as
Ann and I prayed. Into her mind came the words, "Be well,
Paul. Be well, Paul." The group and I were astounded. I had not
said my prayer vocally. It was only in my mind and heart. This
is another example of how powerful the eco-field was in this
healing ceremony.

Robert Lawlor addresses this astounding issue when he
refers to the work of Gregory Bateson and states that the mind
goes beyond the body into the totality of social systems and the
ecology of the planet. (This larger mind is sometimes referred to
as God.) Lawlor explains the reciprocity of mind/Mind. The
Aborigines within their myth have a heightened sense that
through dreams they receive the potencies of the ancestors.
They believe humanity returns this power reciprocally through

daily life in song, ritual and dance. The world consists of the Dreaming of the Ancestors:

> In other words, the interiority of the gods is our external reality, while the interiority of humanity and earthly life is the objective existence of the gods... We are dreaming within a Dream... This, in essence, is the Dreamtime Law: maintaining sensitivity to an invisible, metaphysical prototype, physically sensed and symbolically read in the topography of the land.[20]

This experience on the buffalo robe was a reenforcement of the vision quest experience with the *numinous* and the implicate order that occurred for me in 2006 and is described in chapter nine regarding the direction of the Ancestors.

The traditional ways to pray and meditate expanded in this experience on the buffalo robe. Lawlor explains it this way:

> "The 'infolding' process of prayer and meditation is in stark contrast to Aboriginal spirituality which, through ever-deepening perception, opens outward to empathize and identify with every aspect of a living, active world."[21]

The event on the buffalo robe had a healing influence personally, as well as being a prayer of intention for another. My brother was a Baptist minister in his lifetime and was highly critical of nature-based spirituality until just before his death. His intense rejection of my pathway was painful. He could not understand my inner search, the part of my inner council that Gibson calls *enchantment*. It caused a lonely rift in my heart.

Gibson notes that this search evolves from within due to the cultural impact of consumerism that so isolates us in the cubicles of our world:

> There were always a few mavericks (like me) and romantics who saw such isolation as wrong in sub-

stance and unbearable in spirit... But the current wave of spiritual interest in nature is not simply another outburst of romanticism... (People) respond to the culture of enchantment because it offers them something they need: *transcendence,* a sense of mystery and meaning, glimpses of a numinous world beyond our own.[22]

Some years back, I was sent up for the Episcopal priesthood for the third time and went through the entire process, which is lengthy and difficult. At the last meeting with the Commission on Ministry, the process seemingly ended because I carry a Pipe and claim my nature-based spirituality and honor my genetic lineage.

Something William Stolzman wrote in *The Pipe and Christ* is a comfort to me. He states Christians are, "in God's providential plan, to silently learn from and be blessed by those sacred revelations that preceded the coming of the Gospel, so as to adequately appreciate it in a Christian inculturational manner... It is a key notion in the art of being a fully authentic Lakota (or nature-based) – Christian."[23] It is comforting and healing to me in that it validates my choice to blend my nature-based spirituality with Christianity in the face of the opposition I received from my primary family and a few in my traditional church.

Gibson noted that nearly the entire culture of enchantment is underpinned by Native American spirituality. The Native Americans first reached out to the emerging hippie counterculture. This brought the Native American pathway to a broader society, including the feminist goddess movement. The focus on Earth as God's sacred creation also began to impact Judaism and Christianity.

This impact had not reached fully into the culture. As I was proceeding through the ordination process, the dean and bishop were in accord with my world. However, one could not have anyone on the evaluating committee say, "No." A woman priest I had supported through her process surprised me when she appeared to vote against me because I carry a Pipe. She was uninformed about what that meant and highly suspicious of my spirituality. As James Gibson reported, the social changes that caused anxiety for conservatives (like my brother, the Baptist minister, and the Episcopal priest mentioned previously) in matters like high divorce rates, visibility of gays and lesbians, the global influence of the Internet and abortion clinics at the turn of the century brought forth fears of an imminent apocalypse, reenforced by environmental crises. "The growing popularity of the culture of enchantment within mainstream America struck many conservative religious thinkers as clear evidence of Satan's growing power."[24]

This was not new thinking. Gibson speaks to this issue:

> Christian theologians, the Neoplatonists in particular, made their own contributions to the radical separation between humans and nature. Thinkers from Plotinus (205-70 BCE) to Thomas Aquinas (1225-1274 AD) conceived of a Great Chain of Being, with God—pure reason and spirit—at the apex, animals and plants—pure matter—at the bottom, and humans—creatures of spirit and matter—occupying the middle ground.[25]

This view of the world places humans above and dominant over nature. *Animism,* called a pagan thought or religion, denoted totemic kinship between animal species and tribes. Neoplatonism's influence on Christianity had refuted this commonality and solidarity between humans and animals. God's curse on Adam and Eve extended in Christian doctrine to the natural world. Man's place was higher in the great Chain of Being. Nature as the sacred creation of God, a pathway to recognition of "divine mystery, was completely rejected by Christian orthodoxy and took on the mantle of being heretical."[26]

The indigenous people have not taken this position of removing themselves from a relationship of equality with all living things. They recognize that we are a mammal amongst all other mammals, a part of the One.

There is also a social/cultural impact in a broader context to my personal experiences with nature and the culture. Thirty-two Nobel Laureates and other imminent scientists wrote an "Open Letter to the American Religious Community," desiring the religious communities to accept environmental restoration as a spiritual obligation. In this letter noted by James Gibson, they stated:

> Many of us have profound experiences of awe and reverence before the universe. We recognize that what is regarded as sacred is most likely to be treated with respect. Efforts to safeguard the planetary environment need to be infused with a vision of the sacred and a universal moral priority...[27]

Their initiative and those of other groups resulted in the formation in 1993 of The National Religious Partnership for the Environment (NRPE). This group of mainline religious and educational institutions has grown exponentially. "All told, NRPE claims to encompass faith groups serving over one hundred million Americans."[28]

During the intensive class periods, we discussed many major issues concerning our planet: global warming, giant gyres of debris in our oceans, oil spills, nuclear plants that threaten the environment (as in Japan's tsunami damaged plant). One of our professors dressed as "Gaia," and there was a dialogue regarding these issues and the prospect of potentials, possibilities and hope. I do not know about you the reader, but it seems daunting to me as I read the daily news on the internet, feel overwhelmed, yet long for hope, not just for myself, but for my grandchildren. These issues are crucial, and I wish to address them further in the chapter on the need for reciprocity for Grandmother Earth.

New birth

The experience we had with birthing something new at the juniper tree on Thursday afternoon was a hope in my heart to birth a better future for the generations to come. Robert Lawlor would emphasize the following:

> Dreams, deep collective memories, and imaginings are more potent than religious faith or scientific theories in lifting us above the catastrophic ending that confronts us all. A recollection of our origins—a remembrance of a sense of reality in its pure and primary form—is essential if we are to understand our present circumstances and imagine the possibilities of our collective destiny.[29]

There are several instances in Will Taegel's book wherein he addresses these broader cultural issues regarding the planet and our role in its care and protection. One of them is his fourth proposal, part of which I quote here:

> Unprecedented crisis reveals itself with the basics of the environment... We must re-establish the primal connection... No significant solutions will arise without the nurturing of this connection with the *mysterium tremendum*, that profound sense of awe... I refer here...to radical new practices to recover the Wild Heart birthed in Mother Nature's womb.[30]

In discussing his second proposal, he asserts:

> Beneath the crisis in civilization lies our role in Nature. We are an aspect of the natural order—the rising sun, gravity, pollination, photosynthesis and weather patterns. *We are the environmental crisis*. We

are Nature being aware of Herself in turmoil at this
moment, unless we cover our eyes with rose-
colored glasses.[31]

I am of this time and place. Perhaps, with assistance from
my inner council and others around me with the same mindset,
we can gather from the roots of our forebears and spiritual ancestors the answers for our time. This is my birthing hope for
my grandchildren and this planet.

Robert Lawlor calls us to *re-language* the connection of
time and place with the intention to reenter earth's dreaming in
order to rediscover the channels (passages) within our minds to
reconnect with the earth. Lawlor defines the term indigenous as
an integral part of that process:

> *Indigenous* means "born from" or "being an integral
> part of a place or region on earth." In our time the
> term *indigenous* has come to symbolize the rediscov-
> ery that our race is inseparable from earth and
> nature as a whole.[32]

Lame Deer also calls us to the eco-field in prose of pure
poetry:

> Let's sit down here, all of us, on the open prairie,
> where we can't see a highway or a fence. Let's have
> no blankets to sit on, but feel the ground with our
> bodies, the earth, the yielding shrubs. Let's have the
> grass for a mattress, experiencing its sharpness and
> its softness. Let us become like stones, plants, and
> trees. Let us be animals, think and feel like animals.

> Listen to the air. You can hear it, feel it, smell it, taste
> it. *Woniya wakan*—the holy air—which renews all by
> its breath. *Woniya, woniya wakan*—spirit, life, breath,
> renewal—it means all of that. *Woniya*—we sit togeth-
> er, don't touch, but something is there, we feel it
> between us, as a presence. A good way to start think-

ing about nature, talk about it. Rather talk to it, talk to
the rivers, to the lakes, to the winds as relatives.[33]

And so, my prayer in the direction of the East, "Be well, Paul.
Be well, my beloved planet home. Be well."

Recently, I received a report on Paul from my friend that
prayed with me. The doctors say he is now in total remission
following surgery and chemotherapy. Bear Heart would speak
of this as follows: "When we pray for something and receive it,
one thing that our people are taught to do is say thank you.
When you do that, many more blessings come."[34] I send a prayer of gratitude.

Historically, Christianity seeks *dominion* over the earth,
and for the Native American all things are *equal relatives*. Christianity and Native American spirituality clash on the role of
man in his environment, but as can be gathered from the National Religious Partnership for the Environment, there is hope
for change.

Often as we birth ourselves in the East there is pain and
discomfort. Birthing is messy, but the joy of change, new beginnings, hope and creativity can be great indeed. As my pathway
of nature-based spirituality combined with Christianity unfolds, I have encountered the messiness and pain of birthing a
new spirituality that is appropriate and fulfilling for me and
possibly for others, as well.

Hope, and the hope for new beginnings, is paramount in
prayer. This petitionary form of prayer is one of the earliest,
preceded by gratitude, as we shall discover in the next direction
of the South. I turn my energy and thoughts in that direction.

31

CHAPTER THREE

The Direction of the South:
The Trauma of the Economic Crisis:
The Road to Bankruptcy

The direction of the South is feminine. It is emotional and compassionate. Its attributes are many. They include vulnerability, creativity and humor. There are also the attributes of growth, destiny, reflection, receptivity, the innocence of a child, trust and openness. The trust includes the goodness of the universe.

In the South one is aware, yet accepting, of events. The aspect of destiny is not destination; it's what life's experiences are. However, it does include birth and death in all its forms. I was effected and affected with these attributes of the South in an encounter surrounding major illness and money.

Symbolism of the South

The symbols for the direction of the South are the color white, the vulnerable mouse, the caracara (eagle) and the coyote. The coyote is the "trickster," who tells one to "get off your high horse" and be able to laugh at yourself. The season of the South is summer and its musical instrument the drum (representing the heartbeat). Its element is the fluidity and depth of water. The purpose of water in the lodge is explained by Black Elk:

There is a winged One (the Thunderbird, *Wakinyan Wakan*), there where the sun goes down to rest, who controls those waters to which all living beings owe their lives... When we use the water in the sweatlodge we should think of *Wakan Tanka* who is always flowing, giving his Power and life to everything; we should even be as water...lower than all things, yet stronger even than rocks."[1]

Because the South is emotional and filled with heart, it resonates for me with the Toltec agreement from Ruiz's book, *The Four Agreements*, "Don't take anything personally. Nothing others do is because of you. What others say and do is a projection of their own reality, their own dream. When you are immune to the opinions and actions of others, you won't be the victim of needless suffering."[2] This was a difficult lesson for me to learn. I will speak more on this concept in the direction of the Ancestors and the story of "Liliput."

Trauma of economic crisis: living with vulnerability

My personal trauma and vulnerability that I address in this chapter is the situation of bankruptcy brought about by major illness and is also related to the economic crisis of the larger community, both local and international. The news is filled with situations like mine on both personal and global levels.

As I bring these thoughts to my writing, our federal government is in the process of voting a bill to raise our country's debt ceiling and avoid a default that would take the country toward bankruptcy. These are extremely serious times on the economic front. Greece has already been forced into default, and other countries are on the edge.

Nature and the neo-shaman as healer

I realize that my vision quest in 1992 has deep meaning for me, once again, as I remember facing the financial crisis of bankruptcy. In telling my story, I am utilizing one of the mentoring tools available for a trauma mentor, "the shaman as a storyteller and ceremonialist."[3] I would like to share with you this personal story and the vision quest, one of my deep experiences in nature that still holds great significance for me, and explore how the neo-shaman (mentor) might connect the story of a personal trauma to an experience in nature. First, let us define the term neo-shaman and his/her role:

> If you journey into the heart of Nature and bring your altered states to the current era—while at the same time using the best of modern science—you are neo-shamanizing. The neo-shaman pays more attention to possibility than to trauma. Why? Part of shamanic training consists of creating intentional traumas and stepping into them.[4]

The sweatlodge, the vision quest, the Earthdance that lasts through the night (and any other crisis event) are traumas. These traumas aid in softening the ego and creating space for an encounter with the inner essence. That opens the doorway to possibility and transcendence.

Vulnerability

In February 2008, following an epinephrine/lidocaine shot at the dentist's office in the middle of January, my heart began to be symptomatic. My blood pressure and pulse would escalate rapidly, and I would feel as if the floor dropped out from under my feet, as the pulse would then plummet to barely forty or stop altogether. Ultimately, I spent many weeks in the hospital (approximately six trips and eight days in ICU) and finally was admitted to Austin Heart for surgery. March 21, 2008, I received a pacemaker implant.

At the time of the surgery, I was making a modest salary and had a small, but adequate, savings account. From January to May, I was unable to work. When I did return to work, my employer was in an economic crunch with her business and did not return me to my previous work schedule. I was now making a third of my prior salary.

Financial trauma

It did not occur to me over the years that I should have prepared with more years of savings for serious medical issues. (On a teacher's salary, I do not know how I would have done that anyway.) In my mind, two insurance plans would cover anything I needed. When all was said and done, my Medicare and my teacher's health insurance paid the bulk of well over $225,000 in medical bills, and I paid a difference of approximately twenty percent. The medical bills are ongoing as Austin Heart constantly monitors the activity of the pacemaker.

Three and a half years before I became ill, I bought an RV. As I realized a year and a half after my surgery that I had literally used up all of my savings to financially stay on top of things, I tried to sell the RV. I discovered I could not do that. The RV had become what is called "upside down" in value. (Many people are finding that true about their homes, as well.) To close a pending sale, I was going to have to come up with a very large difference. I did not, of course, have that amount. My son had planned to help me, but it was too much for his family. According to the dealership, the woman desiring to buy the RV wanted to sue me if I did not sell for the lower value.

I called an attorney here in Wimberley. Her advice was to not only let the RV go back to the bank, but also to file bankruptcy. Letting the RV go back to the bank as a repossession would effect me for seven years and so would bankruptcy. Bankruptcy would be a cleaner process, freeing me from judgements and the threatened law suit. My credit rating was nearly 800 points. I was faithfully current on all payments, but would not be so in the coming months without adequate work. I decided to take the attorney's advice and the similar advice of several of my closest friends. The attorney told me that I had an extremely valid reason for the bankruptcy and that most people could not even determine how they found themselves in my predicament. She assured me I had not been radical with my spending.

The judge at my bankruptcy hearing stated in a very gentle, kind voice, "Go home, Lillie. You have done all the right things." It was a wonderful and healing validation I needed to hear with my inner "critic" and "judge."[5] My attorney told me later that she had never known a judge to say that to anyone. However, I disagree with them in one instance. One of my major expenses was the RV. It was a large stressor on my household budget. It was a major mistake to have bought it. Other writers address these issues.

Andrew Bacevich in his book, *The Limits of Power,* calls us to just acknowledge with awareness these compulsive buying habits, not to deplore or celebrate this fact, but simply to acknowledge it," as follows:

> If one were to choose a single word to characterize
> that (American) identity, it would have to be *more*.
> For the majority...the essence of life, liberty, and the
> pursuit of happiness centers on a relentless personal
> quest to acquire, to consume, to indulge, and to
> shed whatever constraints might interfere with
> those endeavors.[6]

He further states, "In 2005, it (the personal savings rate) dropped below zero and remained there. Collectively, Americans were now spending more than they earned."[7]

Reflection

Looking back, I can see that this was true for me. I was in a bonding pattern with my brother. I wanted very much to travel with him, take my grandchild places and in general enjoy my extended family's world. My brother owned two very large bus-type RVs, two large sailboats and at one point an airplane. Not once in all the years had my brother invited me to travel with him, fly, or sail. I was hurt by this, and I think I wanted to prove that I could do some of the things that he was capable of financially achieving.

Hal Stone and Sidra Stone speak of bonding patterns and how they develop in their book, *Embracing Each-Other*:

> The ignition system for these negative bonding pat-
> terns is some injury to the vulnerable child. Its feel-
> ings are hurt; it feels abandoned; it feels left out; it is
> fatigued or hungry. When we are unaware of these
> feelings, that is, when we are not conscious of this
> kind of uneasiness or injury, then we move psycho-
> logically into some kind of power place and identify
> ourselves with a powerful self.[8]

Stone and Stone share the positive, as well as the negative aspects of power and its opposite vulnerability:

> Being in touch with power allows us to get things
> done and be successful. Being in touch with vulner-
> ability allows us to be intimate. Being identified
> with power brings authority to the world and a loss
> of intimacy in relationships. Being identified with
> vulnerability brings a loss of power and a guaran-
> teed identification with victim status.[9]

The very thing I desired was denied to me by the dynam-
ics of a bonding pattern. What I achieved was a fiscal problem rather than further intimacy with my sibling. I did not know that this would be the result. Stone and Winkelman state, "The

developing of awareness is after the fact and not before. We have to live life and then become aware."[10]

Having been employed since I was fourteen years old, my upbringing in the blue meme taught me that you just had to work hard all of your life and things would progress in a positive direction. The orange meme, or business/scientific culture of my younger brother was not familiar, and I ignorantly jumped into the commercial stream with an impulsive purchase that would come back to haunt me. Don Beck and Christopher Cowan speak of these memes, or stages of development, in their book, *Spiral Dynamics*.

Fortunately, I had bought a Honda CRV vehicle that is very economical a few weeks before I became ill, paying cash for it. The bankruptcy will not touch my home or vehicle, but it will take some years to build my credit rating again. My attorney told me that it would not take as long as I think, and she would help me. However, it worried me that something major could go wrong (like the well going dry in the current Texas drouth) before I could reestablish myself. I gave deep consideration to selling my home and using the equity to purchase something smaller, or to invest and rent a condo or small house. In February of 2011, I was able to sell, which was difficult in a buyers' market. I now lease a lovely little three bedroom patio home. I have placed part of the equity from the sale into a CD, which matures each year.

The orange meme of Beck and Cowan's spiral is not a familiar milieu for me, but my current experience is leading me toward a study of the financial world. My blue meme upbringing that one meets all of one's obligations and debts causes me to feel guilty and judgmental of myself. That inner critic is not very helpful at times, but is a very real part of me. I am not alone in my predicament, which helps my inner vulnerable child feel somewhat better.

Stone and Winkelman describe these inner primary selves. They formed as we developed to protect the vulnerable child (or children) within us so the child will never hopefully be wounded. The protector/controller is the primary inner self and works with other primary selves like the perfectionist (our "shoulds"), the critic and its more or less twin, the judge, the pusher that sees that things are done (faster and faster), and the good mother and good father. These primary selves usually drive our psychological car and try to help us maneuver through life unscathed. Stone and Winkelman then discuss how these primary selves define us and reveal another side, as well:

> We *identify* with these selves; it is this group of
> selves which constitutes our personality as we view
> ourselves and as our friends see us. As we have said
> before, for each primary self there is a compliment-
> ary, or opposite, self that is *disowned* or kept out of
> consciousness. For instance, if our protector/con-
> troller is conservative and cautious, we might dis-
> own our gambler or liberal.[11]

This risk taking disowned gambler, spendthrift, was triggered inside me when I was caught in the bonding pattern with my brother.

There is sadness that I can not control my situation, or the similar situations of a friend or two of mine. However, my protector/controller finds infinite relief at my attempts to make adult decisions and find solutions to the stressful events of the past twenty months of my life.

Edward O. Wilson explains how ethics evolve from self-image, to purpose, to value, to moral reasoning in his book, *The Future of Life*:

> The issue...is moral... The ethic from which moral
> decisions spring is a norm or standard of behavior
> in support of a value, and value in turn depends on

purpose. Purpose...urged by conscience or graven in sacred script, expresses the image we hold of ourselves and our society.[12]

It seems to me that until I recognize and incorporate my disowned selves, and the power of all of my inner selves, the ability to make good moral and ethical decisions in any endeavor will be compromised.

The issues surrounding money are still rampant in our society. I am not alone in my experience. William Alden recently wrote in the August 2011 *Huffington Post* an article entitled, "Medical Bills Drive Americans Into Bankruptcy As Many Struggle To Pay Debt" in which he discusses the crisis Americans are facing to make basic payments. A combination of forces have caused these financial issues: medical bills, loss of jobs, a severe decline in real estate values (a primary asset of many people). A Deloite survey noted that a negative credit experience was occurring for a high number of people who had never had serious problems paying their bills before. Alden notes:

> Those payments include medical bills, which increasingly are pushing Americans into personal bankruptcy, the *New York Times* reports. About a fifth of people seeking financial counseling this year and last said debt related to medical bills was their main reason for deciding to enter bankruptcy... One in seven of these previously creditworthy borrowers entered default in the wake of the economic turndown.[13]

Destiny and Growth

Steve McIntosh in the beginning of his book, *Integral Consciousness,* reflects that there often arises a strong desire in people who have been on a spiritual path for a length of time to try to make a meaningful difference and be of service in the world.

However, this desire is often dampened when we remember Gandhi's famous saying that "we must become the change we want to see in the world," which inevitably leads back to the task of working on ourselves.[14]

Vision quest 1992:
The dance between opposites

As I mentioned earlier, one of the mentoring tools is the shaman as storyteller and ceremonialist, and I would like to share at this point one of my vision quests. As I thought about the story of my trauma and vulnerabilities, I remembered and connected this crucial event of medical and financial stress with my vision quest of 1992. That quest (a Native American ceremony) followed the death of my ex-husband the previous weekend, but the message of the quest also relates to this economic story.

The vision quest was to take place at Deer Dancer Ranch in central Texas, near the small village of Cat Springs. The first night in the encampment, I was asked if I had found my vision site. In those days, I was very withdrawn and somewhat shy, and it did not occur to me to ask my supporters to help me. It was becoming dark quickly, and I found after a short distance that I could not see. I was carrying a red cloth tote filled with my prayer items: a Bible, an abalone shell, sage, a lighter, a pen and a blank journal.

Suddenly, a large owl rose up from the ground flying directly in front of my feet from left to right. Startled and deciding this was the signal for where I should be, I set down my prayer bag. In the future I believe I will contemplate on the fact that the owl flew in front of me just as the hawk later in my vision quest would do. I had not thought of that until now. (Vision quests have a tendency to unfold for years after the event.)

The next day, I discovered that I had been walking on a narrow strip of land between two ponds. There was no shade.

(If I had fallen in a pond in the dark, I would have had a funny story to tell.)

The afternoon was hot; the sweatlodge had been even hotter, and I had a slight headache. Entering my tent and thinking about resting to relieve the pain, I stripped down to my underwear and lay down on my sleeping bag. There was the soft sound of something falling outside my tent. Frustrated, I dressed, left my tent and propped the prayer pole that fell back up in the ground. I barely returned to my tent, when I heard it fall again. Deciding there was no opportunity to avoid it, I went back out and dug enough mud and muck out of the edge of the pond to my east to stand the pole upright. Having dirty hands was not on my "I want" list.

When I awakened in the morning, I took a small rug and sat just outside the tent door. The day was very foggy. I thought to myself, "Nothing has happened on this quest. Will they name me *Sits in a Fog*?" I remained where I was. On my left to the west, the pond was surrounded with grass, and trees were growing beyond it. On my right to the east, the second pond was very muddy without grass or shade of any kind, but there were small fish in the pond.

Suddenly, I felt as if I was being watched. I glanced sideways and discovered a blue heron standing in the seemingly dead, muddy pond. It was facing the same direction that I was.

Sensing something to my left, I glanced up and saw a large brown hawk sitting on top of the west pole that I had had so much difficulty placing upright. As soon as I saw the hawk, it swooped down about a foot off of the ground directly in front of my feet, much as the owl had done. Its wings made a loud "whomp – whomp" sound with each beat. The hawk flew directly to the heron, and the two birds flew straight up in a spiraling dance, and then together flew off toward the east.

Soon after, my supporters came for me, and I was returned to the encampment to speak of my experience with the elders. The evening of the naming ceremony, I was given the nature name *Guarded by Hawk*. The nature name is to assist one on the next leg of one's life path. Little did I know that this leg of the journey would reveal itself as still active seventeen years later in my life-time.

Hawk or eagle being symbols of the transcendent, I have interpreted this name to mean that the blessing of the quest is in being guarded by Spirit. I was grieving and very vulnerable at this time in my life. My last child had just left home. I was retiring from my teaching position, and the man I was married to for thirty-one years had just died of cancer the previous week. I held this new nature name very close to my heart.

Reflecting on this vision quest, different segments have meaning for me. I found myself between two ponds. At one point, my mentor asked me, "What are you *between* in your life, Lillie?" Meditating further on my mentor's question, I realized I was between employment/retirement, mothering/an empty nest and had said a prayer of farewell to a significant person in my life (life/death). The pond that appeared alive, lush and verdant green, had no visible life within it. The other pond that appeared as a mud-hole and totally lifeless supported fish to feed the blue heron. This raised the questions in my mind, "What in my life that I thought was *alive* is dead? Conversely, what in my life that I thought was *dead* is alive?"

I had never seen a hawk fly down six inches from my legs and less than a foot above the ground, nor had I ever seen a hawk spiral upward and fly off in companionship with a blue heron. This event definitely caught my attention! Not only that, but they flew *east*. East on the Medicine Wheel is the direction of new beginnings, new insights, first steps, new dawns, seeking a higher perspective, the search for knowledge and wisdom.

44

Teachings of the quest

It is important to note that the prayers in the direction of the South related to my vulnerabilities of bankruptcy and death are still connected within the East of the Medicine Wheel. The Medicine Wheel is a circle that acts as a spiral. We return around the wheel, but in another space along the circumference as we progress.

As a mentor, I might ask, "How does this quest relate to your current issue surrounding bankruptcy?" Upon reflection, I might answer in the following manner. "My financial situation is 'dead.' I have been forced into using all of my savings and the loss of income I previously earned. The pond in my quest, that appeared dead, supported 'life.' How does this situation support life and hope for me?" Then I remember the heron standing deep in the mud of the pond. I remember how it lifted itself straight up and soared with the hawk. I too can lift myself up in hope and trust and turn toward the East of a new beginning.

Creativity

One of the ways I planned to begin was the notion to sell my house which was more than a single person needs. I had a fairly good equity in the house that would allow me to be financially stronger (like the hawk) in the days ahead. My income is extremely modest, and it is necessary to be cautious, but I am blessed with a beautiful environment in which to live.

There are several benefits in the decisions I made. Should I become quite ill again, my daughter will not have to struggle with selling property. I personally will not have to worry about taxes and upkeep like a new roof or digging a new well. The pond that appeared green and living is very much like the confidence I had in my work and savings before major illness and extremely large medical bills. So, I am between where I was, and where I will direct my financial path in the months ahead.

I remember the ceremony of receiving my nature name *Guarded by Hawk* and the blessing of being guarded by Spirit. (Perhaps, the owl and hawk symbolized, "Stop, and enter the West. Look to Spirit to lift you up.") I hold in my hands the medicine bundle I received at that quest and remember the prayers gifted on my behalf. I am not alone. Like the blue heron, I symbolically fly with the hawk. I remember the powerful sound of its wings. Through the grace of Spirit and the love and support of others, I am strong in my hope for a new beginning.

An attorney told me to file bankruptcy, but that engendered no hope, a strong aspect of the East. Nature gives me a perfect metaphor to enrich my choices and to guide my pathway. Utilizing the experiences in nature for a map to guide the way to new perspectives and choices is the ultimate task of an eco-spiritual mentor. That then raises the question, "How can the mentoring of this issue be approached by a *neo-shaman?*"

William Taegel succinctly states in his book, *The Many Colored Buffalo,* how the nature experience of the vision quest, fasting in silence in the wilderness, has guided and assisted me through the years, opening the way for my inner self to connect with the Higher Power and receive the gifts of inner balance and harmony, awe, mystery and gratitude:

> It is the intensity of the vulnerable selves that reminds us that our aware egos must call on sources of nourishment that are beyond the capabilities of our usual selves. It is the spiritual selves that become conduits to transmit the higher, healing energy to the vulnerabilities as they come forward...(to encounter) the larger resources of Mother Earth,...and of Father Sky.[15]

I give thanks for the vision quest of 1992 that still shines its light on my path today.

Money as a spiritual, sacred gift

Recently, I read an article in *Ode* magazine by Charles Eisenstein entitled "Living in the Gift." It gave me a new perspective on money, and its place in my life. He states:

> Money seems to be the enemy of every worthy social and political reform, as corporate power steers legislature toward the aggrandizement of its own profits. Money seems to be destroying the Earth, as we pillage the oceans, the forest, the soil and every species to feed a greed that knows no end.[16]

Eisenstein calls for a "wholesale revolution in money" in order to "make money into something sacred."[17] How then could this occur? Eisenstein reflects, "For several thousand years, the concepts of sacred, holy and divine have referred increasingly to something separate from nature, the world and the flesh."[18] God became something transcendent—above creation and appeared in the world in "miracles—divine intercessions violating or superseding nature's laws."[19] "It is hugely ironic and hugely significant that the one thing on the planet most closely resembling the forgoing conception of the divine is money. It is an invisible, immortal force that surrounds and steers all things, omnipotent and limitless, an 'invisible hand' that, it is said, makes the world go 'round'."[20]

The abstraction of money has even become on-line banking and trading, data in a computer. "It (money) bears the properties of eternal preservation and everlasting increase (interest), both of which are unnatural (exempt from nature's recycling and decay). The natural substance that comes closest to these properties is gold... Early on, gold was therefore used both as money and as a metaphor for the divine soul, that which is incorruptible and changeless."[21]

With the twenty-first century and Wall Street financiers, money became separated from day to day work, production and reality. Eisenstein calls us to look at the god/divine we have created with money and given "sovereignty over the earth:"[22]

> By divorcing soul from the flesh, spirit from matter,
> and God from nature, we have instilled a ruling
> power that is soulless, alienating, ungodly, and un-
> natural. So when I speak of making money sacred, I
> am...reaching back to an earlier time, a time before
> the divorce of matter and spirit, when sacredness
> was endemic to all things.[23]

Eisenstein defines sacred as having two aspects: "uniqueness and relatedness." In ecology, "this is the principle of interdependence: that all things depend for their survival on the web of other beings that surrounds them, ultimately extending out to encompass the planet. The extinction of any species diminishes our own wholeness, our own health, our own selves; something of our very being is lost."[24] (E. O. Wilson speaks profoundly in his book, *The Future of Life*, on this issue.)

Eisenstein calls for the economy to be an extension of the ecology in order to be sacred. Those things produced by industry would return to the ecology after being fully utilized. Anything that is considered "industrial waste" would become another's food or meet a need. "Why do I call such an economy sacred rather than natural or ecological? It is because of the sacredness of gifts. To obey the law of return is to honor the spirit of the Gift because we receive what has been given to us, and from that gift, we give in turn."[25] The original purpose of money was to exchange gifts. It went something like this: I will give you these shells (money) for the gift of your corn. The shells would then be exchanged for someone else's gift of a woven blanket, and so forth.

Helpless infants are pure need with only their love to give in return. All things come to the infant without having done anything to earn them. These are the first experiences of unmerited gift/love, and it births the concept of gratitude. When we mature into adults, we encounter the face of death at some point. Then we have a sense of awe and gratitude for the moment. This gratitude is a clear sign of the presence of the sacred.

There is no spiritual relationship in a financial transaction, as we know it today. However, a gift is an open tie. The giver shares something of self. For example, I have a beautiful owl wing I received some years ago. Every time I look at it I remember the giver with warm feelings in my heart. Because we recognize the sacredness of gifts intuitively, they have special aspects we recognize in ceremonies of gift giving:

> Gifts embody the key qualities of sacredness. First uniqueness:...they partake of the giver. Second, wholeness, interdependency: Gifts expand the circle of self to include the community. Whereas money today embodies the principle "More for me is less for you," in a gift economy, more for you is also more for me because those who have give to those in need.[26]

Compassion and trust

I would like to share with you my personal story of the sacredness of the gift of a monetary transaction that blessed the giver and the receiver with what Eisenstein calls "the mystical realization of participation in something greater than oneself, which, yet, is not separate from oneself."[27]

I spoke of the gratitude for the vision quest in 1992. There is further gratitude. On December 26, 2010, I met with friends I love for a prayer to sell my house. They were wanting to invest in real estate and had looked at a house I liked. Informing me that they intended to buy the house the following week, we prayed, and I was invited to go home and pray again for what I desired. I had trouble with that. It is so easy in my spirit to pray for others, but I was uncertain how to pray for myself. I simply prayed, "Spirit, I do not know how to ask for myself. I ask that whatever is best in your purpose be served." Placing my Pipe beside me under my hand, I went to sleep.

Two weeks later to the day (on a cold, dreary January Sunday), the house was cash purchased by a couple in less than two hours. They looked at it and went to town for lunch, calling me from the restaurant to make a bid on the house "as is." My realtor on such a dark day was still at home in her house shoes. All of us met within the hour. February 9th at 9:00 a.m., I signed the closing. At 10:00 a.m., my friends closed on the house I liked. At 11:00 a.m., the buyers closed and at 12:00 a.m. my movers were backing out of my old driveway.

Arriving at my new home, I found that my friends had been there, turned on the heat on the coldest day of our winter and left me a note of welcome. At 1:00 p.m., they came, and I had the opportunity to tell them how much I love and appreciate them. What I hold dear to my heart is the "immediacy" of Spirit to answer all of our prayers. I had always heard of this "immediacy," but now my friends and I had experienced it. Deep in my heart is more gratitude than I can express. I had received the gift of unmerited love and caring at a time of serious vulnerability and transition.

The South is the direction of vulnerability, compassion and humor. It is filled with the concept of love and compassion. It embodies the Christian golden rule, as well as the Hopi tenets of peaceful coexistence.[28]

As I send my prayer of gratitude on the Medicine Wheel for the positive and blessed ending of an extremely vulnerable time in my life, I turn on the Medicine Wheel to the direction of the West.

CHAPTER FOUR

The Direction of the West: Terrorism

T he direction of the West is focussed on the process of letting go and gratitude. It is the direction of introspection, endings and our dark aspects. It is where our shadow lies. The endings and letting go make space for new things to grow. There are possibilities and potential. In this direction we meet Spirit through "the dark night of the soul."[1] It is a time of slowing down, waiting.

Symbolism of the West

The symbols of the West are the black bear, the thunderbirds and the woodpecker, who has a role in new birth. There is chaos, the abyss, a test needing a crucial turning point. The color for the West is black. Its musical instruments are the rattling of bones, and its element is earth (and rocks).

The season of the West is Fall. Because of the introspection of the West and its call to let go of those things harmful to our soul, it reminds me of the Ruiz's statement of the Toltec agreement: "Don't make assumptions. Find the courage to ask questions and to express what you really want. Communicate with others as clearly as you can to avoid misunderstandings, sadness, and drama."[2] For if we are conscientious in our reflections and letting go, we have extricated ourselves from the drama, internal or external. Then we can experience gratitude for new hope in the change.

Terrorism:
A pursuit of wisdom in troubling times

"What does the pursuit of wisdom mean to me?" I would like to examine the relationship between the history of civilization and the pursuit of wisdom, and acknowledge that history is on-going. Let us examine a simple day in my life. Then, I will choose and examine another day in my personal history and note how my reflections effect and affect my original thoughts.

The day was Saturday, and I spent the day in a sweatlodge. One of our prayers was to ask Sacred Mystery to open the hearts and minds of those persons elected in the coming fall so that they would be even greater in their governing positions than the selves they now are.

When I arrived back home after the sweatlodge, I checked for e-mail and saw the headline news on the internet.

Shock and terror: the dark side of mankind

I was stunned and heartbroken. The Marriott Hotel in Islamabad, Pakistan had been struck by a terrorist bomb. The headline picture was of four men carrying another by his arms and legs. The victim was either dead or dying. It was obvious he was experiencing a bleed out from his chest.[3] My spirit asked, "Where is God in all this cruel chaos?"

As I read his book, I was especially moved by James Garrison's words, "'God has touched me,' is to be able to face the enigma of God's living participation in evil and in the ways we exercise the gift of freedom."[4] Garrison continues this thought:

> Therefore when Isaiah speaks of the Lord creating
> evil as well as peace and when the Deuteronomist
> declares that God wounds, as well as heals, they are

emphasizing the point that the Divine presence is in all aspects of reality. The statement that must come before and after every confession of faith is "I the Lord do all these things."[5]

Struggle between good and evil and relationship with love

We ask ourselves would Spirit be involved in or cause this situation? Where was the loving God I had been taught? I had this reaction to 9/11 and now this new terrorist situation in Pakistan. How can this be? Yet, in my heart of hearts, I know the souls that committed this act in Pakistan had a notion that they were doing something good for their country. After all, the new leaders were supposed to have been in that building, and these newly elected leaders were only spared by a last minute change of plans. The act was to destroy something perceived in the perpetrators' minds as evil.

I perceive as evil the act the terrorist(s) considered good. This difference in the two perceptions reminded me of the statement Garrison made, "The opposite of one truth can be another equally profound truth."[6] I do not have the wisdom to discern what the greater good would be. I know the facts of what happened. I know a little of the religious, political, economic facts. However, it is a very simple knowledge of the situation. I have no wisdom, discernment, or clear understanding of how individually and collectively societies on both sides of this issue can end this strife. Nor do I know if we are even supposed to end it. All I know is in my soul this is not an act of love.

In discussing this issue with my spiritual mentor, he advised me that in the terrorist's mind, it was an act of love on the red meme of Beck and Cowan's concept of spiral dynamics.[7] The terrorist sees it as love of country. What is Spirit's greater purpose in our current behaviors as human beings around the planet? What will change this untransformed power for the greater good? Upon reflection, the only wisdom I might have at this point is "I do not know."

Prayer in the face of seeming insanity

Just as the participants were doing in the sweatlodge, I turn in prayer to a power greater than myself, to the One. My prayer is, "How can we stop this insanity?" Garrison states, "We tend to pray for God to change an external situation, but when the Spirit comes, the transformation takes place within our souls. Though they yearned for vengeance, the prophets were seeking insight. Though they wanted enemies destroyed, they were actually searching for the wisdom to understand."[8]

Terrorism precludes war

One of my first thoughts after I reacted emotionally to the news of the attack was, "Will we go to war again in Pakistan, like Iraq?" Our country is already rattling sabers and casting political insults back and forth with Iran preliminary to a possible war threat. To what extent will war in the Middle East develop? Will and Ariel Durant tell us, "War is one of the constants of history and has not diminished with civilization or democracy. In the last 3,421 years of recorded history only 268 have seen no war."[9] I can not help but note how many wars have occurred just in my lifetime of 75 years. I'm sure I am not alone in this fear regarding war. The Durants call this a "conscription of the soul to international phobia."[10]

My thoughts regarding the possibility of a broader based war led to meditation on Edith Hamilton's commentary on the Stoics relationship to fear from her book, *The Echo of Greece*. The Stoics maintain that there is nothing and no one in all the world to fear. One is safe and free. What is untouchable is your true self, your essence. Only you can harm it. Only you make yourself good or bad.[11] So what do I fear? Deep within I think I must fear the vulnerability of chaos and violence. I am also vulnerable to the separation of family that impacted me when my father left for World War II. (The direction of the South with its focus on vulnerability informs the direction of the West.)

My soul asks my spiritual mentor many questions, and I learn things like I previously mentioned regarding where each level of development connects with the concept of love. In the red meme, if you hurt me or mine, I will strike you. That protection of self and communal others at the red level of Beck and Cowan's spiral is that particular meme's developmental comprehension of love.[12]

Given all this knowledge, then how might I pray? So what should I do, or think, or believe. I was affected by this poem in T. S. Eliot's, *Collected Poems*:

> I said to my soul, be still, and let the dark come
> upon you. Which shall be the darkness of God...Wait
> without thought, for you are not ready for
> thought...[13]

The truth for me is that my soul has no answers, only confusion, and yet I pray. There seems to be no alternative except to be still, and wait.

Psychological shadows within

There is another reflection and owning of a deep shadow within me that can be a warrior, can kill, that is a predator. It is a very scary shadow within that I discovered in an Earthdance long ago. How then can I judge another?

Boundaries and limits: context for ethics

Edith Hamilton writes that "good for humanity was (is) possible only if men were free: body, mind, and spirit, and if each man limited his own freedom."[14] Perhaps, the last few words of that statement, *"if each man limited his own freedom"* are the beginnings of wisdom for our time. Garrison writes to these thoughts on boundaries and limits, as follows:

> The Yahwist makes the point at the beginning that human beings are subject to God's commands unequivocally and that historical existence means existence within limits... We are finite beings. Human life everywhere is lived within limits. Our relation to limits provides the essential context for ethics.[15]

There are no boundaries to human behavior in terrorism in my thinking, although I know that a conclusion comes out of my own value systems and personal ethics. My mind is troubled by the news event. This countering of my value systems is difficult to process in my thinking. Gradually, I am beginning to address the "witness state" of which Marcus Aurelius spoke.[16]

Yet, in the history of my lifetime, the following statement by Garrison seems to have manifested itself, "The twentieth century surpassed every other period in recorded history in brutality, violence, sacrilege, and destructiveness... It has not ceased in the 21st (century)."[17] As a child, however, my family and neighbor families never worried about home invasion with our open screens and unlocked doors. I experienced limits placed on my behaviors and an intensive religious training by my parents and grandparents. After we were successful in World War II, we, as a country, did not seem to fear invasion on our native soil. September 11, 2001 (9/11) was a major shock point. The sense of safety in my personal environment was present in my developmental years, but is now contradicted by the weapons my students carried to class, the street violence and terrorist activities of this generation.

The resolution to these dangerous issues is extremely complex in my mind. Garrison asserts that the feminine "infuses knowledge with faith and transforms power through crucified wisdom..."

> (The) ordering principle of creation, which the feminine represents, offers us a moral basis for knowledge and a moral limit for power... (Positive) and transformational aspects of the feminine...are jointly the gateway to the individuation of the psyche and the grace of the Spirit.[18, 19]

In the Native American tradition the direction of the South is feminine (as is Grandmother Earth). It represents, as was mentioned in the previous chapter, birth, creativity, humor, truth and vulnerability. It will require all of the creativity, humor, and truth that we pray for in the lodge and in the intentions of our communities to change and re-birth the world in which we live. Never has our country seemed so deeply vulnerable since the Civil War.

Political issues and the cruciform nature of reality

To return once again to the sweatlodge and how my day began with prayer regarding the political leadership of our country, Hamilton would say of Plato, "But mark well, this is the true preparation for the political life, because only if a man has knowledge of what is true and good can he lead men to bring about a good state, to change injustice, to put self-control in the place of outside control."[20]

The leadership of our country for the future will depend on our choices. Are the candidates we wish to vote for in the upcoming elections in touch with their inner souls? This raises the question for me, as I prepare to vote, "Do I have the wisdom to discern from all the rhetoric which candidate(s) best meet this criteria of *the true and good*?" It returns my heart and mind again to the shock of reading of the terrorist attack and my deep compassion for the victim in the photograph. Our choice of leadership will be a major force in the unfolding world events we see each day.

Garrison reminds us that "human life is played out on the anvil of tragedy and hope," and he notes that Carl Jung would teach "a fundamental truth about the cruciform nature of reality is that reality is not simply an 'either/or proposition'... Everything in our experience is comprised of opposites, and all things evolve through time within a pattern of life, death, and renewal."[21]

Reflecting on these thoughts, I weigh carefully what information I receive each day as political campaigns and world events unfold. I note the tragedy, and I hope for the good and true. Personally, the pursuit of wisdom means to seek understanding out of knowledge and experience and live with compassion and awareness. Wisdom requires a lifetime of learning and an intention of discernment. It requires a world with limits and ethics, a world where issues can be resolved with understanding and compromise, a world without violence as mankind evolves above the red meme of anger and war.[22] If enough of us set our intentions in that direction, I believe it is potentially possible. Mankind can evolve to a higher plane. That, as I have prayed often, is my hope.

Terrorism is ongoing, shaping our unconscious minds and psychological responses.

Some weeks after the attack on the hotel in Pakistan, I woke on Thanksgiving morning following a dream. In the dream, it is night; we are being attacked by men in helicopters:

> My young brother fled to the woods at my command, where I knew he would be safe. I ran for a small single-car garage, much like the one my

grandfather had on his property. As the searchlight swept the grounds and across the garage window, I stacked paint cans in front of the front bumper of an old truck and quickly cast a paint tarp over the cans and crawled underneath to hide. The helicopter landed, just as I hid. Praying I was fully covered, I waited. The men came to the garage and swept the beam of a flashlight under the old truck. One man said, "There is nothing here but an old truck and some old paint cans." The men left for the house which was fully lit. I was wondering if it was safe to climb into the truck to sleep and awoke from the dream. (Author, 2008)

I have a Yorkshire terrier named Brennan, so I arose and took him outside. After fixing breakfast, I checked my e-mail.

To my horror, once again there had been a terrorist attack. This time it was in Mumbai, India. The terrorists had attacked two hotels, the train station, a hospital and a Jewish center. People were hostages in the luxury hotels. "Authorities said 119 people died and 288 were injured when suspected Islamic militants—armed with assault rifles, hand grenades and explosives—launched a highly coordinated attack against ten sites in the city Wednesday night... The attackers had specifically targeted Britons and Americans inside the hotels, witnesses said... Dozens of people were also apparently hiding..."[23]

Several nationalities were killed, including Australian, Japanese, Italian and German victims. Some of the people huddled under tables in the dark, trying not to be seen. Police and military personnel began rescue efforts immediately. Fire ladders were used to pluck people off of balconies; helicopters circled. Chaos reigned with desperate efforts.

There was a picture of a young mother. She was standing outside the attacked hospital waiting for the bodies of her two small children. My heart went out to her. There can be no consolation for such a loss.

At the same time, the Jewish center was attacked, and Rabbi Gabriel Holtzberg and his wife Rivka were later discovered assassinated with three others. A cook heard their two year old son screaming. She risked her life, opened the door, grabbed the toddler, whose pants were soaked with blood, and ran out of the building. In the main hotel, a male cook was carrying a small baby. Evidently, very small children and workers were not included in the assault.[24]

I saw pictures of two of the assailants. They were very young, in their twenties, and smiling. They had carried bags of almonds into the points of attack for sustenance, much like teenagers carry snacks to school and events.[25] When I later mentioned their age to my mentor, he taught me that the teenage years have an increase in sociopathic tendencies, which makes it easy to indoctrinate and influence them to violence.[26]

One of my thoughts was the attack was possibly toward the Jewish community and the Americans who support Israel, and to avoid a possible response from Israel, a diversion was created by the other attacks. There seemed to be no point in trying to rationalize the events, but the mind tries to do that. I felt I had come almost full circle from the day I read the news and considered the first attack, so I decided to look at what changes may have occurred in my thinking. Garrison elaborates, "The supreme command of the Greeks was that of the Delphic oracle, made immortal by Socrates: 'Know thyself.' Out of this profound insight came the first democratic impulse in history and the flowering of a culture centered around the pursuit of truth, beauty, and goodness that influences us to the present day."[27] How can one possibly find "truth, beauty, and goodness" in the intent of these events? (Though it is evident in the story of the cook, who rescued the toddler.)

My heart, mind and soul find it difficult to accept these events with any equanimity. One thought is helpful:

> It must be said that any wisdom gained in trying to understand momentous events, particularly those in which one is actually involved, is often elusive... (Understanding) comes slowly, painfully, and only after deep reflection... (Our) thoughts change as our subjective interactions with the event deepens, as they will...with the passage of time and America's own maturation...[28]

After reading the news so close after my dream, I felt I must have touched into Rupert Sheldrake's "morphic resonance" field in some manner, or an eco-field that included guns and helicopters.[29] I had a similar experience prior to the 9/11 attack. My parents used to tell me that if I had a premonition prior to a trip, they would not travel. Evidently, this is a sensitivity with which I was born. I don't know the origin. I just know it occurs.

There is another sensitivity that appears in my mind to be occurring. Garrison speaks of this phenomenon. "Especially since 9/11, Americans have been extremely sensitized to real or perceived threats and have tended to divide the world into forces of good and evil, seeking finality and victory over the forces of darkness."[30]

My heart is very troubled by the wounding and deaths. As I write this book, a young man in Norway has bombed a building and attacked and killed many children in a summer island encampment. The news media wants to debate whether he is sane or insane.[31] It is the eternal question, "Why?," which is not a question, but a psychological cry of pain. I do not believe I am alone in this thinking.

In March 2008, as I came near death in the emergency room, I was calm and accepting of the thought of my death at that moment. What makes this type of death so different for me is the utter chaos, sudden violence and lack of constraint on human behavior. I am returned to my original struggle to accept that the terrorist(s) is expressing the good from the point of love of country or ideals; I keep looking for the goodness of Spirit.

In my reading, as I thought on these matters, the following words resonated with me, as Garrison speaks of what motivates us most of the time is a sincere desire to do good, to manifest the light, and motivates our religious traditions:

> If we look back over time, the pattern we see is
> whereas the quest for light provides the biggest in-
> spiration, the quest for power—as the ancient
> Hebrew understood—(is) the ultimate seduction. The
> drive for power lies at the root of competitiveness,
> ...the impetus for knowledge,...the goal of ambition,...
> (and) compels us to violate the wisdom of limits.[32]

When Power becomes force.

This is true, but psychologically, we have a shadow side, which manifests out of our ambitions, and light or goodness becomes corrupted. The light is sacrificed for our own ends and expediency. Power is used for its own sake, and then becomes force. Power becoming force lies at the heart of empire.

Upon reflection, I remember again the owning of a deep shadow within me that can be a warrior, can kill, that is a predator. That warrior is extremely powerful and invincible. It is a very scary shadow that I would prefer did not exist. What is this darkness built into our psyches?

In my personal thinking, I believe this is partially the basis of terrorism, as well. (*We can scare you into submission to our power.*) For me the terrorist is seeking power through force, the dark side of man's soul, the dark, war and bloodshed side of the red meme.[33] This is a deep journey into the West.

The terrorists were singling out British, United States citizens and Jewish people, as a priority. Garrison speaks of this emotional reaction of the Arabic world following French and British colonialism that effects the Palestinians so profoundly:

> From the point of view of their enemies (in these
> cases, the terrorists) Americans are guilty of major
> crimes against them, thus their hatred and violence
> against the United States... In the Middle East in particular... The crowning insult came in 1948 when the
> state of Israel was established by Western fiat and
> European Jews were given Arab land in Palestine.[34]

As I contemplate, it occurs to me that I was twelve years old when Israel was formed. I remember people around me discussing how terrible the holocaust was. I remember seeing films and reading *Anne Frank*. The choices America was making seemed so good and right, so greatly needed.

Now I perceive the evil that can come out of seemingly good choices. (The power of our country's choices became force in the eyes of the Palestinians and others.) I have no right to judge a terrorist without understanding his heart; yet, I judge the act. It brings humility to my self-righteous anger, as I observe these terrorist acts unfold almost daily.

Garrison asserts, "Terrorism does not arise in a vacuum. It is rooted in historical, political, social, and economic dysfunctions so deep, so cruel, and so institutionalized that they create and sustain discontent until it spills over into desperation."[35] Acts like those of September 11, Pakistan and Mumbai, require meticulously planned, methodical precision of groups that are sophisticated and committed with their lives to a vision of something more than individual hatreds. Most of us do not live with that depth of hatred or religious fervor. Garrison relates this terrorism to the more than four thousand Kamikaze pilots of World War II, who knew they would die in their mission.[36]

Osama bin Laden has now been assassinated by the United States government. It remains for the future what impact his death will have on the world of terrorism and al-Qaeda.

In my dream, the attacking helicopter crew did not seem like a Robin Hood situation, nor did the news from Mumbai. It brought to my mind the "big bad wolf and the three little pigs," or another tale of *Little Red Riding Hood* (the archetypes of hunter and prey).

In the beginning of this chapter, I wondered if we would fight again as a nation on yet another front in Pakistan. Garrison states, "Few acknowledged that the nation was in the grip of a Jacksonian act of vengeance, that it might be affected by a form of post-traumatic stress disorder."[37] And if we were not suffering PTSD, then CNN every night with a blow by blow sound and picture of war would bring it about. The question was, "Would our new President Barack Obama follow in the footsteps of President George Bush in a Jacksonian manner?" Garrison noted the following:

> In defining the American response to 9/11 as a war, the Bush administration was able to use the occasion to refine American foreign policy and enunciate the Bush doctrine henceforth, the United States will engage in "anticipatory self-defense" and "preemptive deterrence"...to combat the evils of terrorism, and it was the opportunity to expand American military power massively around the world.[38]

As I experienced 9/11, it was the same reaction I experienced in the past with Pearl Harbor. Our nation is at war. President Bush's reaction is highly understandable, but personally, I can not see that it was effective. In my mind it only creates more chaos and hatred. It is like when one slaps a child and says, "Do not hit." It is illogical. Garrison succinctly stated this concept:

When you fight fire with fire, the fire is not always
vanquished. It can lead instead to a conflagration
that burns beyond any borders, particularly if you
are fighting a fire that is considered holy, and doing
so in a world without boundaries.[39]

There were other choices, but these choices were not considered. I have read of these choices in other news articles and
in points made by Garrison, "The point was made that in the af-
termath of trauma there is often a bifurcation in the affected
group between community and lawlessness."[40] This split led to
the decision by President Bush and our leaders for immediate
vengeance. These articles and Garrison suggest we could have
used military reprisals in conjunction with the United Nations
and not proceeded as a nation alone. Thus, "Defining the events
as crimes against humanity would have relegated Osama bin
Laden and al-Qaeda to the status of common criminals and
mass murderers."[41] This would have allowed military action,
time for international reaction, and also explored the underlying social human rights and humanitarian issues that are now
before the United Nations.[42]

Andrew Bacevich addressed this issue in his 2008 interview with Bill Moyers:

They (*the terrorists*) succeeded because we let our
guard down and we were stupid. We need to recognize that the threat posed by violent Islamic radical-
ism, by terrorist organizations, al-Qaeda, really is
akin to a criminal conspiracy, a dangerous conspiracy. But it's a criminal enterprise. And the primary
response to a criminal enterprise is policing.[43]

The situation seems to me overwhelming with no favor-
able end in sight. Yet, I continue to pray, as I did in learning
about the first incident in Pakistan following the sweatlodge.

Seeking light, hope and coherence in the transformation of chaos

The night before the presidential election in 2008, Will Taegel invited people to join him in prayer for the leadership of this country at the 2:00 a.m. Pipe ceremony. I arose and lifted my Pipe to join with his. My intention was that whomever our new leaders would be, they would seek a new path for our nation and seek a global solution to all the masculine violence. I prayed that the static feminine traits of waiting, compassion and stillness would emerge on this planet.

The next day, I learned that Barack Obama had been elected President of the United States in an unprecedented landslide vote. For me, this was a momentous step for our nation. It was so important in my spirit that I rose again the next morning at 2:00 a.m. to pray again. It seems to me that as a people we have projected an archetype on this man much like the king spoken of in Bacon's *New Atlantis*:

> There raigned in this Island, about 1900 yeares agoe,
> a King, whose memory of all others we most adore;
> Not Superstitiously, but as Divine Instrument,
> though a Mortall Man: His Name was Solamona:
> And we esteeeme him as the Law-giver of our Nation. This King had a large heart, inscrutable for
> good; And was wholly bent to make his Kingdome
> and People Happy.[44]

We look for President Barack Obama to be as wise as Solomon of the Bible, to be the Solamona of Atlantis. In his acceptance speech, President Obama stated:

> And to all those watching tonight from beyond our
> shores...our stories are singular, but our destiny is
> shared... And to all those who have wondered if
> America's beacon still burns as bright...the true
> strength of our nation comes from the enduring

power of our ideals: democracy, liberty, opportunity, and unyielding hope.[45]

The inner question is, "What is America's beacon?" Garrison states:

> ...the United States has sought to bring freedom to an unfree world. Envisioning a nation of light did not mean being naïve about society or governance- Following the teachings of Bacon and the political philosopher Thomas Hobbes, the founding fathers were profoundly realistic about human nature; understanding that government had to take it into account, not try to change it.[46]

If the nation is to be a beacon of light, Garrison calls the nation to remember the fall of Atlantis at the height of its power in the current face of the crises of the planet at this time and to go back to our originating principles before the nation pursued power. "It is America's failure to grasp this necessity that constitutes the major part of the world's current danger."[47]

These dangers spill over into all aspects of our lives. In recent weeks, I have watched intently the ongoing struggle with our lawmakers and the President to come to terms with the national budget. The country was/is facing serious risk of default and bankruptcy. Chaos seemed to reign in the meetings. It remains to be seen if the compromises that resulted in a bill to raise the debt ceiling will be effective. Our military will be downsized, and some medical cuts will be made which will impact medical providers and the public. Things are serious. The only seemingly reasonable voice I noted came from Senator Reid, but I realize many voices were not heard by the media. President Obama seemed to be struggling with his decisions regarding how to solve an imminent problem with the chaos of the political factions. The light seems very dim.

It seems good that we will be reducing our military oblig-ations and calling troops back home, but is it? Will a military financial cut place us in greater danger from terrorists? Will we try to balance our out of control national debt and still cause further chaos? These are unanswerable questions in my mind.

President Obama and all of us were/are seeking the light for our country. When I speak of light, I think of my tendency to pray about incidents in my life. What I am becoming more aware of is that prayer is what the terrorists and others are do-ing, as well.

For instance, what promoted Osama Bin Laden's appeal to his constituents and troops was his dedication to his religion. He was from his viewpoint not engaging in terrorism (the wan-ton destruction of civilians), per se. Bin Laden was leading *jihad*, a holy war, against what he considered infidels. This attitude comes from the deepest roots of Islam, wherein the prophet Muhammad divided the world into believers and non-believ-ers. People of the United States and other Western countries were in his mind not sacred and a threat to Islamic believers.

This attitude or perspective is also true of the Jewish and Christian apocalyptic traditions. All three monotheistic reli-gions within their fundamentalists maintain essentially the same views, although with different emphases and details; "God is on our side, and in the end will destroy the infidels."[48] Therefore, the mixture of perceived humiliation in the Middle East at the hands of the United States and deep theological be-liefs of the Islamic world will continue to motivate al-Qaeda and other Islamic terrorist groups to continue a holy war against impurities within their religion and against the infidel to obtain the redemption they believe is their just reward.[49]

Osama bin Laden fought on until he was killed in his home May 2011. Others will assume his leadership, because it is a *jihad*. This was his pathway:

If this were not true, why believe? As the credo of the
Muslim Brotherhood states: "God is our objective; the
Quran is our constitution; the Prophet is our leader;
struggle is our way; and death for the sake of God is
the highest of our aspirations (*Therefore, the young terrorists in Mumbai smile, as they go out to kill.*)."[50]

This leads me to reflect on my own pathway. Do I not try
to seek the highest good? Do I not try to live a godly life? Just
how fundamentalist am I? Do these desires differ from those of
Osama bin Laden and the terrorist? Where in my inner council,
deep in the shadows, is my own inner terrorist? When I start
asking these questions, then I know I can not "cast the first
stone," as I was taught in Sunday School when a child. Once
again, I must return to the wisdom of Socrates:

If, therefore, one wishes to find out the cause of anything, how it is generated or perishes or exists...all
that is proper for man to seek about this and
everything is only the perfect and the best; but the
same man necessarily knows the worse, too, for the
same knowledge includes both.[51]

So then, what choices can we make regarding 9/11 and
the traumas I have been concerned with in the news recently?
Garrison calls us as a nation to be more empathetic to the griev-
ances held by the terrorists and suggests the following:

If Americans can prove as willing to combat the
roots of terrorism as they are the terrorists themselves, then light will have come from the darkness
and wisdom will have come from the excesses of
hatred and war. America will have learned the wisdom of limits,...(in) an increasingly complex and in-
terdependent world, no country is an island and no
nation has a monopoly on either sorrow or virtue.
(*Nor, do I believe I/we have God in our personal pocket.*)[52]

My thinking returns to the election of President Obama, and the hopes we have for leadership, as I originally joined in praying for earlier in this chapter. I reiterate. We hope for a Solomon to lead us. We hope for a leader that will guide us to a global community of peace and prosperity. Only time will tell if there will be success or failure with regard to our national hope. Beyond our own national boundaries other nation states are struggling. Greece is in a financial disaster. Somalian and Ethiopian citizens are starving from massive drought. The world needs hope and light in so many areas. We are truly in the dark depths of the direction of the West.

There has been a great amount of thought going through my mind as I monitor the news each day. These were not issues that were usually in the forefront of my awareness. I still find terrorism evil, but I recognize that there is a deep seated religious stance within me that I must own. That stance gives me some empathy for the soul of the terrorist. I can not condone terrorism because in my mind it is a crime committed against innocents. In noting this, I realize I must let go of my innocence. That is a basic tension between psychology and my childhood Christian upbringing that all God created is good. There is a need to let go of my belief that people are basically good and face the reality that we all have a dark side, and sometimes it may dominate our ego.

This thought gives me more breathing room. I was taught from my earliest years to be good, and that God, the great Father in the sky, was in heaven keeping a ledger of when I was not. That was terrifying to me as a child. I truly believe only each individual aspiring to know their inner world and motivations and recognizing those of others will bring us into community with one another.

I return to my original longing for greater compassion and awareness. I continue to set my prayer and intention on a world less filled with darkness. My heart is filled with gratitude for those glimmers of light I see in the cook that rescued the toddler from the Jewish center in Pakistan, and the men trying to save the wounded man in Mumbai.

How then would one look at the shadow side of man? How is gratitude expressed when man turns from a dark path, or what seems evil becomes good? Can we turn from vengeance and war? Can we turn from the concept of "my God is the only path?"

Hope, compassion and transformation

There is a spiritual response that brings light for my soul into this dark aspect of our souls called terrorism. In response to the September 11, 2001 terrorist attacks, citizens of the United States have formed non-profit groups to assist others in times of trauma as a commemoration for the loved ones who died in the attacks we call 9/11.

"When Jeff Parness heard Mayor Rudy Giuliani say in 2003 that people were forgetting the meaning of September 11, 2001, forgetting about the love and support that strangers showed one another...he thought about...the friend he lost, Hagay Shefi."[53] Parness wanted to teach his son about compassion and sharing. His son had been effected by the news of the California wildfires. The child wanted to send his old toys to the children. "That's when Parness realized that he could help both those who had been directly affected by September 11, and those who have been overcome by other tragedies. Parness decided that 'New York Says Thank You' would serve as more than just an inspiring banner."[54] He gathered together 100 survivors of victims as volunteers, and they have provided assistance with U-Haul trailers of supplies, rebuilding a barn for rehabilitation of special needs children and many other ministries. The group has grown to more than a thousand volunteers.

71

The compassion of these citizens, who are in a sense victims, gives me hope in the light for the future.

"You can tell the character of a man by what he does for the man who can offer him nothing," wrote Bradley Fetchet in his journal three years before he died in the south tower on 9/11."[55] In his memory a non-profit group called *Voices* was formed within a month of the attack and provides social services support for families and works toward promotion of security changes.

Bear Heart would say, "It's time to stress the things we have in common... We might be surprised to find we are really all brothers and sisters in this universe, and most important; that we have to maintain that relationship in order to survive."[56] These are helpful thoughts to me from the indigenous nature-based world, as I struggle in my mind with the Christian perspective that "God is in His heaven, and all is right in this world."

Terrorism is the shadow side of man manifested in tension with the light of love and goodness. I am well aware both aspects are within me, and they are also manifested in the terrorists that cause me deep pain and trouble my soul. There is gratitude within me that I can see the goodness of humankind in the efforts to help others and work toward a better world for all. It is a struggle between deep opposites.

Black Elk had a vision on Harney Peak that shines a ray of hope:

> (Round) about beneath me was the whole hoop of the world. And while I stood there I saw more than I can tell and I understood more than I saw... And I saw that the sacred hoop of my people was one of many hoops that made one circle,...and in the center grew one mighty flowering tree to shelter all the children of one mother and one father. And I saw that it was holy.[57]

Would that all people could have Black Elk's vision and begin to have compassion for the belief systems of each other.

Still considering and praying about these issues, I turn in prayer to the North on the Medicine Wheel and reflect on war, a more overt terrorism. I think of the young warrior, the masculine energy.

CHAPTER FIVE

The Direction of the North: Finding My Path Through War, Violence and Spiritual Emergency

The direction of the North is masculine in intent. Its attributes are discipline, practice and practicality, strength, organization, purpose, meditation and healing (cleansing winds of change and purification). It is a mental direction, as well as physical.

Symbolism of the North

The symbols of the North are the color red and the buffalo (abundance). Its musical instrument is the rattle of seeds or small stones (like those from anthills). The element of the North is air (and wind).

Black Elk addresses a prayer to the North:

Behold, O you Baldheaded Eagle; there where the giant *Waziah* (north) has his lodge! Wakan Tanka has placed you there to control this Path (north to south —the "good red road"); you are there to guard the health of the people, that they may live. Help us with your cleansing wind! May it make us pure so that we may walk the sacred path in a holy manner, pleasing to Wakan Tanka.[1]

Dave Abram in *The Spell of the Sensuous* notes the following, "The Navajo elders suggest that that which we call 'mind' *is not ours,* is not a human possession. Rather mind as Wind is a property of the encompassing world."[2] "The Greek word psyche signified not merely the 'soul,' or the 'mind,' but also a 'breath,' or a 'gust of wind'."[3] When I breathe, or the wind touches my body, or echoes in my ears, I am hearing and sensing the breath of "All That Is." It is interesting to me that the culture speaks of "the winds of war" and at the same time connects wind and breath with Spirit.

I think this direction fits the Toltec agreement "to always do your best. Your best is going to change from moment to moment. It will be different when you are healthy as opposed to sick. Under any circumstance simply do your best and you will avoid self judgement, self abuse, and regret."[4] This direction has an investigative open-mindedness.

War, mentoring and the soul

The issue of "war, mentoring and the soul" is perhaps a more difficult topic to address. My tendency has been to think in terms of war as "over there." September 11, 2001 (9/11) was an occurrence that tended to continue to remove my "blinders," as did the media with its ongoing filming of the recent wars and sending it to our televisions via satellite technology. The terrorist war incident was literally the "elephant in the middle of the living room."

It is my privilege to have a friend, Larry Winters, who is a veteran of Vietnam, willing to share his experiences and feelings with others. At the conclusion of a talk by Larry, he presented a poem that he had written that had been combined with music and sung by a vocal artist. It was an incredibly moving and beautiful insight into the soul of a warrior. I suggest that his book, *The Making and Unmaking of a Marine,* was and is very worthwhile to read.

Larry Winters returned to Viet Nam on a healing mission for himself and other veterans. One of the veterans asked in a meeting with Viet Nam officers, "General Diep (who was sixty-eight years old and had been in the military for fifty years), Sir, how do you feel about the men you have known that were killed by Americans?"[5] Winters reports what the general, who had fought the French, Chinese and Americans, replied:

> (War) is not in the hearts of our people... When I was fighting in Cambodia my troops had surrounded 5,000 Chinese soldiers. I had seen so much death at this point; there was no need for more... I (told) them to retreat back to China and I would not follow... The suffering of our enemy contributes to the suffering of us all...

"A tear dropped from his eye."[6]

Personal encounter with the threat of war

As we spoke of war and its impact on our lives, I began to recall incidents in my own personal history. My husband was a warrior in the Signal Corps of the United States Army. In early spring of 1958, my husband John and five others were sent to Jordan to install radio equipment in thirty-three tanks King Hussein had bought with monies supposedly allotted for Syrian refugees fleeing their political situation.[7]

In February of 1958, Iraq and Jordan had formed an alliance in response to Syria and Egypt creating the United Arab Republic. The United States was supporting this alliance. Although John and others were attached to the Signal corps in Pirmasens, Germany, their passports designated the men as civilians to prevent notice. Beck and Cowan would entitle and define these military groupings part of the red meme:

> RED-dominated periods are marked by warlords, exploration, exploitation, empires, and the idea that

nature is there to be exploited... RED stubbornly res-
ists power exercised over it...this raw self-assertive
power contributes to a positive sense of control, lets
the group break away from constraining pro forma
traditions, and energizes a society to reach the very
ends of the earth.[8]

Before John left Jordan, King Hussein gave a party for the six men on his palace grounds. Only the king and high-ranking military officers were there. The feast was similar to a Texas barbecue. A sheep's head was served on a platter of rice with natural gravy poured over it. It was eaten with the hands. As a delicacy, the guest of honor received the eyeballs. My husband told me that he was never so pleased to be outranked.

John returned to Germany in May, and at his request, I flew overseas to join him. At twenty-one years of age, I was totally ignorant of the political climate surrounding me. My life was centered on being a new wife, finding work and returning to my parents' home, when my new husband was drafted and going through his training and assignments. We then lived in Augusta, Georgia for a few months, until John was reassigned to Germany. I was to ultimately live in Germany for the next twelve to thirteen months.

It would be fifty years and researching this topic before I would learn of the politics surrounding the events of 1958. On July 14th, King Hussein's cousin, King Faisal II of Iraq, was assas-sinated along with several members of his family.[9] King Faisal was born May 2 of 1935 and had already survived a coup in 1941. His father had been slain in a suspicious car accident when Faisal was three years old. King Hussein was born on November 14, 1935.[10] My husband was born August 2, 1934, and I was born November 15, 1936. All of us were in our early twenties, very young and innocent. The brain itself has not fully formed at that age. The United States immediately mobilized and sent troops into Lebanon to prevent invasion in that country and to provide a buffer, as well, for King Hussein in Jordan.[11]

Our first inkling that this event was occurring was in the early morning hours of July 15th. Somewhere between two and four a.m., two military policemen entered our second floor bedroom without knocking and commanded John to put on his battle gear and appear at the gate. They were going to pick up another soldier in Muenchweiler and would be back in fifteen minutes. I was nearly hysterical and nervously laughing because I could not hook John's canteen into his web belt. I asked him how he would carry his rifle. John told me that it was strapped on top of his radio equipment. I remember thinking that was no help.

The military police told me that I and other dependents were to appear at the base the next morning for instructions. When we assembled, we were told to place water, non-perishable food we could carry, comfortable clothing, a coat, a blanket and a flashlight by our bedsides. We were given IBM punch cards that identified us. If sirens were heard, or the balloons were mounted above the base, we were to dress quickly, wear walking shoes and start the journey across western Germany, France, and on to the coast. Hopefully, ships would be there to evacuate us. If a mother had more than two children, we were instructed to take the cards of one of them and help her escort her family to safety. If people had cars, they were to take as many as possible, drive until the gasoline tank was empty, and then abandon the car. I walked alone back to the farmhouse where we lived. We waited.

My father sent a message requesting that I come home. The flights had been commandeered to move military personnel, and I was stranded in Germany. I did not speak German or French.

Daily, I watched as missiles and other ordinance bedded in straw were being moved continuously on the road in front of the house in the countryside where I lived. The Russians moved tanks to the border of Eastern and Western Germany. The military base was on full alert. I was afraid, but acted as if I was not.

A few days later, John came home for dinner. His Signal Corps unit was attached to a French unit, so he was not flown out with the rest of the base during the night of the 15th with the unit assigned in Germany. We continued to wait. It was several months before the situation in the Middle East calmed down, and the troops were removed from Lebanon that fall. The base returned to normal status. If John knew what was occurring politically, he was not allowed to tell me.

Spiritual warriors and the bond of violence

In the winter, Frau Ebert, my German landlady, told me laundry was hung in the attic of the farmhouse. When I went up the stairs to the third level, I discovered a full German dress uniform and a duffel bag hanging there. I asked Frau Ebert, as we made anise cookies for Christmas one day, whose uniform it was. It belonged to her son, who was killed at Bastogne. To my surprise Frau Ebert informed me that his widow had married an American soldier during the occupation and was now living in Kentucky with their grandchildren.

I find this amazing. Some of the people in Pirmasens were very bitter toward the Americans. Pirmasens was a shoe making town and made boots for the German army. The town had been leveled three times during World War II. Most of the citizens, however, were very kind and friendly.

Edward Tick speaks of this phenomenon in his book, *War and the Soul*:

> The idea of killing as creating a sacred bond may startle, but the truth is that war is an intimate act.

> Whether we intend it or not, we achieve a perman-
> ent shared history with those we battle... We also
> cannot separate the history of the modern era from
> that of Nazi Germany, or...Korea or Viet Nam. We
> are all in the Spanish peasant's sense of the word,
> "married" through our mutual violence.[12]

Fred Gustafson in *Dancing Between Two Worlds: Jung and the Native American Soul* speaks to this issue of the bond created by violence, as follows: "It is a law of the soul that it is impossible to heap such violence on another person or people without simultaneously heaping it on ourselves..., so a people who violate the earth and others who dwell on it violate themselves as fellow inhabitants."[13]

When the crisis ended, I was like a young adult/child again. Herr and Frau Ebert were very good to me. They treated me like part of their family. I was as welcome there, as the veterans that returned to Viet Nam with Edward Tick. The Eberts were an example of his reference to the compassion of everyday people that can occur on a larger scale. Edward Tick calls us to pull our hearts and minds from vengeance and to become spiritual warriors that have compassion and redress for everyone's suffering:

> We must rely on rationality at all times, we must
> revere all beings, especially those who differ from us
> in ways that threaten us, and we must remain
> humble before those powers that should never be
> under our fallible control... The World Court, not
> world war. The council chamber, not the war coun-
> cil. The appeal to reason, not the power of force.[14]

I was too young to comprehend the spiritual warrior depth of the Eberts, but I recognize it today.

Herr Ebert was always teasing me about riding on the back of his treasured motorcycle. Affectionately, he teased me in other ways, as well. When I first arrived in Germany and went to live on the farm, I kept hearing this strange sound (sort of a popping noise). I came cautiously down the stairs. Herr Ebert must have thought the look on my face was funny, because he teased me, "The Russkis are coming. The Russkis are going to get you." It was the bubbling, popping sounds of new wine fermenting in the kegs. Another time, I tried to make home-made bread. It was so hard and flat, we put it out for the chickens. Herr Ebert cut the shape of a shoe out of it. There was love and humor in our lives.

Edward Tick states, "Post-traumatic stress symptoms, then, can diminish or disappear when we reconcile with our deepest moral and spiritual convictions about the sacredness of life."[15]

Cyclical, generational history of war

Some years later, I was to experience the same feeling of anxiety that occurred with the entry of the military police, as my son, then in the Marines, was to be deployed to the Gulf War from Cherry Point, North Carolina. Fearing for his safety in this war threat to my son, I drove to Cherry Point from Texas in two days time, thinking it was possibly the last time I might ever see him. Again, I saw military personnel being transported in civilian Greyhound buses all along Interstate 20. When I reached Cherry Point, huge helicopters were ferrying war ordinance and personnel on to the decks of immense war ships in a continuous stream. Once again, my loved one was spared. President Bush changed my son's attachment orders and left the personnel already in place overseas for an extended tour of duty. My son then spent the next months tracking personnel and war supplies by computer.

War has constantly touched the lives of my family. My great, great grandfather was a Union physician and died helping others on the battlefield at Gettysburg. My grandfather was in World War I, and one of my great uncles suffered from mustard gas in that war. My other great, great grandfather was on the Confederate side of the war and brought his family from south of Shiloh and Harden County, Tennessee to Texas. When I was a child, that branch of my family still stood when Dixie was played. I have another grandfather several generations removed who died in the War for Independence.

When I was five years old, my father left for World War II and returned the spring before I turned ten years old. I remember going to San Antonio when he finished boot camp. I could not find him in all the hundreds of men marching. I remember the radio announcements of Pearl Harbor and being afraid because my parents were afraid. I also remember black-out shades, rationing, and making bandages and small boxes of personal items at school to be shipped overseas.

Some of my classmates in high school died in Korea.

My life has been touched often by war, rumors of war and family stories of war. My coping skill has been to try to put it at the back of my mind and not think about it if possible. This book and others I mention brought these memories and thoughts to a conscious level. There seems to be no end to the conflict in the Middle East. It has continued over my entire lifetime. War seems to be what constantly involves the United States. Bogart noted in his study that we have been in conflict or mobilized "159 times from October 1945 through December 2006."[16]

Inner spiritual and psychological changes

Consideration of the spiritual ramifications of these events is something new in my awareness. As a child, I prayed for the safety of my father and worried and grieved his loss. I prayed to be reunited with my husband and for the safety of my son. My prayer life became broader with the television news of the Gulf War, and later, Desert Storm. I began to pray for the soldiers and their families, and the civilians caught in the maelstrom on both sides of the conflict. My heart ached for them. There is an even larger spiritual story beginning to unfold for me. What is the meaning and purpose of all this war and aggression—death and threats of death? How fruitless it is for a healer like my ancestor to die on a "killing field."

John and I were young and innocent as our lives were impacted by events beyond our control, as was my son and my father. King Faisal was barely more than a boy, as was King Hussein, yet the machinations of power and control were molding our lives.

Edward Tick has one possible answer for me:

> Our goal is not just to awaken the soul; that is what childhood religion and secular education is meant to do. Rather, our goal is to *grow* the soul large enough, to help it become wise and strong enough so that it can surround the dominating wound we call trauma.[17]

Tick believes that in growing the soul large enough Post Traumatic Stress Disorder will be healed and disappear, and people like the Eberts and Mr. Tiger in Viet Nam, will "be devoted to the peaceful cultivation of the earth and to international friendship and reconciliation."[18]

We do not have in this culture a means of reintegrating the returning warrior. We say, "Welcome home. Find a job and raise your family." The Native American culture would welcome the warrior home. There would be a feast and an opportunity to tell and act out the story of the warrior's experience (a time of catharsis). There would be a sweatlodge and time with the elders for spiritual integration. Young men were sent out on a vision quest to seek their vision of how to become men. Our culture sends our youth to war to become men, then expects them to integrate their experiences on their own. Then we are insensitive when they show signs of post-traumatic stress. The individuality of our nation leaves a gap in the support and intimacy of small communities.

Muriel James' book, *Born to Win*, has been an inspiration to me, as I have studied her work, practiced with my mentor toward integration through the Parent/Adult/Child model, and explored the transactions that occur between people. I will later speak of this work more comprehensively. Hal Stone and Sidra Winkelman Stone's work is similar, though more varied in parts of the self. As I investigate these parts of the self, it is a certainty to me that these inner reflections of self also mirror the outside behaviors of the world. If changes in the inner world of enough people occur (like it seems to have changed in the Eberts), the outer world will reflect the same. The world soul can *grow* and *integrate its awareness*.[19] Then the door to compassion for and in the world is opened.

Robert Lawlor in *Voices of the First Day* speaks of the Australian aboriginal belief that the dreamtime (unconscious) and the external (conscious) world are interrelated and reflect each other.[20] I spoke of his interesting work on the indigenous mind in chapter two and will add more in the direction of Grandmother Earth.

Spiritually, my prayer life had expanded to include others beyond my immediate groups of family, friends and church associates to include those one might call enemies; yet, they are our fellow human beings. It is a discipline in my mind to separate the behavior from the individual or group I want to reject.

Christianity teaches to love one another, forgive and turn the other cheek; yet, the Bible is filled in the Old Testament with war and the righteousness of conquering a land and removing religious practices and objects that are not acceptable to Jehovah. There is the same tension regarding war that I found as I struggled with the issue of terrorism.

Nature-based spirituality teaches that all are created equal, as well. *Mitakuye o'yasin* means all things and beings are related. History notes that the indigenous people also engaged in war. There is the call for peaceful coexistence, as well. Whatever the spiritual base of a people it seems there is this tension between good and evil, light and dark, peace and war, internally and externally.

I turn now in prayer to the direction of Grandmother Earth, as I remember moments of lying on her "face" and being restored in spirit by my environment.

CHAPTER SIX

The Direction of Grandmother Earth: A Vision Quest, Nature's Blessings

The direction of Grandmother Earth is sustaining, one of nurture, balance and grounding. In the Native American and Australian Aboriginal minds, the earth is a living entity. We are a living part of that entity. One of the songs we sing in the Earthtribe is "Mother I feel you under my feet. Mother I feel your heart beat." The drum is a symbol of that heart beat. Often the name "Grandmother Earth" is interchanged in my writing as "Mother Earth." They are two aspects of the one: *unchi* and *ina*.

Black Elk prays to Grandmother Earth:

> Grandmother Earth, You are wakan and have holy ears; hear me! We have come from You, we are a part of You, and we know that our bodies will return to You at that time when our spirits travel upon the great path..., but above all I think of *Wakan Tanka*, with whom our spirits become as one. By purifying myself in this way (sweatlodge), I wish to make myself worthy of You, O *Wakan Tanka*, that my people may live![1]

There are four stories that I would like to share with you in this chapter. All probe the meaning of Earth as a direction. In each of them the healing nurture of Mother Earth in bringing emotional, physical, psychological and spiritual balance can be observed. The first story is about being a supporter at a vision quest. The second is a time when I was in the hospital. The third story is about the healing nature of Mother Earth for a trauma client of mine I'll call Sara. The fourth is a recent vision quest in April 2011.

In gratitude for the gifts of Mother Earth, I would like to speak of reciprocity for the generosity of our planet home, and how we might heal and protect her. This issue I will address in chapter eleven.

Song: Grandmother the Earth

Some years ago, I went with four other women to the Adirondacks as a support person for a vision quest. On the last day of the quest, I was asked to supervise the children present with crafts and games so that the questers would not be interrupted as they were brought back in silence to meet with the elders. Late in the afternoon, the children became restless, so I taught them some songs. One of the songs had come to me in a dream. That evening, Sophia, Edward Tick's daughter, sang it with me to the group at the naming ceremony. I sang the verses, as Sophia sat on my lap and sang the refrain. This is the song of my dream:

> *Ho, Grandmother! Ho, First Mother.*
>   *Ho, Grandmother the Earth.*

> Heart fires burning, deep passions churning.
>   For your creatures on earth.

> *Ho, Grandmother! Ho, First Mother.*
>   *Ho, Grandmother the Earth.*

> Spin with your night star, wheeling and turning,
>   waltzing the dawn a new day.

> *Ho, Grandmother! Ho, First Mother.*
>   *Ho, Grandmother the Earth.*

Changing your raiment, donning the springtime,
  bringing new hope and new birth.

Ho, Grandmother! Ho, First Mother.
  Ho, Grandmother the Earth.

Spread forth your mantle, filled with your bounty.
  Feeding your children so small.

Ho, Grandmother! Ho, First Mother.
  Ho, Grandmother the Earth.

May I be thankful, ever respectful. May I walk
  humbly in truth.

Ho, Grandmother! Ho, First Mother.
  Ho, Grandmother the Earth.

May I lie at your breast, fall into rest,
  blessed by the Father of All.

Ho, Grandmother! Ho, First Mother.
  Ho, Grandmother the Earth.

Heart fires burning, deep passions churning,
  for your creatures on earth.

(Author, 1995)

Little did I know that small Sophia that I taught would be a foreshadowing of my journey in a search for Sophia (Wisdom). This search for meaning and wisdom would be the catalyst that connected my thoughts on nature-based spirituality and Christianity and the genesis of this book.

Healing nature of Grandmother Earth: finding balance and nurture

The next story I would like to share occurred in February 2008. I was hospitalized in an effort to discover why my heart was symptomatic. This was my second admittance for this issue, and it was decided by the cardiology team that I needed a heart catherization procedure to rule out any blockages or valve issues within the heart and surrounding arteries. It was anxiety provoking to be hospitalized once again.

Psychological aspects and mentoring tools for the trauma

In this story I examine eco-spiritual mentoring and the shamanic path through trauma. To do this, I will begin with the role of the *witness state* as it assists the *aware ego* to make an informed decision and then take an action.

Utilizing Hal and Sidra Stone's work on "voice dialogue," I will explore what parts of the self were speaking in the hospital event. Then I would like to delve deeper and investigate the process of accessing the aware ego and witness state to locate a balance between the sub-selves in the story. This process leads to a decision the aware ego could or would create for a future step to take or practice and then develop.

To begin, I will define the terms that I am using for this section of my thought processes. Hal and Sidra Stone in their book, *Embracing Our Selves*, describe how this process works: "Consciousness evolves on three different levels. The first is the level of awareness. The second level is the *experience* of the different selves, sub-personalities or energy patterns. The third level is the development of an aware ego."[2]

I particularly liked the definition of sub-selves as energy patterns. I know that there have been moments when I felt my vulnerable inner child was in charge of my actions and acting as my operating ego. These sub-personalities or energy forms can be called many names. The ones used by the Stones include "the inner pusher, the pleaser, the frightened (or vulnerable) child, and the critic."[3] From our early childhood, we develop a protector/controller. It is what we usually mean as we say, "I." Hal and Sidra Stone define the protector/controller, as follows:

This protective controller is subjective in its obser-
vations. It is always deeply concerned with our impact on others. It always has a specific goal in
mind. It is generally quite rational and very much
determines what we perceive and the way we
think and behave.[4]

This part of our personality works with our limbic brain
and feelings that the operating ego protects; therefore, it is not
fully objective. That leads me to the part that can be difficult to
grasp, the aware ego and its relationship with the witness state.

First, let us look at Hal and Sidra Stone's definition of
awareness:

Awareness is the capacity to witness life in all its aspects without evaluating or judging the energy patterns...and without needing to control the outcome.
It is otherwise referred to in spiritual and esoteric
writings as the "witness state" or "consciousness,"...
a position of non-attachment...neither rational nor,
conversely, emotional. It is simply a point of reference that objectively witnesses what is.[5]

The difference between the witness state or witness and
the aware ego is the distinction I struggled at first to discern.
The following quotation from the Stones helped clarify this
more succinctly in my mind:

In its traditional definition the ego has been referred
to as the *executive function* of the psyche, or the
choice maker... (The) ego receives its information
from both the awareness level and the experience of
the different energy patterns. As our consciousness
evolves, the ego becomes a more aware ego...(with)
a better position to make real choices.[6]

However, our ego can be led to operate by one of the
primary selves mentioned earlier. These primary energy sys-

tems (like the protector/controller, perfectionist, critic, etc.) or sub-personalities can perceive our world and enter the data for processing, then direct our lives. Stone and Stone explain the result, as follows:

> When this happens, our ego has *identified* with these particular patterns. Most people believe that they have free will because they choose to do a particular thing... Unless we awaken to the consciousness process, the vast majority of us are run by the energy patterns with which we are identified or by those which we have disowned.[7]

Having noted this particular psychological information, I would like to return to my original story and explore how this information applies to the hospital situation.

Medical trauma

A day or two before the hospital procedure, the cardiologist in charge gave instructions that I was to be informed by hospital personnel the risks that could be involved, and I was required to read and sign release forms. The personnel informed me of the worst possible scenarios, including issues like the risk of death, heart attack, stroke, or hemorrhaging after returning home. To read the release forms is a trauma in and of itself, much less the fright of being ill enough to be hospitalized and need a heart procedure.

The night before I was scheduled for the 6:00 a.m. test, I was very anxious. I tried to do breathing exercises and calm myself. The reality was I was very frightened. My family was two hundred or so miles away in Houston. Every fifteen minutes around the clock the blood pressure machine activated. Every four hours someone took blood to see if I had signs of a heart attack. There were pills to take and shots in the abdomen each day to prevent clotting. It seemed endless. My friends and mentor visited me, and that helped during the day, but at night I felt very alone.

About 5:00 a.m., the morning of the procedure, I awoke thirsty and hungry, as a nurse took my vital signs and added drugs to the IVs. I began to watch the door for the gurney to arrive to move me to the testing area. Awakened by the nurse's presence, my roommate turned on the television.

What followed changed the entire experience and outcome for me. CTMC is a hospital owned by a religious organization. The hospital has made tapes for a special in-house television channel. The channel was displaying beautiful scenes taken from nature. One after another, scenes appeared of rivers, woods, mountains, rain, birds, flowers, deer, all types of butterflies and other wildlife. The background sound was of familiar hymns without words that I knew well. One that remains in my memory was "I will put my hand in the hand of the man who stilled the waters... I will put my hand in the hand of the man from Galilee." I remembered the tenets of my belief system, and I remembered the support of my spiritual mentor. Gradually, I began to relax.

A nurse came in and changed my IV, disconnected the blood pressure cuff on the other arm and said we were nearly ready. I was not aware the new IV held my anesthesia, which was beginning to drip into my system. I relaxed further into a half sleep still watching the lovely scenes from nature flow across the video screen. The hospital team came for me and moved me to the testing site. The nurses began to prepare me for the procedure, and I drifted out of awareness. I noticed a large piece of equipment move across my vision above my face. I asked, "Are we ready to begin?" The staff and doctor laughed. We were already done, and I was returned to my room.

Christian and nature-based healing

The songs and scenes from the video tapes remained in my spirit. I watched them for lengthy periods before I was released to go home. At home, I healed swiftly with no side effects. I was told I would have dark bruising from the groin to the knee, but none occurred. I had no pain whatsoever. I attribute the lack of bruising and pain to how relaxed my spirit was as I entered the procedure, to the calmness of watching the beauty of nature and listening to the soft sounds of music.

With the Earthtribe, I have traveled to many sites in nature for vision quests and events. In my mind and spirit these past events and the scenes of the television connected into my sense of well-being. My frightening hospital event in February became a quiet memory. My spirit had an anchor in Grandmother Earth, as well as my Christian faith, through the familiar hymns.

The experience of approximately six trips to the hospital over the spring of 2008 is helpful information as I explored the process of trauma mentoring for others. McFarland speaks to what I experienced:

> Any...experience that happens outside the realm of normalcy, the devastation to the psyche is unspeakable...often at those times (or later when the trauma is integrated) a deep spiritual experience balances the horror. If the psyche can withstand the onslaught and be open to Nature's guidance..., the affected person can eventually use the insights gained to discover her/his soul's path.[8]

Keeping this in mind, let us now turn to another story of Grandmother Earth's assistance in healing.

Grandmother Earth and mentoring

The third story occurred in 2009. I was working with a person who experienced several severe traumas, one of which was a hospital error. Each time Sara (a fictitious name for the purposes of confidentiality) came for mentoring, we sat outside on my four acres of land under a very large cedar tree. Small wind chimes lent their soft music to our sessions. Butterflies and birds were abundant.

We spent a little time placing our bare feet on the earth, or turned our attention to the breeze or sun on our faces. At first Sara was afraid outdoors and afraid of taking off her shoes. I took Native American tobacco and invited her to make a safe circle around herself. We only needed to do that once for her to be comfortable.

One day, we went and stood barefooted on a smooth out-cropping of dark limestone. It had a center cave deep into the earth. Sara asked me, "Why did we do this?" I answered, "So that we can feel grounded and connected to Mother Earth. It is good to remember the joy of being alive and barefoot like a child." Sara had been so distraught that she contemplated end-ing her life. It was a happy moment in my heart to see her smile and wiggle her toes on the surface of the rock and in the soft earth around it. She is now out of a wheelchair, wearing leg supports and beginning to walk around a little faster.

Sara would not look up or speak above a whisper when I first met her. One day, as she made colorful prayer ties, she burst out into giggles. I had taught her this skill to objectively project her inner thoughts out into prayers as part of the pro-cess to draw her out of her depression. Sara spoke of her love for her husband and twelve year old son. Shyly, she began to bring small samples of her artwork in leather and painting. Her paintings included birds and a wolf, a Medicine Wheel, clouds and stars.

This courageous woman told me her desire and determination was to never go back into the wheelchair and to walk the wooded paths around Wimberley that she had loved since she was a little girl. Sara had originally been told by her doctors that she would never walk again. With courage, she overcame her morning paralysis and arose out of bed. Sara wanted to show me a waterfall that she said people here in Wimberley were not aware existed. I no longer heard comments that it was too hard to remain alive. Like my response to the hospital, Sara's spirit was reaching out through her love of the natural beauty around her.

In his book, *The Many Colored Buffalo*, William Taegel addresses what occurred for Sara and myself in these words: "There would be a time when the two of them would learn how to wrap the energy of the leaves, the warmth of the sun, and the music of the creek around the bruises and cuts on (the) wounded inner child..."[9]

As I observed Sara in our work together, I was convinced that she would recover not only from her serious injuries encountered in three separate events (two of which were her near death from attempted murder), but that she would use what she was learning for her own personal and spiritual growth for the benefit and healing of others. Peter Levine states in his book, *Healing Trauma*, "I have come to the conclusion that human beings are born with an innate capacity to triumph over trauma. I believe not only that trauma is curable, but the healing process can be a catalyst for profound awakening—a portal opening to emotional and genuine spiritual transformation."[10]

Sara and I are blessed by the gift of imagery from Mother Earth. It is our grounding and hope. (Also, both of us like to oil paint what we see in nature.)

Naparstek in *Invisible heroes: Survivors of Trauma and How They Heal* speaks to the gift of imagery:

> Imagery is highly compatible with religious belief
> but doesn't insist upon it. It offers the gift of open-
> ing up even the most cynical trauma survivor to
> the spaciousness of the wider perspective, a felt
> sense of the mystical, and glimpses of long-shut
> spiritual doorways.[11]

Naparstek then addresses the traumas that both Sara and I have encountered that were serious and debilitating for both of us:

> After we experience...heart-shattering events, enter-
> ing (a) vaster perspective allows us to apprehend
> the larger truth that everything really is, at some
> level of reality, still all right. This is not the same
> thing as denying the ugliness—we understand that
> what happened is hideous. But from this other view
> we can hold both truths at the same time, derive
> comfort, and maintain hope.[12]

So, as Sara and I met and spent our time outside, lifted our faces to the wind, the gentle rains and the sun, bared our feet to the earth, we were learning to live and breathe fully present in each moment. William Taegel in *The Many Colored Buffalo* speaks to this issue:

> No learning experience—whether psychotherapy,
> collegiate, or religious—will be transformative un-
> less the body is required to be there and be awake.
> Most deeply spiritual selves play hooky when the
> body can coast through an experience.[13]

Sara and I will still physically live with her recent diagnosis with cancer, her leg injuries and my pacemaker, but we have the opportunity with great consciousness to live fully in each moment, fully alive and in tune with "All That Is."

Let us turn then to the fourth story in the direction of Grandmother Earth.

A vision quest 2011: Nature's blessings

On my recent vision quest in 2011, eight others and I went out to fast and meditate alone for varied lengths of time. I chose to go out for two days and nights and returned to the encampment midday of the third day.

One of the issues that unexpectedly rose up for me the first day and night was the term *lonely*. At this time in my life, my children are scattered across the country and rearing half-grown children of their own. My parents and only sibling are deceased. My cousin Mary with whom I spent so much time died unexpectedly this past year. At first, when your supporters take you to your prayer site and leave, there is this deep sense and awareness of "I am alone."

Day one

In the beginning, I looked about and oriented myself to my environment. There was a lake in front of me, a very large old oak above my tent, and a broad meadow behind me with groves of trees around the edges. There was a companion oak and a tall pine tree at my site, as well.

I first began to feel present with the wind (a gift from Grandfather Sky). I removed clothing and let the wind caress my skin in the ninety degree heat of the day. Then I noted the clouds and the birds. I savored these things for a good while, especially the wind that seemed to sing, then fell asleep for the night.

Part of my process was to keep a journal or log of my experiences. In the night, I woke and in a half-dream state was meditating on how lonely I felt and what that meant for me. I quote the following from my meditations:

Night thoughts:

I woke and watched the moon come up thinking about being lonely. I was thinking about all the creatures I could hear: frogs, cicadas, crickets, coyotes in the distance, the

*wind—so much life. I realized lonely is a soul wound, not
a scratch, a deep wound to the soul; but it expresses a
yearning for connection, a first step toward connection. I
remember being a child and spending lengths of time no-
ticing the tiny white star-faced flowers beneath the grass,
the "doodle bugs." If the innocent soul-free connection
ability of a child is lost, how can we connect with others,
or trust, or love with that clarity and honesty—that is
the yearning of "lonely."* (Author, 2011)

Something woke me—someone is walking with heavy
footfalls up to my tent in the dry leaves. Deborah?! No one
answered. The footfalls stopped at my prayer ties by the west
corner wall of my tent. I heard the footsteps leave, but I could
not see anyone. I lay back down and put my hand on my Pipe.
Energy flowed strongly through my left arm.

Day two

The morning is soft. The wind is still blowing strong. The sun
popped out and turned the world gold. The wind on the water
gives the lake the appearance of a moving river.

I smell smoke. There are trucks and cars and a dirt mover
racing up and down the road. I heard sirens. I hope Lisa is safe.
I heard her drum earlier. Jeff was really driving fast out to her
site. I thought I saw William's car, too, and Jack on the all-ter-
rain. What is going on? Deborah came and said there was a fire,
but everything is okay, and Lisa is safe.

A cardinal returned and called from above me. I see a
woodpecker on the pine tree. He taps and peels bark, then taps
some more. He is pretty big. He flew away now to the east.

This oak tree is so peaceful. It is very old with moss growing on it, some dead limbs, but new leaves on others. Reminds
me a little of myself—some things dying, body now old, new
leaves growing in my thoughts and heart. It has sheltered me

well with shade and the birds have come to sing and visit here. Old as it is, it still bends flexibly to the wind.

I know the wind is a danger with the fire, but it has been my joy here. It sings, ebbs and flows, keeps me cool in the early summer heat. The tree and the wind are like blessings.

I was lying on my back with my head on my Pipe when a strong wind blew a cloud shaped like a perfect cardinal before me, then the wind elongated the cloud into the shape of a hawk swooping, then the cloud morphed into a long-necked water-fowl—amazing and beautiful.

I have been watching these tree asps fall on my tent. The temptation is to knock them off, but they just want to go home. The hairs shine white against the sun, a contrast to the big dark eyes.

Suddenly, I heard the loud speakers of the fire department. I made out the words "half a mile north/south, fire is out, we are lucky." I am grateful. The conditions are so right for a catastrophe.

Two times the *Being* has awakened me. The first time it walked up and sat down with a light thump at my head. To-night, I did not speak, but all was quiet. The second time it woke me it was pushing at my tent by my head. That was a little more startling, but I just pushed back slightly, and it stopped. The first time the moon was not up yet. The second time the moon was about thirty-five to forty degrees up the sky. I watched the moon a while and hearing nothing else I went back to sleep. Before dawn I woke and noticed that where the branches of the two oaks met there was the form of a warrior.

I woke again, and it was morning with the wind rising and the sun coming up. Birds were calling, and I felt rested. Mother Earth is very hard from this drought, but I could find a comfortable curve in the ground last night to sleep.

Curious, I went outside the tent and looked at where the Being kept coming. The black silk flag and my prayer ties were touching the West corner of my tent. They were undisturbed. The leaves had not been ruffled. I wish I knew its message. My spirit longs to understand the messages, though it is a blessing in and of itself that it appeared. (I discovered later that the Being had walked near two other questers.)

I have been watching these three Peace Eagles play and swoop in the wind, the sunshine, the birds. The wind is singing in the trees. It is a perfect day. I was thinking that I had not seen flowers, but in front of me a bright fuchsia one has bloomed overnight. I have a song forming in my heart, a song of gratitude.

Looking back at the experience I begin to see a map unfolding for myself. An issue with emotional impact rose to the surface. The eco-field around me came into my awareness. I became a part of that field and realized I am part of creation and never alone. I felt held with the Creator's larger plan.

Will Taegel speaks to what I felt:

> The Grand Attractor, a mysterious and impossible to define Force, pulls you out of the confines of culture (and in my case belief) into the hands of the Divine Wild Heart... It is the same wildness pushing the edges of the Universe. Once you clasp this forceful hand and continue to hold on for dear life, you can be led to your true nature within nature.[14]

Then I began to remember my early connections to the eco-field as a child and saw that early connection as a step forward to cathecting with all things, including other humans. It was a tie for me of going back to reclaim my early rooting in Mother Earth and the gradual growth to becoming an adult human on the planet. I did not feel lonely the rest of my quest.

Taegel in his book, *The Sacred Council of Your Wild Heart*, refers to this process that I experienced, as follows:

> *soul retrieval*... I will propose that our hope for mov-
> ing through planetary and personal traumas resides
> in a return to our awareness zone of the Nature-
> based self, that dormant side of ourselves just wait-
> ing to council us as we connect with sitting in oak
> trees in urban parks and touching our feet to grass
> at the edge of golf courses.[15]

Reflecting, I ask myself inner questions: "How does my small common issue on my vision quest effect or affect the crises of our planet? What of the drying lake I sat and observed? What of the fire on the ranch that was started by a falling tree that had died in the drought? What of the oil company that wants to drill on the sacred land on which I prayed?"

Robert Lawlor in his book, *Voices of the First Day*, asserts:

> Dreams, deep collective memories, and imaginings
> are more potent than religious beliefs or scientific
> theories in lifting us above the catastrophic ending
> that confronts us all. A recollection of our origins—a
> remembrance of a sense of reality in its pure and
> primary form—is essential if we are to understand
> our present circumstance and imagine the possibilit-
> ies of our collective destiny.[16]

Or, as Will Taegel asserts even more strongly in his book, *The Sacred Council of Your Wild Heart*, with his fourth proposal, "Earth's unprecedented crisis reveals itself with the basics of the environment (*the drying up lake of my vision quest site*)... (We) must return to the loins of Mother Nature. We must re-establish the primal connection. That is our first order of business."[17]

Taegel further asserts in his proposal:

> No significant solution will arise without this connec-
> tion with the *mysterium tremendum*, that profound
> sense of awe we feel lying on the Earth looking at the
> night sky. I refer here not to an occasional peak exper-

ience but to radical new practices to recover the Wild Heart birthed in Mother Nature's womb.[18]

This small psychological change in how I perceived *lonely* is but an example of the changes that can occur on many more profound issues.

Lawlor calls to us to change our language (For instance, such personal thoughts as, *"We have always done it this way. We must have fossil fuels. I'll always be lonely:"*

> Our fixed inner and outer worlds mutually support and incestuously feed on each other, disfiguring mind and nature alike. A transformation of our world view requires that we completely change our concept of language from a fixed, consistent, absolute structure to a mutable, spontaneous communion between being in a living place and moment.[19]

Remember that I was half asleep and meditating or dreaming about the topic of lonely. The Aborigine of Australia connects the unconscious with the conscious as dreaming. To Lawlor that means the following:

> *The qualities by which things are categorized are never separated from living reality.* For the Aborigines, every quality that exists on a physical level relates to a quality manifested on psychic or metaphysical levels... Every objective quality or state has a subjective component, since the visible world is everywhere fused with the Dreaming.[20]

Therefore, within my soul, when I told myself I was lonely, yet I was surrounded with abundant active life forms, a dissonance formed. The pain of lonely was actually in my way of thinking the pain of that dissonance. Only when I accepted that I was one with all of creation did my discomfort disappear.

The Western tradition has created the concept that in order for the spirit to be free, it must be disassociated from, or transcendent of the physical body and physical world. We look in Christianity toward Heaven. For me, Spirit and my inner encompassing of spirituality include both the explicate and the implicate orders.

In my mind, this passage from Lawlor reflects the *mysterium tremendum*, The Grand Attractor or Force, incarnate in the natural world:

> Spirit is movement; it is invisible animator and motivator of all growth and change. It is the urge to extend, encompass, transform and become... By maintaining self and society alive within expanding, flowing forms and processes, the Aborigines...conceive of Spirit as the constant lusting consort of the physical world.[21]

It is not that "someday, I'll go to heaven. Heaven is now." That translates into a wondrous condition. Spirit and the world (and that includes me) are one—now!

For the indigenous tribes, Grandmother Earth is the total gift of the transcendent, to be honored as sacred. Lawlor would speak of the earth as the reciprocal manifestation of the Dreamtime of the transcendent for the Australian Aborigine.[22]

For Christianity, man is dominant over nature and can either exploit it or conserve it. This contradictory difference in approach from the indigenous tribes in my mind is part of the crises we are facing on the planet. The industrial revolution has brought deep exploitation of the natural resources of the earth. This despoiling of natural habitats has resulted in the extinction of many species and threatens our own species.

I like my car and the ability to go easily from place to place. Yet, I know that the mining of metals, production of plastics and fuels are major contributors to the current environmental crises.

These are powerful spiritual issues surrounding my desires versus the healthy care of the planet. This is just one example of the spiritual issues confronting my priorities. It calls into my awareness that these crises need our full attention not only with prayer, but with participatory prayer (action as we are able).

We have looked at mentoring tools (vision quest, imagery and dreams, nature-based experiences outside, meditation that also includes song and poetry, the support of community and a guide (vision quest), and psychological tools like voice dialogue in this chapter. Sara was supported in our work by nature-based spirituality, and I was supported in my journey by both nature-based spirituality and Christianity (with the re-membered hymns at the hospital).

Song: Gratitude

Out of my vision quest came this song called "Gratitude" that I wish to send as a prayer in the direction of Grandmother Earth:

Gratitude fills my heart.
Gratitude fills my heart.

Born of Light, Born from Dark,
A tiny flicker of the Universe.
Grateful deep humility,
I was meant to be.

Gratitude fills my heart.
Gratitude fills my heart.

All that is, all I see,
Blessings of Great Mystery.
Abundant Life in rainbow's hues,
All was meant to be.

Gratitude fills my heart.
Gratitude fills my heart.

Let us now turn our intention or prayer to the direction of the Sky, the direction of transcendence.

CHAPTER SEVEN

The Direction of Grandfather Sky: Quantum Leaps and Evolutionary Spirituality

T he direction of the Sky on the Medicine Wheel is the mature male, the grandfather. It is the direction of the transcendent. It sees events and conditions from a higher perspective with detachment. The task of transcending our personal stories and inner voices is ongoing throughout our lives.

In this chapter I explore the journey from the grounding of the direction of Mother Earth to the transcendent awareness of the direction of Grandfather Sky. I look at it from my personal experiences in my search for meaning and connection to Spirit and my personal concepts of God. As tools, I will explore Taegel and Yost's psychological and developmental tools of evolutionary waves, Ken Wilber's four lenses from the perspective of his book, *Integral Spirituality*, and Beck and Cowan's book, *Spiral Dynamics*, the upward spiral of values that leads to the turquoise level that I associate with Sky and the transcendent. I will also investigate the role of myth and story as a projection of the evolvement and development of human beings and the use of language in the form of pronouns as a working model for evolutionary development.

Symbolism of the Sky

The sky is the direction of the eagle, soaring toward the heavens with the greatest view of all. The eagle in Native American tradition is a guide to the Ultimate Reality, the Ultimate Awareness. In this direction one prays to God, the Other, Sacred Mystery, the One, All That Is, the Named, the Nameless, the *mysterium tremendum*. The eagle bone whistle is the musical instrument often used. The eagle's beautiful tail feather is frequently used for healing and a symbol of connection to Sacred Mystery.

Transcendence and Greater Awareness

The human being grows through stages of development and matures into the possibility of seeing an event through different lenses.[1] Another method of looking for transcendence is through anticipating the recognition of levels of the spiral and the quantum leaps that might lead us individually and collectively to what Don Beck and Christopher Cowan call the second tier.[2] When I speak of memes and levels of the spiral, I am referring to their work.

Personal experiences of evolution

Looking back in time to the 1980s when I was divorced, I lost all sense of psychological and spiritual balance. I was so depressed I could barely speak above a whisper. My minister recommended a psychotherapist in the city in which I resided. I began a slow, painful process at first. I was mentally and emotionally in the beige level of the spiral.

During my own training as a psychotherapist, I became interested and involved in the Earthtribe. As I mentioned in the beginning chapter, I began to go outdoors to sweatlodges and later to vision quests and Earthdances. These attractors led me to begin once again to seek my spiritual roots and my sense of being psychologically balanced. An attractor is defined by Taegel as "an invariant set that attracts the trajectories of all near points... The attractors in evolution use life conditions like travel, illness, hurricanes, earthquakes, stock market crashes, war and geography as a springboard to the 2nd Tier."[3]

The attractors of nature, my Native American roots and this new (in my case) way of praying began to pull me out of my negative thoughts and emotions. I began a new pathway toward healing for myself and others.

My Christian tradition accepts, but does not condone, divorce. I felt totally isolated from my traditional Christian community. There was this deep sense of judgement. Part of this was my own inner judgement of going against my value system and the vows I had made when I married. The other part came from some members of the community who were close to my husband, who was on the church vestry. Another part of the alienation from the community came from the rector's good intentions regarding the rite of reconciliation. That rite left me feeling more wounded than anything else. My prayers in church were intense but isolated within my own inner world. The journey out of my depression would lead me toward a clearer view, a pathway to the aspects of awareness and Sky energy.

I attended several sweatlodges. As the participants in the sweatlodge would pray through the first four directions of the Medicine Wheel, I would remain silent in the direction of the West. At first, the energy of anger expressed in that direction of prayers was somewhat shocking and overwhelming. Then one Saturday, as the prayers in the West were expressed by others, I found myself weeping silently in the dark lodge. Not too many lodges after that I found my anger in a growling animal sound from deep in my throat. I was able to locate the red meme of the warrior or hunter in my soul.

Sometimes people unused to the manner of the Earthtribe lodge are surprised or shocked by the growls or anger and expressed emotions that are contained safely within our lodges. Once, I remember as a Christian chaplain and Lay Eucharistic Minister at Hermann Hospital in Houston, a mother came to me crying and upset. Their teenage daughter had just died of a closed head injury, just like her older sister had done exactly ten years before. The wife was immensely distressed because her husband was cursing God. My explanation was that that expression is a prayer, as well. We do not become that deeply angry with someone with whom we do not have a relationship. I have found personally and in my work with others that these frightening (culturally unacceptable) voices must be heard. Taegel notes, "The sweatlodge offers an opportunity for many of the selves that have been expressed in traditional psycho-therapy to be experienced in greater depth."[18]

Humility is a sub-personality that shows up in the purifying experience of the lodge. My experience is that you crawl into the lodge on hands and knees in little clothing, usually a bathing suit, with all the spider veins, extra weight and messed up hair revealed. One does not wear jewelry because the heated metal would burn the skin. There is nothing within the lodge but the basic self.

As the four directions are prayed or given intention, subpersonalities emerge and tend to seek balance. This sometimes requires the guidance of a therapist or shaman. One of the things taught to me as a Pipe carrier was to be imminently conscious of where everyone was mentally, physically, emotionally and spiritually in the lodge, and to monitor that with my own body, mind and spirit. It is a profound and serious task to provide that safety.

Inner growth tends to move in a spiral. Sometimes it appears one is back at the beginning, but there is a higher perspective each time the issue returns. I liken it to a well, wherein our wounds are held. As we move up the spiral, the well is still in the pathway, but we are no longer sitting on the rim or diving into that well. It is a point on the path in our memories. We can look back, see that it was there, but are no longer captured by it.

Rupert Sheldrake, Terence McKenna and Ralph Abraham speak to this phenomenon of the use of animal voices in the West in *The Evolutionary Mind*:

> (Whatever) the causal mechanism—the stimulation of psilocybin or modeling the behavior of the top predators that we competed with—the domain in which change was born, and in which we live,...is the domain of the imagination. That is what we created that is uniquely human,...the cradle of humanness,...so it also is the domain in which our trans-human metamorphosis will occur.[4]

Earthdance

Soon after that, the warrior energy emerged again while taking part in an Earthdance. Late in the night, half asleep, I was invited to dance with a woman who lit two torches. Astoundingly, that inner warrior (born in my imagination and inner council) was very powerful to the point of fearlessly invincible as we each "fought" with the lit torches. My hand actually passed through the flame of her torch and was not burned. A fierceness arose that I suddenly realized frightened the other woman. Onlookers were calling out, "Kill her. Kill her." Appalled and becoming aware of this strong dark energy, I decided it was time to halt. Raising my torch and touching the top of the other dancer's torch ended the dance. No longer was I a victim of a divorce. Deep inside was a powerful will and strength, a warrior. Occasionally, it will peek out of the inner council slightly hidden as stubborn.

William Taegel states, "I propose that a new atmosphere of evolutionary ideas is crucial to the leap. The old map and practices, no matter how inspiring (or in my case overwhelming) are simply not sufficient for us on this planet."[5]

The sweatlodges and vision quests still had a magical purple meme aspect for me at that point of my life, and I was struggling with the blue meme of rules from my family and religion of origin: *It is a sin to divorce*. My mother noticed the "Honor Song" taped to my bathroom mirror. Convinced that I was joining a cult, it took her a while to accept that my process was a legitimate way to pray. In the eyes of my mother and Baptist minister brother, I was involved with pagan, non-Christian spirituality, and my soul was in danger.

Many fundamentalist Christians appear to have this religious world view. Christianity is a transcendent religion that denies the body in many ways. One lives and prays for a life in the hereafter. I needed an embodied spiritual life in the present. For me it was not a matter of leaving Christianity, it was a matter of bringing spirituality into my physical world. I needed the *here*, as well as the *hereafter*.

It also seems strange to me that no one seems to pay much attention to the fact that Christ went out into the desert and fasted (vision quest) before he began his life's work. He also went out into the garden to pray (not in a dark room) prior to the events that led to his death. Jesus prepared himself in nature for major life transitions. This indicates to me that He had a nature-based spirituality and also taught from that perspective. Living in the hill country, I connect with the stories of the mustard seed and fallow and stony ground.

Sheldrake, McKenna and Abraham address this issue of shamanic practices, the sacralization of time and reconnecting ourselves with religious traditions in their book, *Chaos, Creativity and Cosmic Consciousness*:

> (The) most important aspect of this process...is to
> find the pre-Christian roots that underlie the timing
> and quality of existing forms and festivals. We need
> to ground the new religion in the old...a continuous
> living strand that goes right back to the pre-Christi-
> an shamanic societies of Europe and the pre-Jewish
> shamanic societies of the Middle East.[6]

The day I was requested by my therapist to take off my wedding band will never be forgotten and is part of the example of how retreating back to this nature-based (shamanic) pathway and community was of assistance to me. It was a major hurdle and a physical/psychological acceptance of my new identity, a *divorcee*. The green meme of the Earthtribe community was beginning to pull me along the spiral, but I had a long way to go in my personal growth.

What Taegel says about clearly seeing our usual behavior patterns from an objective distance, and the freedom we gain in the sweatlodge or on a vision quest from these habits or thought patterns, has deep meaning for me as I live in the daily routines (ruts and grooves) of my life:

> You really can never be satisfied after you experi-
> ence what it is like to shake loose from the
> ordinary... The person you were in the circle calls
> you in your new name... If you develop new prac-
> tices and persist, then you set the stage for a
> quantum leap. A new center of gravity is not just
> possible, it is probable. Persist.[7]

It would be a few years before I recognized my freedom. One day my therapist and I went for a walk outdoors, as we often did in our sessions. A dog was sitting just outside a board missing from a fence that bordered the dog's backyard. The dog was looking back into the yard and not wandering off. It was a small lesson from nature that I was now free, but still looking backward into my past and the divorce. Nature is a powerful mentor indeed.

Love, trauma and our many births

One day my mentor asked a group of us, "How do our profound traumas fit with love? Even deeper, is love possible without upset—without sometimes overwhelming experiences, which we are calling trauma?" We spoke about our actual birth and moments when we experienced a "new birth," noting if any challenge, upset or difficulty was in the situation. The following is what I wrote for the day:

> I was born at home in a small apartment near the stockyards in Fort Worth, Texas to a fifteen year old mother and an eighteen year old father. My premature birth weight was two pounds and thirteen ounces. My father grew up on a farm in the panhandle of Texas on what is called the "Llano Estacado." He knew that I needed an incubator, so my father ran in a blowing Texas "blue norther" to a nearby all night grocery store and obtained an apple crate. He took the arm off of a lamp that he had made in his high school metal shop and attached it to the crate, creating an improvised incubator to keep me alive. I am told I had extremely long black hair and fit on my father's broad, short hand. I was fed with an eyedropper. My father named me for my two grandmothers. Later, my mother told me she didn't like the name and would have named me something else. I knew she didn't like my father's mother. In my spirit, it seemed my mother over the years never liked me, and I was deeply resented except by my father and his parents.

I experienced a "new birth" in my life and my belief system when we were having long discussions about God in spiritual mentoring class and my private mentoring sessions. I heard the terms "couldn't care less" and "ultimate awareness." These were not terms I had heard in Sunday school class in the Baptist or the Episcopal churches I had attended. How could the loving God the Father I had been taught stand in a totally observing "couldn't care less" witness position? It radically challenged my inner belief system. It was very painful and scary. It sounded almost blasphemous to me from my "blue level meme" of the spiral.

The conclusion I came to after we talked about our births as a group I noted and sent in a follow-up e-mail to these friends, as follows:

> The subject of "birthing" and "births" was very enriching. There was such a sense of similarity and continuity in our experiences. Something that "bubbled up" for me was the individuality of the fetus, even with the symbiosis of the birth process. I thought also of seeds birthing and breaking forth to form new trees or plants. On a personal basis, it was a new awareness of my birth mother's vulnerability and separateness from my self in the process. What her personality was had not yet truly impacted the new born. I saw her without the lens of looking through her personality and/or mine. It was very freeing. There was a clear sense of gratitude for her process and freedom for my soul from that process. It was so energizing I went for a walk at lunch. In that walk, I was glorying in the beauty of the grass, wind, trees, the fleeting sun and scents surrounding me. There was a connection with the next layer of mother, "Mother Earth." I was rather reluctant to return to class at the sound of the conch shell. A deep longing emerged to remain detached, to savor this new sense of individuation for myself and for my birth mother.

Thinking about trauma and love, I'm wondering how that "freeing" process of slipping past the ego might help in work with veterans returning from our wars (and with others traumatized by some event). Would there not be a separation due to the trauma from the next layer, "Mother Earth?" That points toward a door for healing in my thinking. The question would also beg as to how to prevent the quiet and meditation times from possibly encouraging the "traumatized" to "dig in" to memories and not "wade through" them to the other side. Much reflection is going on in my mind.

When I freed myself from needing to relate to mother's personality, I was given the ability to open my heart and begin to love her as an individual separate from our relationship formed by birth. It was an especially strong return to an inner peace surrounding my upbringing. I had a much greater perspective regarding my mother's life story.

A perspective regarding God

New birth in my life and my belief system was engendered when we were having long discussions about God in spiritual mentoring class and in my private mentoring sessions with the terms "couldn't care less" and "ultimate witness." For several more days, I processed these new concepts back and forth in a dialogue with my mentor in a series of e-mails. I'll try to recapture that process and what I learned from it. My mentor and I were discussing the soul. When we go back far enough in our own personal witness state, the process brings us to our soul, or our *ultimate awareness*. An essence of my teacher's responses to my meditations are in italics. They are very important to my comprehension of God as *Ultimate Witness*.

E-mails with my mentor:

> Author: If the soul is "ultimate awareness" and not knowable, we have spoken of "God" as the "Ultimate Witness" — that in the tautology must be what you mean when you say, "We are God." So then in some way "soul" is "God," and always present? What about revelations?

> Mentor: *Soul is within God..., a vehicle of the Ever Present Witness..., the Subject that is not an object. The formless is present everywhere in relation to form—that is the meaning of the non-dual. The 1st chapter of John is an attempt at moving beyond separation of formlessness and form.*
> *Revelations can be experienced as evolutionary Spirit seeking openings through humans in the unfolding of Spirit into greater awareness. When you become aware, you are the universe becoming aware.*
> (Author and mentor, 2007)

From these discussions, my thinking about what God *Is* was radically changed from the God as Father image of my childhood. I had thought of God more clearly as Spirit as an adult, but not in terms of an Ultimate Awareness. Nor had I ever conceived the notion I was "God" (born "in the image of" from the creation of the universe and the *awareness* of all particles of the universe).

This concept of God for me removes God from the punishing or loving Father (more like a grandfather), the *Abba* of my earlier thinking, to a deeper broader concept that is known in my intuition and experience and yet not known (both/and).

Evolutionary waves applied to myth and story

Psychologically, I can understand the development of humans including myself and how we evolve and transcend with tools like evolutionary waves, spiral dynamics and the four lenses. I would like to address these perspectives. There are evolution-ary waves (orbits) of human development.[8] These sub-selves appear along the developmental levels of Beck and Cowan's spiral dynamics.[9]

Myth: The Golden Compass

An example of how these waves and sub-selves evolve can be applied to myths. Philip Pullman's The Golden Compass is a story in which we can observe these value levels. We can ob-serve the center of gravity on the spiral in the myth, then see what lens the compass itself was providing for the reader to look through. We can connect the myth to our own life issues and observe how Sacred Spirit speaks to us through the myth in relation to our story and the greater story of our culture.

The Golden Compass was written on the levels of the beige, red and purple memes. The characters were in a battle (red meme) for their very souls, or life force (beige meme). The young girl protagonist, Lyra, and her friends were guided by the magical wisdom of the compass (purple meme).

In the story, Lyra requires her love for her soul and the love from her soul to keep her balance and survive. Her mother and others were taking the souls from disappearing children. The myth is a mirror to reveal to us that I/we need those who understand and love us in order to stay connected to our souls and ultimately Sacred Spirit. Our souls can be threatened and wounded, even killed. There is a need for courage to meet our challenges and sometimes the individual person's soul is not strong enough alone. (We need relationship and community.)

The young girl chooses to follow the compass and go into the unknown. The elements are bitter cold. At the end of the myth, Lyra must choose to go across to the "other side," even though she does not know what is there, and the "bridge" to return will collapse behind her. Lyra looks back at her mother, who is calling, but chooses to go forward.[10]

As a young girl, I had a mother essentially like Lyra's and had to find my own way to avoid her and remain intact within my core spirit, or soul. One of my tasks is to understand and love my mother from a different perspective than our two personalties. Taegel and Yost speak to this issue:

> First there was this churning upset,...followed by the creation of a gravitational bond holding each thing in the universe to everything else. As we, the Universe, meditate on ourselves, we note that in some fundamental way we hold within ourselves a paradox. Our situation tells us that the very hurt that we endure...participates in the creation of bonding, an important aspect of love.[11]

In the myth, *The Golden Compass*, the compass is expressing the yellow meme of objective awareness. Because the compass leads Lyra and her friends toward the salvation of their souls, I also think it touches the turquoise level of objectivity (Sky) combined with the subjectivity of compassion or caring. I am not certain of the lens through which the compass is looking.[12] It is dominantly looking from the objective "it" or scientific plural "its." Also, there is an aspect of the plural "we" of Sacred Spirit and the protagonist Lyra. Possibly, it could be viewed as all of these lenses at different moments. I believe that the turquoise meme I noted is the cultural truth that we need to seek individually and as a nation in the world.

We as individuals and cultures are filled with potential, a potential to serve and to be Sacred Spirit in action. Taegel and Yost in *90 Days with Nature* speak to us from the point of view of the Universe:

> There is nothing in the universe that was not there (at the Big Bang), including you... We came together

119

in just the right way. This coming together, this allurement into elementary particles hinted at the potential of love in the very fiber of our being. This event was also full of upset and disturbance, even trauma. Infinite potential emerged out of the grand upset of things.[13]

Finding meaning and evolution in our personal story

My mentor gave me the question, "What is the point of my life?" This was my written response:

> Interesting question, I do not have a clue, and yet I do. We have studied about being the awareness of Mother Earth and the awareness of Spirit—so how does that "fit" for me? As a young girl, I wanted to marry and have children. I would pretend with my doll, as my little friends and I played. Over time, I fulfilled that role. From that respect, I was fruitful physically. I wanted to be a spiritual person from about age five and honor the Creator, so I was an active church member. That process also fulfilled many spiritual tasks. However, I felt a void in myself from the teachings of organized religion. Intuitively, I believed there was something missing—in the church, in me? I wasn't sure. I began to explore other paths to Spirit. I found the Earthtribe. I studied psychology. I began to have a thirst to expand the limitations of my mind. In the face of family oppositions, I continued graduate work, studied four years of theology from the University of the South. I was involved with the formation of the spiritual direction school for The Episcopal Diocese of Texas, taught there for several years and during that period mentored a clergy group. I had some small input in the formation of the Eco-spiritual Mentoring School. Now, I am involved in study at Wisdom University. One of my aims is obviously to expand my knowledge base and awareness. Another aim is to expand my compassion—to grow beyond my

ego's demands in order to reach out to others. In
that direction, I have done many things: psychotherapist, spiritual mentor, chaplain, educator in private
and public schools. I accept my mortality and wish
to honor each new day as a gift.

As a Christian church member, I developed a profound
spiritual belief in the existence of God. I tended to perceive
Christ as my teacher and a pathway to understanding God as
Father. It was my belief that if I followed the ten command-
ments and lived as best I could a godly life that all would be
well. This process worked well for many years until my mid-
thirties to mid-forties. Then a series of psychological/emotional
blows sent me into depression and loss of my sense of spiritual
balance and hope. The blows were rapid fire from the death of
my son, the death of my father, my divorce, financial collapse
and a mild heart attack that sent me to bed for six weeks.

As I mentioned from some encounters in my church community and my primary family, I received rejection and judgement. For instance, my mother told me, "I just do not understand you, Lillie Pearl. No one else in our family has ever let a
child die." I withdrew into a deep lonely place. There was no
one, not even a loving God of which I had been taught, that
could lead me out of where I retreated for a time.

From my nature-based community of the Earthtribe and
the guidance of my mentor, I began to connect with my life
force once again through sweatlodges and vision quests. I
began to have sensory feelings once more and began to see with
my artist's eyes the colors and beauty around me. Tentatively, I
began to reconnect. I blended these experiences into my original traditional faith. I began to question and seek awareness
strengthened by the compassion of my mentor and others in the
Earthtribe, as they also told their stories.

Slowly, I began to develop a spiritual center again and found a pathway that worked for me. I began to look beneath the church rules for the essence of what God/Spirit meant to me and began to embody this belief through my encounters with the beauty of creation. I began to perceive the creative force in all things. It took many years in gradual but stronger and firmer steps as I became secure in being a part of creation, a part of the Creator's plan, a part of the Creator. It is Isaiah who speaks of being an arrow in God's quiver: "The Lord called me from the womb, from the body of my mother he named my name... He made me a polished arrow, in his quiver he hid me away. And he said to me, 'You are my servant'..." (Isaiah 49:1-3).[14] I, too, am an arrow on a trajectory through the experiences of my life that include the range of despair through hope that is the human condition.

I see these events now from the direction of the Sky, the direction of awareness that transcends the actual events. All of these events have led me and shaped me into the elder I have become. Christ is still my teacher. God, Sacred Mystery, Spirit, the Creative Force, the Ultimate Reality is present in all things for me, even in the abyss. I found this truth from my roots in both Christianity and nature-based spirituality. They are not mutually exclusive for me; they meld into a powerful totality. Each pathway provides me deeper glimpses of the *mysterium tremendum*.

Language as development and evolution for transcendence

The development of pronouns helps to describe the lenses (perspectives) with which we can observe, and also their relationship with the levels (memes) of the spiral.[15,16] Taegel and Yost propose "Pronouns (are) signifiers of expanding awareness and expression."[17]

William Taegel describes the *pre-ego* stage as beige and purple. The pronouns are collapsed in an undifferentiated ego mass of survival. The group acts and thinks as one to survive. Anything unusual (like an eclipse or a storm) is magic. On a personal, developmental level, I would be age one or less. Perhaps that lack of differentiation is why we do not remember those early months of our lives.

The next level is the *ego-centric* (purple and red memes). The power of "I" emerges into awareness. We see this in our two year old children. The sense of subjective occurs, and the child stamps his/her foot and says a clear "No," or "Yes." My small son at age two would become so frustrated (red meme) he would throw himself on the floor and bang his head. I wonder now if it was an effort to clear his thinking from rage, or to punish himself for defying me. Charles indicated the early stages of the purple mystical meme one early morning at the beach. We were walking along the jetty, and he saw the fiddler crabs lined up against the pier at high tide mark. Charles said, "Look Mommy, they are all lined up to sing." He was associating seeing the choir line up at church with the physical position of the fiddler crabs. This stage or set of memes remains with us all of our lives.

I remember an Earthdance a few years ago, when the leader gave each of us a hand mirror. We would walk up to each other, holding the mirror facing ourselves (between our face and the other person's face); and then we would say, "It's all about me." That statement came up many times among my friends in the Earthtribe. It was extremely funny, but profoundly true, and it resonated throughout the group for months.

The third level is the *ethno-centric* (blue and orange memes). The individual "I" begins to note a "you," and then form the concept of "we" (intersubjective). "We" is limited to immediate family, friends, Sunday school class. "Love extends only to the boundary of the group."[18] My mother took a picture of me when I was about two and a half years old. I had a new pail and shovel, and I am offering them to a little boy that I played with in the neighborhood. It was one of my earliest attempts to share and recognize a "you," and a playmate "we."

From that age until the present, I have lived much of my life in the blue and orange memes of rules, education, science (I love my computer and e-mail) and occasionally money. I remember having a small coin purse as a little girl to hold my allowance, and my first job at a hardware store at age fourteen. I still have my first W-2 form. I had earned $14.00 at a minimum wage of twenty-five cents an hour and was quite proud of myself. This is the level I was in when I longed for a family, as I played dolls with my little friends, and as I raised a family as an adult. I honored my father for serving in the military and my husband and son for doing the same. I remember being excited about supporting the election of President Eisenhower and the first successful moon landing some years later.

William Taegel states, "This perspective is immensely important. We have to love those near-by before we can love all sentient beings."[19] I belonged to the organized church and attended faithfully. I loved my family, my country and my religion. What I was taught was *right,* and I did not question it for several decades. Then came the 1960s, when I was in my late twenties, and a new level of the spiral strongly emerged in the culture.

The next level is *world-centric* in the orange and green memes. "The 3rd person (upper right "it" of the lenses) and the 4th person (lower right "its" of the lenses) perspectives evolve through science, the Renaissance, the industrial revolution and later the information age."[20] This level came in waves: Greece, the Renaissance, then emerged "the industrial age and representative democracy with full maturity."[21] In the process of questioning all the rules and behaviors I had been taught prior to the upheaval of my divorce, I entered psychotherapy and began to look at my world through the right lenses or perspectives. I sought objectivity from my therapist in order to comprehend the inner turmoil and contradictions of my existence. I began to study and to wrestle with new concepts I had never encountered. I still was using a major amount of the blue meme of education and the orange meme of psychotherapy and science to learn. Shocked and wounded, I was a far cry from understanding intimacy. I was in full retreat for some time emotionally. Retreating down the spiral to beige again to learn trust would be part of my pathway, as well as redefining the blue meme of my inner beliefs and rules.

At this point we have four different perspectives or stages from Ken Wilber's lenses to look at the development of human beings and five stages from spiral dynamics (beige, red, purple, blue and orange memes). The inquirer may take any lens (pronoun position) and look at a developmental level on the spiral. That opens the door to twenty viewpoints or even combinations thereof.

From this level on, we can reach even higher to the *Kos-mo-centric*. This level is the developing 2nd tier of spiral dynamics. This 5th tier person perspective in wisdom traditions is called the *Witness (Visionary) State*. We have gone beyond the first four pronouns. In the blue meme this witness is our inner critic. Remember my statement from my church and family that "divorce is a sin." Taegel and Yost assert that "Making friends with your inner critic is a path to establishing a center of gravity in the witness state. Our proposal: all roads to higher levels move through the critic."[22]

Part of my journey would be to reconcile my inner thinking and emotions surrounding judgement from my external critics and my internal critic, before I could move forward on my path. Deep within me is the internalized critical mother

125

with which I lived as a child. As I'm thinking about this critic, I believe it moves us through our traumas, because it pushes us to question, not only to question, but to *question everything*.

We have moments of greater awareness and move along the spiral, but an amnesia seems to occur. It feels like we are back where we started. This is a wake-up call to community, as explained by Taegel and Yost:

> To understand this process, note your own peak spiritual experience, especially vision quests... You receive a higher vision of yourself and life in general, maybe the Universe. Yet, you return to your usual life, and the 5th person perspective may fade. "Why?"... (Our) dominant orange/green culture acts like a magnet to pull you down from the heights of the witness/visionary state.[23]

In the safety of the Earthtribe community, I could look at how I felt judged by my traditional Christian faith and my family over my divorce. My brother went so far as to call me an adulteress for being divorced. (That was a little far-fetched, since I'm boring and have had only one partner in my entire life.) I could question my life and absorb into my inner world the gifts of my quests. I was not an irredeemable sinner. I was surrounded by the love of the community and Spirit. I did not need to throw stones of judgement at anyone else either. They were free to make their own life choices.

In this 2nd tier, the first level is the yellow meme. It is an objective level that permits one to see a bigger picture without judgement or feelings. The goal is the good for the larger whole. In my vision quests, the experiences I had were not only a gift to my spirit, but a message for all in the community and beyond. The 5th person perspective would allow the recognition of that aspect, but also recognize what meaning that message had not only for the soul on the personal level on many levels of the spiral, but also the meaning for the larger community.

There is a sixth person level (perspective) called the *integral era* denoted as the turquoise level that includes all the stages that went before. It is a meme that includes *agape*. Taegel defined this level, as follows:

> ...(The) spiral shaman (is capable of) moving between the orbits of evolution. In the up and down movement a profound wisdom arises... You don't over identify with anything, so you are free to embrace whatever arises (5th perspective), but embrace it, learn from it (6th perspective), then let go. Cleanly.[24]

The turquoise, or 6th person perspective, was a relief to me, because I first judged the 5th perspective as so distant as to be cold and callous. I asked my mentor, "Where is the compassion?" He explained that the compassion was in letting the observed be totally free to *be* without having the need to change or fix it. The 5th perspective is so objective it can just walk away. What is so freeing is what follows:

> The sixth perspective allows you to hold all the previous five perspectives in your circle at one time... Or one at a time,... You are no longer bound with the glue of your personal story to a particular map (perspective). Your story comes into your circle. You mourn. You brag. You learn. You don't take it too seriously. Then, you let it go.[25]

This quote is a good prayer outline in my mind for the direction of the West (letting go and gratitude) that we previously discussed. (Note how the direction of the Sky of the 2nd tier with its greater awareness informs the Medicine Wheel. Every direction on the Medicine Wheel interrelates with the others.) What a wonderful means to escape from our dramas. These perspectives allow us to look at history with new awareness. Doorways are open to experiences like my vision quest (told in chapter nine), when I sensed something beyond the stories/dramas I carried with me into my vision site.

This part of the journey up the spiral leads to the 7th perspective, *Sacred Mystery*, a perspective beyond words. Dr. Taegel eloquently described this state in this manner:

> ...Each night, you drift into sleep, a state supported by your causal body. In that state (perspective) you cease to be an object.
> You are purely subjective.
> You are the Subject that has no object.
> You are that which has no opposite.
> You are the Original Face before the Universe was created.
>
> That is, you drift in mysterious spaciousness... I believe what folks experience with a shaman, a guru, or a sage is this 7th perspective. Another name might be "enduring grace."[26]

In the Christian tradition, this would be called infused contemplation.

Ken Wilber's four lenses and the perspectives for change and transcendence

A personal experience to look at through the first four lenses from Ken Wilber's work would be my vision quest in the spring of 2006, when I received the nature name *Beauty's Breath*.[27] I will share more with you in chapter nine concerning this four day quest and the incidents that led to this name.

When I look at this incident through the lenses, I note the following:

> From the upper left lens of "I," these are my thoughts:

I am alone and feel sad.
I am praying with my hand on my Pipe.
I feel wounded by someone I deeply love.
I feel I am a "no-thing."
I am frightened by the sound of breathing, not my own.
I have an experience of Spirit.
I feel safe and totally at peace, deeply loved.

From the lower left lens of "we," I note:

I hear the "breath of something other."
There is a "we" of breath within the tent.

From the upper right lens of objective "it," I observe:

Lillie has spoken of being abandoned over her lifetime.
Lillie thinks her friend has abandoned her.
Lillie is praying in her tent after three days of fasting.
Lillie is in a weakened physical state, too weak to persev-
erate on her feelings.
Lillie puts her hand on her Pipe bag.

From the fourth lens "Its," lower right, I observe:

Experiences of this type have been documented by others
that quest and meditate in other ways throughout history
by people like Teresa of Avila, Julian of Norwich.
Vision questers are given names according to these
events.

In this chapter, I have journeyed back through many memories as examples of our life processes: some funny, some sad, some profound.

Lake Medicine:
The ceremony of remembering

I truly enjoy a meditation entitled *Lake Medicine*. It reminds me of Christ mixing dirt and spit to heal the blind man's eyes. The meditation is a strong connection for me of nature-based spirituality and the story of Christ's healing work.

The Ceremony of Remembering:

> Move through and beyond your current body and personality in a death. This ceremony can be used either for small deaths to new levels of evolution or the major death, the big journey beyond.
>
> In either case you journey to the great Medicine Lake, the Lake of Memory.
>
> Look at the cold water, how clear it ripples before you. Pause there, and breathe until you are ready to speak. The waters from deep in the Earth fill the Lake not only with spring water but with the profound wisdom of the Earth.
>
> *The Lake listens as we speak the ancient words.*
>
> **Leader:** I am a child of the earth and of the starry Heaven.
> **Group:** I am a child of the earth and of the starry Heaven.
>
> **Leader:** I am parched with thirst from my long journey.
> **Group:** I am parched with thirst from my long journey.
>
> **Leader:** Give me quickly the cold water of memory or I perish.
> **Group:** Give me quickly the cold water of memory or I perish.
>
> **Lake Medicine:** I touch you with the cold water of the deep memory of who you really are.
> **Group:** The cold water awakens in me who I really am.
>
> **Each person:** Wash away the dust. Let me see.[28]

The traumas of my life, including the inner child Liliput, created a dust or filter through which I unconsciously viewed life. To cleanse the filters through my journey with nature-based spirituality has given me a new awareness of who I really am, a loved being of the Creator, fully engaged in the pathway before me. With deep gratitude, I am able to see the world with new perspective and hope for myself and others, no longer blinded and captured by some of my unconscious energies. The traumas of my life are memories that teach me, no more than that.

We have looked at several mentoring tools in this chapter: nature walks, journalling and meditation, storytelling and myth, psychological and developmental tools. The mentoring tools included in this chapter are the values and stages (lenses, orbits, levels, and perspectives) from Ken Wilber and Beck and Cowan, the use of myth and storytelling, and ceremony (Lake Medicine, Earthdance, sweatlodge). I also include a discussion with my mentor of what God *Is* that was a major turning point in my Christianity. I was able to conceive of God more as Spirit and Creative Force, rather than the anthropomorphic, judgmental God the Father of my cultural upbringing, yet, include both concepts.

The work to transcend our personal stories and voices is ongoing throughout our lives. Yet, when we have some awareness of our own stories and inner voices, then we can relate to others with intimacy.

There have been so many changes in my journey that have led me to greater awareness and compassion. My mind, heart and spirit can hardly encompass them all at once. Perhaps, I can express it best in my paintings, poetry, or song. Out of my heart in the beginning of my journey, out of depression so long ago came this poem that speaks of my world today. I offer this voice to Grandfather Sky in gratitude for the journey:

Reflections

Fruit and flowering shrubs strewing petals,
Soft colors carpeting tender firstborn grass,

Rain clouds hovering, scent of weeping dew,
All the Earth created new.

Ancient trees with broken boughs,
Decked in Spring's bright hope,
Sheltered with birdsong—
    concealed, windblown sigh,
Eternity glimpsed in age and rue.

Sing out my heart to the raven's cry—
Awake! And see what is real
Flashing dark light in dove grey heaven,
Now settling gently out of view.

When storm and shower cleanse the world,
    Sudden the rainbow's hue,
Vibrant, glimmering stream gathering the
    shadowed sky,
Reflecting the light anew.

(Author, March 26, 1984)

Note again how the direction of the Sky of the 2nd tier with its greater awareness informs the Medicine Wheel, for instance the West. Every direction on the Medicine Wheel connects like spokes with the others. It is time to turn in prayer and intention to the direction of All of my Relations (*mitakuye o'yasin*).

CHAPTER EIGHT

The Direction of All My Relations: Sacred Leadership, Building Resilient Community

The direction of the relations includes all things created. In previous chapters and the chapter to come, I speak of relationships to people, animals, birds, snakes and wind.

All living things are one

Lame Deer teaches us the following:

> Nothing is so small and unimportant but it has a spirit given to it by Wakan Tanka. Tankan is what you might call a stone god, but he is also part of the Great Spirit. The gods are separate beings, but they are all united in Wakan Tanka. It is...something like the Holy Trinity. You can't explain it except by going back to the "circles within circles" idea, the spirit spinning itself up into stones, trees, tiny insects even, making them all *wakan* (sacred) by his ever-presence. And in turn all these myriad of things which makes up the universe flowing back to their source, united in the one Grandfather Spirit.[1]

In this chapter, I will first explore taking the responsibility of leadership and the building of a community, based on all things are *wakan*, sacred; and secondly, the structure and tenets of leadership that evolved in my thinking, as I researched information, contemplated and practiced community leadership. One of the blessings of the Earth Circle group is the non-denominational aspect. It offers the opportunity to form intimacy with those of different traditional belief systems.

Sacred leadership:
Building community in an Earth Circle

Some years back, I formed a spiritual community called an "Earth Circle." It was so named, because our prayers and stories center around our connection with the Earth and our relationship to Spirit and nature. The small group centers on an aspect of nature each month and meets to discuss how that particular aspect relates to our individual life stories. Then the question is given, "How does this reflect Spirit's action in your particular life journey?" The small circle is a microcosm of how even larger circles might form or disintegrate. A strong bond has formed between members as they shared the intimacy of their lives. A strong affinity to Spirit has developed. A few of the stories from the group are indicative of the meaningfulness of the nature-based spiritual group, so I would like to share them with you.

Grief and death

One of the members had experienced the death of her husband. As she shared her story, the other women spoke of losses and grief. In a few months she began to look around her and see beauty in life once more. She was especially moved in a meeting when "storms" was the topic. She spoke intensely of the storms and near drowning from emotions. She became aware that storms end. They replenish and cleanse. Spirit could and would replenish her. The etchings of grief are no longer visible in her face. Her conversation is more diverse.

Margaret Wheatley states in her book, *Leadership and the New Science*, "It would seem that the more participants we engage in this participative universe, the more we can access its potentials and the wiser we can become...evoking multiple meanings through our powers of observation."[2]

Medical issues and anxiety

A second member of the group was undergoing medical tests for sleep apnea and confronted also by the need for surgery on her hands. She was captured by these issues for weeks. One month, we were discussing the birds and winged creatures in our environment. She suddenly looked at the group and said, "I don't want to be a grackle." Everyone laughed, but honored the sincerity of her desire.

Finding a lost child

A third member of the group was very excited. At first she was hesitant, but the joy of the news led her to share. As a young unmarried woman, she had given up a daughter for adoption. Through a group that assists in the location of children and combining them with birth parents, the half-sister had located the adoptee. The mother was re-united with this long lost child. She had carried the infant's birth bracelet in her purse all these years. As part of the preliminary meeting, she sent this bracelet to her daughter and verified how she loved and longed for her. The member also discovered she had twin grandchildren, a boy and girl, age six.

We all celebrated her joy and were delighted with pictures she began to bring to the group. This is a perfect example of the love of a community without judgement, a community with compassion. This member connected her joy with the seasons, especially spring. Margaret Wheatley in her book, *Finding Our Way*, speaks to the new story this group member was creating with her lost daughter. "Those who carry a new story and who risk speaking it abroad have played a crucial role in times of historic shift. Before a new era can come into form there must be a new story."[3]

Cancer diagnosis and the family

A fourth member was diagnosed with breast cancer. She trusted that a connection with Mother Earth would heal her. Her daughters requested a sweatlodge ceremony for her healing. Discussing this with the sweatlodge leader, it was decided that we would require a preparation time. I met with the family on a Saturday. After discussing with them that healing might be the reality of physical death, we made prayer ties. The mother was at peace with the prospect of possible death, but the daughters were not. On the appointed day, we brought the mother briefly into the lodge for the ceremony, being mindful that she was in intense chemotherapy. To our amazement and joy, the mother was later diagnosed free of cancer, and both of her daughters have since graduated from college and married.

The mother returned to the Earth Circle and shared how she felt as she sat on Mother Earth and said her prayers. Her complete trust in Spirit was beautiful to see and most likely provided a major contribution to her return to health. Once healed, she left the group and continued her previous life. I saw her a month or two ago still radiant and happy with her beautiful thick hair grown back and waiting for her daughters to join her and her husband for dinner.

The cancer victim had descended to the beige meme of survival. In the family's steps to ascend the spiral, they began by ascending to the purple meme of magic and shamanism in the sweatlodge (nature-based spirituality). Don Beck and Christopher Cowan describe this level, as follows:

• Obey desires of the mystical spirit beings.

- Show allegiance to elders, custom, clan.

- Preserve sacred place, objects, ritual.

- Bond together to endure and find safety.

- Live in an enchanted, magical village.

- Seek harmony with nature's power.[4]

After the cancer victim's healing, the family then ascended further along the spiral to the blue meme of their membership in the local Baptist church. Will Taegel denotes how the person's ability to move down the spiral also relates to our physical health. This was a new and interesting concept to me. I had never considered that the cells of our bodies (We can even think in terms of the sub-atomic particles, or even a discrete unit of energy like a quantum wave.) have a consciousness, an awareness, which scientists have proven. All of these discrete energies function within the whole.[5] Taegel then relates these levels of our physical development (cells, organs, whole body) to the functioning of the levels of mysticism and says, "So it is with non-dual or integral mysticism, which depends upon deity mysticism, which then depends on Nature mysticism. Without Nature-based mysticism, non-dual mysticism cannot function."[6] We address these stages of mysticism again in chapter nine.

Family unity, making a connection to the Earthtribe through the Earth Circle, the creation of prayer ties and attending a sweatlodge were crucial steps in the family's progress through the purple meme. The family then returned to the traditional blue meme of the Baptist Church.[7]

Perspectives on leadership: Noting strengths and weaknesses in leadership

It is extremely important to evaluate one's leadership strengths and weaknesses. Personally, I spend a day or two after each group meeting thinking about all that occurred. I meet with my mentor on a regular basis and bring up questions and concerns as they arise for me (for example, my encounter with the cancer victim). Wheatley addresses the needs of leadership with the following statement:

> To live in a quantum world... We will need to become very savvy about how to build relationships, how to nurture growing, evolving things. All of us will need better skills in listening, communicating, and facilitating groups, because these are the talents that build strong relationship.[8]

Through the years, I found strengths in inviting others into the group and encouraging participation. They appear to feel safe and trusting with me. I am careful to maintain confidentiality. Wimberley is a small town, which means "news travels fast."

My weakness tends to be that I want to *fix* issues for people, what Muriel James in her book, *Born to Win*, calls a Parent/Child transaction.[9] It is difficult and incumbent upon me to monitor my mothering tendencies. Another issue for me is that I genuinely like others and want to communicate with them. In that process, I tend to join in and speak quickly. There needs to be "wait time" for others to come up with their own solutions. It is a task to guard against being impulsive with one's thoughts and comments. They are born out of caring, yet may have the opposite effect on the recipient.

The following quote from T. S. Eliot once again seems to apply to me:

I said to my soul, be still, and wait without hope for
hope would be hope for the wrong thing, wait
without love, for love would be love of the wrong
thing; there is yet faith,... But the faith and the love
and the hope are all in the waiting.[10]

Another weakness that I constantly fight is allowing my
busy schedule to interfere with timely announcement of meetings. Occasionally, this causes difficulty for others as they plan
their schedule. They know the meetings are the second Sunday
of the month; however, announcements are helpful.

One might well ask me, "What is the rationale behind the
formation of an Earth Circle?" Will Taegel in his book, *The Sacred Council of Your Wild Heart: Nature's Hope In Earth's Crisis*,
speaks of the spiritual benefits I believe are attained, as follows:

The fresh air and weather act as hot water on freeze
dried crystals being poured over your innards. Deli-
cious smells, like that of fresh coffee or, better,
mountain laurel in the Spring, waft through you.
Powers you didn't dream you had are drawn forth
by your contact with The Wild Heart. These very
powers are essential ingredients to address the current crisis in the human journey.[11]

Aspects of leadership

I turn my attention now to a class on leadership I experienced
at Wisdom University. In my mind, five major incidents that
demonstrate leadership skills stand out regarding the intensive
I attended. There were other wonderful moments, but I especially relate to these five.

Transparency

The first is "transparency." The President of Wisdom University
(now the Graduate School of Ubiquity University), two board

members and the faculty (including the Dean of Students and a Vice President) met together in the center of the classroom in a "fish bowl." In that setting, they discussed the struggles and goal setting for the past, present and future of the university. I was deeply moved. In the process of attaining two master's degrees, I have never experienced this type of openness shared with the student body. In the sharing of the differences in goals and personality that help shape the university for the future and the underlying spiritual belief system, we as a student body were offered an opportunity to intimately know the motivations and personalities of our leaders. We were offered an opportunity to share in a co-creative process that gives hope for the future of this university and its tenets.

The university has a two-fold mission: intellectual stimulation and the spiritual, psychological and physical growth of each student (objective and subjective). Never before in my educational experience has the faculty of a university, much less its presidents and board, been overtly interested in the evolution of my soul. That intent in and of itself is motivation enough to attend this particular university. It is also a profound teaching about leadership in the group context.

Conflict and goals

The second momentous challenge occurred in a dialogue with President Garrison, wherein he addresses his own personal efforts to form two world forums for the purpose of a prophetic warning to the human race that we are destroying this planet's capabilities to sustain life for our species. I appreciated his vulnerability and transparency in this discussion.

It is a shocking warning that eighty to ninety percent of the population will be dead before the end of this century. This discussion also raises my awareness of the starvation in Somalia, Ethiopia and other parts of the world. My instant thoughts were of my grandchildren who would be in the very middle of this chaotic event. It struck deep fear in my heart that I would psychologically resist. Another board member Jim Hickman addressed the class that evening and stated that he had a more hopeful alternative view.

These two ends of the seesaw of viewpoints reminded me of an event in the 1980s, when I was visiting Eva and Mike in California. My friends took me on a hike in an unfamiliar park to enjoy the redwoods. Somehow, we became separated. Calling for them and receiving no answer, I walked further along and found a fire lane cut through the forest. I turned and decided to walk down hill to find a place where this fire lane might connect with the road on which we arrived, hoping that I would discover other people there and locate my friends.

A forest ranger came along the fire lane in a jeep. He asked me if I was lost. I told him I was going to walk down the lane to find the road. I must have been going in the right direction, because he left.

My thoughts after this incident were as follows:

Are we lost, when someone else thinks we are?
Are we lost, when we think we are?
Or, are we lost without any knowing?

For me, this metaphor seemed to fit what I was hearing. Are we doomed as prophesied? Are we doomed, when our fears think we are? Or, are we doomed without any knowledge and awareness? This raises the question and hypothesis as to how to approach this imminent global disaster.

During the class, we talked about sustainability for the planet. We discussed using solar energy, rather than carbon products, gardening and rain water collection to offset drought from global warming. These collaborative discussions gave insights into how to manifest hope for our species.

141

Limits and potential for change

The third moment that stands out in my mind is our class trip to Enchanted Rock. This approach to connect back with our human roots of development with a deep shamanic connection with Mother Earth is a pathway I have been following for some years now in the Earthtribe. We are connected to a deep nature-based spirituality.

On this trip, I sat on an embankment in the creek bed below the rock. I encountered three rattlesnakes. The first warned me when I came within six feet of it. I stopped and oriented myself to its sound and direction, then stepped backwards to another tree. When I sat down in the shade the snake continued to rattle another five or six minutes. Then a second snake began to rattle across the creek about twelve or fifteen feet away. A third snake rattled from the opposite direction from the first snake about thirty feet upstream. This encounter is a teaching from Mother Earth. There are limits. There are dangers. There are warnings. We need, like I was at the stream, to be respectful and watch out for the boundaries of what we do.

When the rattle snakes I encountered settled down and permitted my presence, I first noticed the variety of rocks: Cambrian granite, white and grey limestone, sandstone, quartz and feldspar. In my heart, I honored the diversity of Mother Earth. Then I noticed how many types of plants were visible. I thought of the gift of abundance. Then I looked higher and watched the breeze move the branches of the trees. Suddenly, like a rain shower, leaves blew down to the earth. I thought of the concept of change. With Mother Earth there is always the potential of change. This encounter was a teacher, like the ones we discuss in the Earth Circle each month. Relationships and communities require limits and the potential for change.

Collaboration and roles

The fourth incident I encountered was the class assignment we received wherein we met in groups of four at the base of Enchanted Rock. Our assignment was for each member of the small group to assume one leadership role. My role was to organize a consensus from the group about what we would do and where we would go. Another member of the group was responsible for leading us to individual sites for meditation. The third leader was to keep track of where everyone was located. The fourth leader was to monitor the time and bring us all back to the main group safely. I found this assignment easy to accomplish.

We had four strong leaders in our group, but we were able to adjust to each other's needs for control. One leader wanted to go up on the rock, but generously gave up her position for the good of the whole. Two of us were physically not capable of such a strenuous climb. There seemed to be a genuine positive bonding of the group and little if any tension I could ascertain. I think it resulted in a willingness on everyone's part to collaborate as a group and set aside our individual strong personalities thereby forming the basis for a small tribe.

Need for Community

The fifth powerful and heartwarming incident was the morning we walked the labyrinth. I have done this several times over the years in different settings. One incident I had enjoyed in the past was leading one another through the labyrinth in dyads with one partner being blindfolded. That was an extremely moving encounter, but this morning walk was very powerful.

Part of this large group arrived at the center of the labyrinth and stood for a while. As they started moving back out of the labyrinth path they were facing those of us still walking toward the center. It was a moment of face to face encounter with each approaching person. It was like the Native American

143

phrase, *Heh A Nah* (I see you, or greet you.). There was no possibility of staying isolated in one's own reverie or altered state. It was like an obvious wake up call to connection and community.

Summary thoughts on relationships and community

The Earth Circle is an ongoing community. I find that my own spiritual life improves as I prepare topics for each month's meetings and meditate and reflect on them myself. The deep sharing of the group builds a strong sense of caring for one another. It was hard on some members of the Earth Circle for me to become vulnerable and ill for a space of time. One member left because of this. Her vulnerability is a fear of being trapped into becoming a caregiver.

In the beginning, the members expect constant strength in the leader. I believe it is important to build strong leadership throughout the group (like the small group of four at Enchanted Rock), so one does not carry a role of perfection, or "guru" like persona. The shared leadership of the small group experience is freeing. One can be leader and a follower at the same time. Margaret Wheatley speaks to this issue, as follows:

> Ownership describes personal links to the organization, the charge emotion driving feeling that can inspire people. A tried and true maxim of my field of organizational behavior (O.B.) is that "people support what they create"… In quantum logic, it is impossible to expect any plan or idea to be real to… (participants) if they do not have the opportunity to personally interact with it.[12]

For example, it was important that the member with cancer and her daughters develop the awareness that her healing would not be a magical event, like a rabbit's foot, but Spirit's natural flow in her life span. It is also conversely imperative that I monitor my ego states and not satisfy my ego needs as a leader. I consider my range of thoughts and emotions continuously with my own mentor. It is a personal suggestion that if you mentor others, it is nearly impossible to do so without a mentor of your own due to the processes of transference and countertransference.

My spirit feels moved to expand the group's thinking a little further. As I announce the time of the meeting and the topic, it would be fruitful to introduce such topics as carbon footprints, global warming, the threat of extinction of our species and methods of sustainability. If in fact these warnings reach a "tipping point," all of us will need resilience. Brian Walker and David Salt in their book, *Resilience Thinking: Sustaining Ecosystems and People in a Changing World*, define resilience and its need, as follows: "Resilience is the capacity of a system to absorb disturbance and still retain its basic function and structure."[13] Their conclusions from a statement by Walter V. Reid, Director of the Millennium Ecosystems Assessment, Stanford University in the foreword of their book are, as follows:

> It is widely apparent that humanity's use of the biosphere is not sustainable... (The) human species is living beyond its means on a planet with finite resources; demand is out of balance with supply. Environmental problems...will not be solved using the failed approaches of the past. But they can be solved if we embrace resilience thinking.[14]

No one person can hold all the answers. Together, perhaps our species can find the answers to the chaos and danger we are creating with our profligate and negligent use of our planet's abundance. Awareness from our inner council, forming resilient communities, addressing the issues needed to protect our planetary home in these times of chaos on the economic front and the threat to the survival of our species and others on the planet with climate change that includes drouth is our "world-work."[15]

One way I am approaching this excess is partially altruistic and partially pragmatic. As I have mentioned earlier, I downsized my residence and disposed of many of my personal belongings. I am amazed at how much *stuff* I have purchased over the years and thought I needed. As I express my evolving sense of freedom from this orange meme, my friends are beginning to say they need to do the same thing.[16] It is a small moment of leadership I did not premeditate. There is a good feeling in the process. As I let go of my relationship with my possessions, there is a sense of spiritual growth. My first reaction to this process was, "Oh, no;" but now it is a strong, "Oh, yes!"

The Christian church teaches that one can not serve God and mammon (or the world). It also teaches to go out and have dominion over the world. In my thinking this is a conflict of duality. This attitude of dominion is slowly beginning to change. I will address this Christian tendency toward change in chapter eleven on reciprocity towards the earth. Nature-based spirituality has been recognized as Franciscan in nature and mostly ignored, minimized, or rejected. Christian community is related to praying together and focussing on the life to come, not the relationship to all living things. One's relationship to God is a preparation for the hereafter—to live with God in an eternal heaven of many mansions. There is argument for God both with us and in the eternal. God with us however is expressed more as the incarnate Christ who has ascended. This focus on the afterlife tends to reject our place as a species among others on the planet now and negate interest in the planet's crises.

Nature-based or indigenous spirituality, perceiving us as a species among species, calls, even demands, attention to the planetary crises for we are part of the crises. Spirit (God) is totally enmeshed in the environment. To neglect the environment is to neglect our relationship to Spirit. Interestingly, Christianity would call that separation "sin."

The indigenous tribes concretely honor that we are a species among species (*Mitakuye O'yasin*, all my relatives). The Lakota tradition as I learned it from my grandmother was to use what one needed with thanksgiving and not waste anything. She always taught me to give to others whatever I could to ease their path (food, clothing, emotional support). These teachings are basic tenets of community resilience. My grandmother's teachings also resonate with the Christian tradition and injunction: "You shall love your neighbor as one's self" (Leviticus 19:18).[17] Are not our neighbors also other species? My prayer to Spirit about relations is that we bridge the separation of humans from nature and ever be mindful of all living things and take deep care of Mother Earth, our planetary home.

In this chapter, I have addressed the issue of sacred leadership and how to build a nature-based spiritual community. The mentoring tools utilized are nature-based community, the sweatlodge, the development of values from Beck and Cowan, authenticity and transparency, and the labyrinth.

Spiritually, I connect with the healing of Spirit, and the gift of Spirit's nature-based teachings of change, abundance, limits and potential. On a Christian level, I am grateful for the incidents of healing I mention in this chapter. I was taught by my traditional church to go into the world and be Christ's hands and feet. The Native American tradition calls for us to live in relationship. For me, that means to open myself to be a channel for Spirit's work.

The deep connection with nature through relationship, especially formed in vision quest encounters, leads me to moments of mysticism. Our spirituality and mysticism is founded on Nature Mystics, from which evolved Deity Mystics, the Unity Mystics (one with the One), and the Non-dual mystic, who integrates all of the levels. This integration has been a major part of my pathway for nearly thirty years, and really began when I was five years old sitting on my grandmother's front steps.

We had been to evening church services, and I was waiting outside before my grandmother prepared a light supper of biscuits and buttermilk before bedtime. I asked God, "Why do grownups tell me you are way up there in the sky in heaven, and yet you feel like you are right here?" My journey with Christianity and nature-based religion was in early stages; yet, I was taking beginning steps.

Mitakuye O'yasin, All My Relations
Puha, The Sacred Wind breathes through us.

I speak of the concept *mitakuye o'yasin* and *puha* many times in the book. They are the essence of my writing.

Earlier in this chapter, I spoke of the threat of death to the cancer victim. The term *death* calls us into the direction of the Ancestors. I turn my prayers and intention in that direction.

CHAPTER NINE

The Direction of the Ancestors: Who, Me? A Mystic?!

The eighth direction of the Medicine Wheel honors the Ancestors. Prayers in this direction are informed by the wisdom of those that have died and gone before us to the implicate order. They include our personal and spiritual ancestors. Most importantly to me, it includes that which I call "God, Sacred Mystery, the One, All That Is."

In this chapter, I would like to reflect upon my personal near-death experience March 2008 and my vision quest (called the "little death") in April 2006. When I meditate on these incidents, I am aware others have also experienced these spiritual events. Because one is encountering the *numinous*, those who speak of this process are often called mystics.

Michael Cox writes in his book, *Mysticism: The Direct Experience of God*, the following definition for "mystik"(German term):

> (Mystik)…is generally taken as authentic mysticism… (It) begins in a fundamental consciousness of a beyond, of a Reality, changeless and eternal, that permeates and gives meaning… The mystic…apprehends a truth that is beyond the grasp of the rational intellect… He grasps the abiding unity of all things, perceiving the co-immanence of the eternal and temporal. For the religious mystic,…this apprehen-

sion becomes the direct experience of the Presence of God.[1]

Four levels of the development of the mystic can be delineated:

- The first mystics in the human story were Nature Mystics. They practiced their spiritual connections in the forests, mountains and desert...

- Next the Deity Mystics come into view. These are the Judaeo-Christian/Islamic monotheists who emphasize spiritual oneness with Deity, the Other...

- Next in the evolution of spirituality, Unity Mystics teach students to become One with the One as in Hindu mysticism...

- Finally, emerges the Non-dual Mystic who integrates essential elements from all of the above.[2]

My experiences touched on these levels of development on my vision quest and in my near-death experience, (as they have on other quests and in meditation moments) and I will discuss them later in the chapter. For now, let us look at a medical emergency that was life threatening.

An encounter with death and the ancestors

In January 2008, exactly a year after my brother's death, following a dental appointment where I received an epinephrine and lidocaine injection, I began to have recurring symptoms of atrial fibrillation and incidents of erratic heart failures. I was in and out of the hospital several times over the next three months with heart tests and medications. None of these treatments showed the problem clearly, nor were they effective. The cardiologist kept saying following all the tests that I had a healthy heart and would send me home.

In mid-March, I again was rushed to the hospital emergency room. The nurse said, "Lady, you have a 'funky' heart!" In the next few minutes my heart began to stop. It did this three times. Just as the medical team was rushing in with the crash cart and heart paddles, my heart started beating again.

While my heart was stopped for a period of several minutes, I had the following experiences. I saw a lot of white light. I was in the light. I curled into a fetal position on my right side. (In reality, I was lying prone on my back with a lot of monitors and tubes.) As I lay on my side, my mother's presence was behind me and near the foot of my gurney. I told my mother I felt okay about crossing over. My children's lives were going well. Paula had won her custody battle for her son, and Charles David had married in December. I told her there was enough money in the bank for the children to bury me. Then I said, "But, I just registered at Wisdom University, and I would really like to go there and acquire my degree." Then I became conscious of the medical personnel rushing towards me, and someone saying, "She started again."

The next thing I knew I was in ICU, where I would be semi-conscious for the next eight days. Two different nurses told me confidentially that I needed to be moved to Austin Heart Hospital. My cell phone was in my bed, and I called my daughter. That evening she met with my first cardiologist, who was having trouble diagnosing me, and demanded that I be moved to Austin.

The next day I was taken by ambulance to Austin Heart Hospital. I was given an electrical cardiologist. I could hear him discussing my situation from the monitor at the nurse's station outside my room. "Do you see this. It is not striking here and here. It's striking in the wrong places." On the third day, I received a pacemaker. My heart was not damaged. I needed a replacement for the node that times and fires the electrical impulses. The physician's assistant to my new cardiologist told me that due to the injection at the dentist's office I had developed in seven weeks a condition that usually takes seven years.

In retrospect, the dentist's error was a blessing. Atrial fibrillation over a period of time enlarges the heart. This had not occurred for me.

My experiences in the emergency room are far from unique. In the preface of Dr. Raymond Moody's book, *Life After Life*, Dr. Melvin Morse states, "...virtually every conscious researcher and medical scientist in the field agrees that these experiences are a real and natural part of the dying process—not caused by drugs or lack of oxygen to the brain."[3]

> We do not simply die... We die conscious, with an expanded awareness of the reality coupled with a greater understanding of our lives. By understanding near-death experiences, we connect ourselves with the wisdom of tribal shamans, the insights of the *Tibetan Book of the Dead*, and the origins of the great religions of the world.[4]

Dr. Morse also speaks of Dr. Elizabeth Kubler Ross's concepts that a religious figure (coinciding with personal religious beliefs) or a relative come to assist the dying, and that many have an experience of being out of their bodies and observing their death with a quiet sense of peace and wholeness.[5] This was true for me and for my brother, as I observed his death. He calmly and acceptingly told his wife and I that Jesus was standing in the corner of his room, and that he was going home.

I was very joyous when I registered at Wisdom University January 8, 2008 to seek a Doctor of Ministry degree. Dr. Moody speaks to near death experiences and my personal desire to go to the university with this statement:

> (Persons) have told me that, though they were comfortable and secure in their disembodied exist-

ence and were enjoying it, they felt happy to be
able to return to physical life since they had left
some important task undone. In a few cases, this
has taken the form of a desire to complete an unfin-
ished education.[6]

My journey into the border between life and the after life
reminds me of Plato's allegory of the cave for I knew the presence of my deceased mother and sensed the reality of the other
side or implicate order in my mind's eye like the shadows on
the cave's wall in the allegory.[7] There was a greater reality I
could sense behind me where my mother's presence stood, that
I could only glimpse in the shadows. I could not yet see and experience this reality, but I was very close to the instant moment
of turning to face it.

William Taegel in his book, *The Many Colored Buffalo*, explains what I told my mother's presence on that hospital gurney:

What many aspects of our selves (inner council of
selves) strive after face to the background when
death is near. As they fade, other spiritual energies
come forward. They are the ones that say things
like,… "Your son and daughter will be okay. They
will have to run their lives without your input." The
nearness of death brings forth a quiet spiritual energy, one that is content with very little.[8]

Personally, I found it would be so gentle to just turn and
step into the implicate order. What was difficult to accept was
the medical process, the fears and "jangling" of my nerves
with alarm bells and fifteen minute blood pressure checks,
multiple blood tests through the day and night, IVs and injec-
tions in the stomach.

Dancing with the Ancestors

We often do not want to accept death. During a fall Earthdance that a friend and I led for the direction of the Ancestors, the following occurred:

> I had placed a rope on the ground. On the other side of the rope representing the domain of death was a lantern. Each dancer was given a candle. When the dancer was ready, the candle was to be blown out, and the dancer would step across the rope to the lantern, symbolizing the implicate order, the realm of Spirit. A few of the dancers wanted to tease me and not "cross over." A cool front was due to arrive that night. Just as the small group of dancers decided they would keep their candles burning, the north wind arrived and blew all of the candles out at once. The only remaining light was the lantern. It was a powerful, if humorous, teaching.

A "*dark night of the soul*"

There is another death that is not physical. It is a spiritual death. The mystics like St. John of the Cross speak eloquently of this form of death.

In 2005, I was to prepare for a vision quest in the spring of 2006. During this period, I found myself in a "dark night of the soul."[9] The vision quest itself is called the "little death," and questers are led out by their supporters beneath a shroud. They are brought back to the community at the end of their quest under the shroud, and it is removed for a symbolic new birth.

In preparation for a vision quest, the quester meets with a mentor/guide for a year prior to the event and for a subsequent year to process some of the vision's unfolding. This unfolding often occurs over a period of years.

The vision quest is a period of time, when the quester goes out alone to fast and pray for a connection to Spirit. One prepares personally with a circle of 405 prayer ties that sur-round the site of the quest. The preparation of these ties begins the spiritual focussing of the quester and provides a spiritual "safety net" of energy at the time of the quest.

For me the major teaching of the quest in April 2006 came the day after Christmas 2005. I was walking along a narrow path behind my mentor on an extraordinarily beautiful day. As is common in Texas that time of year, it was warm and sunny.

Suddenly, my mentor stopped on the path, looked back at me and said, "Lillie, I could care less what you think or feel." It struck me like a physical blow. I was so stunned I went into some sort of altered state. I do not know how the meeting ended, or how I drove home. In this "dark night of the soul," I did not know how to pray. I did not know the words of John of the Cross I would read later:

> God turns all this light of theirs into darkness...so completely in the dark that they know not whither to go with their sensible imagination and medita-tion,... (They) experience no pleasure and consola-tion in the spiritual things... (On) the contrary they find insipidity and bitterness...[10]

I not only found myself numb, but I could not feel the bit-terness, nor seem to find my soul. At this point, I could only grieve in greater depth than I ever thought I would feel again since the death of my son many years before. Peers in *John of the Cross* goes on to say, "However greatly the soul labours, it can-not actively purify itself so as to be in the least degree prepared for the divine union of perfection of love, if God takes not its hand and purges it not in the dark fire."[11]

A few days later on New Year's Day, I sat in a swing on my deck overlooking the woods. I began to cry. I went to a very dark place within myself where I was lost for days. My mentor and I met again, and it was explained that the comment was in relationship to a teaching and only meant for the moment, but my inner child to the depths of my soul could not hear the words of explanation. This inner child felt like a "no-thing." This deep sadness and grief would last for months, actually more than two years, until about the time of my heart incident and my first classes for certification in trauma mentoring.

Many of the prayers offered as I created my ties were related to this grief and sense of abandonment, or rejection, from my guide that my inner child believed had occurred. Thomas Merton in his book, *Contemplative Prayer,* also addresses the mental, emotional and spiritual state I found myself living:

> During the dark night...anxiety is felt in prayer, often acutely. This is necessary because the spiritual night marks the transfer of the full, free control of our inner life into the hands of a superior power. This means too that the time of darkness is, in reality, a time of hazard and difficult options.[12]

Then Merton sets the stage for the little Child within me that felt I was sitting on a rock in the midst of a fast moving river with only darkness surrounding me:

> If we set out into this darkness, we have to meet these inexorable forces. We will have to face fears and doubts... And, at this moment, precisely, all spiritual light is darkened, all values lose their shape and reality and we remain, so to speak, in the void.[13]

Muriel James in her book, *Born to Win,* describes this inner Child that rose up out of the depths of my psyche. I could not convince this part of myself with my inner Adult or Parent that anyone cared for the inner Child.[14] This quest would lead me into the depths of the abandoned Child that I was at age three and a half, when I was left by my divorcing parents in an orphanage for more than a year. All of the explanations of my parents in later years had not been enough to comfort that buried grief.

My guide had opened my oldest and deepest wound with that small comment, "Lillie, I could care less what you think or feel." In this moment the light of healing and awareness had an opportunity to occur, although it did not seem like it at the time.

Breath of "All That Is," Vision Quest 2006: Turning point

The vision quest in the spring of 2006 was the turning point for the resolution of this incident (and the event of my early child-hood) and for my inner healing. It would take many months, but it was the most important step in that process. I went out to my vision site to pray and fast for a period of four days.

The last afternoon before my return to the encampment I heard the drums and conch bringing in some of the questers. I decided to light my Pipe. My intent was to pray for them and a friend of mine I knew was in the process of dying that week. When I had completed my prayers, I lay face down with my left hand on my Pipe bundle.

I must have gone to sleep. I woke to the sound of deep breathing outside the tent near my head. I thought it was one of the buffalo on the ranch and rose up to look for it, thinking the buffalo was coming for a drink from one of the two ponds on each side of my tent. Because it was now dark night, I discovered that I could see nothing.

I lay back down, again placing my hand on the Pipe bag. Suddenly, I heard the breathing *inside* my tent. I could hear my own breathing. The other breathing was a different tone and rate. Frightened, I sat up. The breathing instantly stopped. Cautiously, I lay back down. Then the breathing returned. It wrapped around me like a warm cloak.

Spontaneously the words came, "It's the breath of *All That Is*." I was so startled and awed that I had spoken the words aloud. They rang with truth. Other powerful events occurred on this vision quest, but this one was life and spirit-changing for me.

The next day, when I was brought back to the encampment by my supporters and processed this quest with the elders, I stood at the end of my story and faced my vision guide. I looked into my guide's eyes and knew a profound peace. It did not matter what had wounded me so deeply. What mattered was the deep foundation we had forged together over a period of more than twenty years and the deep trust and affection I felt for this person. I thought, "It doesn't matter if this person could care less what I think, or feel." What matters is that I can trust someone this totally.

William Taegel in his work explains, "For years there is no aspect of the person there to listen, and then the ego begins the journey of expanding awareness by listening to the voices of the parts, hence the phrase—voice dialogue."[15] He then states, as follows, and addresses the depths of my inner despair and the later owning of "trust" that occurred:

> One way I have suggested that this inner nourishing of the individual takes place is through the expanding of the aware ego. The sub-personalities strain to express themselves. When we listen to the observer and patient selves, the awareness level is then taken to the ego in an ever-expanding process. Then, the aware ego can better utilize the parts.[16]

Taegel then states, "This moving to a higher level of awareness is what I call the transforming process."[17]

I was able to perceive myself and my mentor in new ways. In *Why Not Be A Mystic?*, Frank Tuoti speaks of the wisdom of Karl Rahner and Thomas Merton. "In this new age we must begin to 'see' as God 'sees'—inwardly. We must perceive —through a graced experience of the heart—the reality of things, most of all the inner truth of every person."[18] We seek but are not capable of union or understanding with one another on the deepest level until the inner self can confront in intimacy the inner self of the other, and this meeting must be in mutual trust.

The ability to bring my inner Child to trust opened the door for my spiritual self to begin to change. As I was preparing to write and meditating in the night, another healing moment came for me five years after this quest. I realized that God, Sacred Mystery, cared for me. I had been wrapped in Spirit's breath and comforted.

Within our many selves are the little children we once were. I acknowledge this truth regarding my inner shadow child I call Liliput. We also have other sub-selves that are pushed back because our value system and culture denote them as "bad," or not acceptable in some manner. For Taegel, the "meaning is clear. Through awareness of the deeper instincts lies the pathway to God."[19]

Recently, I read in Bear Heart's book, *The Wind Is My Mother,* something that really moved me. Bear Heart stated, "The Christians of our tribe call (God) *Him, He-sah ketah nese,* 'The Master of Breath.' Whatever name we use, there's a feeling of warmth and closeness."[20] *Puha* means this sacred breath.

Since, I was five years old, I had believed in what my elders taught me about a loving God, but I could never actually believe the reciprocity of that love. My early childhood "gods," my parents, had left me, so why would God love me? On this vision quest, I was gifted with the experience of being held by Spirit. The teachings of my elders and the traditional church had not been enough. The abandoned little girl in my inner council needed to experience this love. Through the generosity and grace of Spirit on this quest, I received that unmerited gift.

These words from the *Cloud of Unknowing* speak to my experience of the breath of *All That Is*. "Then perhaps He may touch you with a ray of His divine light which will pierce *the cloud of unknowing* between you and Him. He will let you glimpse something of the ineffable secrets of his divine wisdom and your affection will seem on fire with His love."[21]

In *The Many Colored Buffalo*, William Taegel again addresses the depths of my inner struggle:

> It is the intensity of the vulnerable selves that reminds us that our aware egos must call on sources of nourishment that are beyond the capabilities of our usual selves. It is the spiritual selves that become conduits to transmit the higher, healing energy to the vulnerabilities as they come forward.[22]

Never in my deepest imagination would I have thought I would encounter Spirit in my physical senses, embodied in the Breath of *All That Is* in the world of nature and have been so blessed. Taegel further states the following:

> This spiritual self (or selves) points out that there are
> many aspects of life beyond the realm of usual
> thinking, that there are connections and rhythms operating in this universe we can only guess about,
> and the creativity emerges out of these connections.
> This transpersonal spiritual energy balances the
> skeptic...[23]

Transcendent change

These two major events in my life have changed me in many ways. I believe there is an implicate order. I have experienced the proximity of it. The veil is very thin. There is an Ultimate Reality that I call "All That Is," or "Sacred Mystery," or "God."

I have learned to not only hear these things from my mentors, but own them from my own experiences. As I told my mentor one day walking on the road, "Love is much bigger than you (I) think."

On a relationship level, I have learned to trust not only others, but my own inner council. I have learned that there is a time to just observe and not be emotionally involved ("couldn't care less," if you will). From this witness state, I can perceive more clearly the experiences of my life.

The shock of the few words spoken on a sunny day that opened the wounds of my inner Child was a voice from Spirit, as well as my vision guide. I could have chosen to never return to see my guide rather than face my inner pain, but I chose to blunder through it the best I could. This choice led me to my vision quest's opportunity for healing. There is no doubt in my mind that the experience of my conversation with my mother in the hospital emergency room and the experience of the "Breath of Spirit" were pure reality.

Pathway of a mystic

Matthew Cox discusses the difference between those fleeting moments of awe we all experience and the reality of the mystic. We only approach the borders of the mystical state in fleeting experiences of awe. However, there comes a time when there is a feeling of identity between what is perceived and the mind. When this harmony is total between the mind and thing it perceives, such experiences may loosely be called mystical. There is a difference for the mystic. The inability to understand or apprehend the nature and significance of the experience; the vagueness and element of incoherence disappear in a veritable flood of certainty. One can recognize the true mystic, because "His sensations and reactions are focused by supreme and inalienable certitude and he is uplifted by the utter authenticity of his vision. The mystic therefore tells his story with absolute assurance: he *knows* what others simply believe."[24]

The stages of development of a mystic mentioned in Taegel's work can be seen in my vision quest and near-death experience. In the hospital, by accepting the reality of my mother's presence and the subsequent conversation, I entered the second stage of development (Deity Mystics). There is a heaven or implicate order, and my mother is there. On my vision quest, the stages are a little clearer. I entered the first stage (Nature Mystics) by going out to fast and pray under pine trees between two ponds. I connected to Spirit in the wilderness of a ranch. There was a connection with the second stage of a mystic (Deity Mystics) with my experience of *All That Is*, a Supreme Being. My spirit approached the third stage (Unity Mystics), or perhaps entered it, when I was wrapped in Spirit's breath. The acceptance of all of these realities perhaps places me for a moment in the fourth Non-dual stage of the mystic.[25] Will Taegel further points out these relationships or stages are a process: "So it is with non-dual or integrated mysticism, which depends on unity mysticism, which depends on deity mysticism, which then depends on nature mysticism."[26]

However, the question arises, "What does one do with the natural doubts that arise over time following an event?" Matthew Cox in his book on mysticism alluded to Coventry Patmore regarding the tendency to question an experience and ascribes it to the concepts of the modern scientific mind. Cox observes that mysticism in an absolute sense is a science in that it seeks knowledge of an Ultimate Reality. An all-consuming quest for perfect and supreme understanding or *knowing*. This reality is what theology acknowledges with the term God. [27]

Living on the Medicine Wheel

Let us now turn to May of 2009. In a class at Wisdom University, the students were invited to write a story or poem about their life. For a little more background, as I previously mentioned, I was born at home in north central Texas during a blowing "blue norther," a two pound, thirteen ounce premature baby. The following is what I wrote entitled *Living on the Medicine Wheel*:

> Born on a North Wind, sharp and strong, in a
> limestone studded land, far too small to live, yet
> live I did.
>
> Stumbling through years of being the "wrong"
> gender, servant to all, yet free and full of a
> joyful Spirit.
>
> Hidden from others deep within,
> I walked the path of daughter, wife and mother.
> For a span of years, I did not count, yet walked
> my path unaware.
>
> Then, a marker in the road, a split in the path:
> I noted I was fifty and lost my way in a divorce.
> "What way do I go?" The forest is deep and dark.
> "Should I die and end this pain, this loss of way?"
> I stumbled along in the dark, dead yet alive.
>
> A mentor came from a path I did not know.
> "This way," said my guide.
> I followed tentatively, still lost.
>
> Slowly, I began to notice: a lizard, a rainbow, an oak
> tree outside my window.
> My head and heart began to lift.
> I found the words to pray.
>
> I sat in my sweat on Grandmother Earth;
> I reached for Grandfather Sky—
> My guide stayed steady on the path, and I began
> to smile,
>
> "Death where is your sting?"

I began to live on the gentle practice of the Medicine
Wheel.
My heart called me to quest and seek to learn
again to sing,
"Wind blow on our troubled souls. Wind blow,
North Wind blow."

Not long ago, deep in the night, the breath of "All
That Is" surrounded my soul.
I knew beyond my fearful self that I was filled
with trust,
Surrounded in the love of "All That Is."

I was ready to move on again in the strength of the
North Wind's course!
My soul goes to meet others with all it has
learned.

"Mitakuye o'yasin," we all are one.

My guide nods with all he has taught me, and I too
learn to become a guide.

Puha! (Sacred Breath flowing through us)

      Butterfly Woman (1985)
      Guarded by Hawk (1992)
      Tiger Lily (1997)
      Grandmother Song (2000)
      Beauty's Breath (2006)
      Wise Wind (2011)

One can not help but note the progression of the nature
names I received from my quests. There is vulnerable, fragile
Butterfly Woman (facing a divorce), protected by Spirit in
Guarded by Hawk (at the death of my ex-husband and major
transitions in my life). Then more growth develops in *Tiger Lily*,
who faces her fears; *Grandmother Song*, who received a Pipe and
sang for her mother, rather than dissolve into tears at her
mother's death. Then came *Beauty's Breath*, as I learned about
trust and intimacy, and the name *Wise Wind* that is the next leg

of my journey. My life continues to unfold and evolve (one might say revolves) on the Medicine Wheel.

Taegel denotes the following about the major alliances and unfolding maps that develop with the nature names one acquires over a series of quests:

> From the aware ego position the seeker makes
> choices about which energy name is called for in
> which situation. Slowly, it becomes clear which
> name fits the whole person, and from the aware ego
> position (chooses). The names that the person re-
> ceives from the encounters form a map of the inner
> totem of selves; it is not the total map... All of the
> sub-personalities are (not) represented.[28]

The melding of these energies would form what Taegel calls *totem balancing*.[29]

Bear Heart, Native American mystic, shaman and Road-man, speaks to our seeking connection to a Higher Intelligence, whether through introspection, contemplation, or a vision quest. I, or we, might be looking within trying to discover: "Who am I? What do I truly feel or believe about this (our personal question)?" In his book, *The Wind Is My Mother*, Bear Heart speaks what is relevant to my experiences:

> There is a path for each of us to follow—that's what
> life is all about… "Questing" is something all people
> have done since childhood. You have quested for
> knowledge ever since preschool and kindergarten,
> on up through the university. Traditionally, the
> Creek people's primary focus wasn't on how smart
> we became. Our focus was on wisdom—how we
> used what little we had.[30]

Somewhere on this journey, my prayer is that I have gained some measure of wisdom. I know I face life with the knowledge that I am wrapped in the breath and love of Spirit. I am connected to all living things. I have learned to trust, that basic gift a child (and an adult) needs for survival and relationships. These are great teachings. As I faced my mortality, I have learned that I value education and the learning process through my experience with my mother. These are moments of awareness that remain with me. Perhaps, sometimes, I will forget the intensity of these moments, but in times of meditation each day I remember, and I am filled with gratitude.

Let us turn now to that reality we all tend to avoid, the reality of death.

Death and the soul

The Indigenous tribes and Christian religion have individual perspectives on death and the "Other Side," the side of the Ancestors. All of the ceremonies include the petitions and gratitude prayers spoken through the Pipe in the directions of the Medicine Wheel. I find it profound that the first ceremonial rite of the Oglala Sioux, the keeping of the soul, has to do with death.

Lame Deer speaks of remembering the ancestors in the sweatlodge:

> In the center of the lodge we scoop out a circular hole into which the stones will be put later. We pray to the Great Spirit as we do this. His power will be there in this little pit, which, when it is used in a sacred manner, will become the center of the whole world... The center pit also represents *wakicagapi*—the beloved, the dead relative who has returned to the earth. You have to remember him when you put the rocks into the hole.[31]

The Oglala Sioux have a ceremony for the soul, *hokshichankiya* (spiritual influence, or seed). The keeping of the soul, usually for a year, is a *sacred seed* that grows in the heart so that the people will "walk in a sacred manner." It also represents the seed for the tree of life at the center of the nation's hoop. "It is good," Black Elk has said, "to have a reminder of death before us, for it helps us to understand the impermanence of life on this earth, and this understanding may aid us in preparing for our own death. He who is well prepared is he who knows that he is nothing compared with *Wakan Tanka*, who is everything; then he knows that world which is real."[32]

The soul, usually represented by a lock of hair, is purified with the smoke of sweet grass and wrapped in a sacred buckskin. It is kept in a special place in the tipi. The body of the deceased is taken to a scaffold in a tree and given back to the elements, the creatures and the earth. The keeper of the soul is sacred and must keep that intent night and day in prayer. The keeper of the soul is not allowed to hunt or use a knife. He does go on the hunt and sits nearby with the Pipe in prayer. The buffalo cow killed near him is his and the shoulder meat is prepared with wild cherries as food for the soul. There is a woman chosen to care for the sacred bundle, as well. When the weather permits, the soul is suspended from a tripod with a thong hanging down to the earth. Facing the south, the bundle and tripod are covered with the robe made from the buffalo cow killed in the hunt. People bring gifts to the soul and pray there.

On the day the soul is released, four virgins share in the ceremonial meal. They are commissioned to raise their future children in a sacred manner to be sacred leaders for the tribe. The Pipe is smoked and the soul is released to the south. The family may keep the bundle, now free of the soul, as a remembrance.[33] Lame Deer speaks of the direction the soul takes to the south. "Going south, in our language means dying, because the soul travels from north to south along the Milky Way to the Spirit Land."[34]

For the Hopi, the road of life is the path of the sun. The man (soul) travels west and reenters the *sipapuni* (navel of the earth) where he is reborn like a baby to live through the other three worlds of the universe. If he lived a ritually pure life in this world, he can omit the three worlds and go on to the multi-worlds of the universe as a *kachina*, or spirit. If he lived an evil life, he must remain in the underworld for a long period of time. Waters in his book about the Hopi explains, "Life and death, then, are considered not as two separate stages completing man's temporal and post-earthly existence; but as complementary phases in an ever-recurring cycle; a continuity that remains unbroken until mankind passes through the seven successive worlds of each of the seven successive universes, completing at last the forty-nine stages of his complete existence."[35] The kachinas emerge from the underworld or other worlds at the winter solstice and remain to help the people during the time of seed and growth until the summer solstice, when they leave and return to their other world.[36] This reminds me of the Australian Aborigines belief in the dreamtime and its connection to the physical world.

Robert Lawlor speaks of the death process of the Australian Aborigine. The Aborigines believe that one moves through the realms of the unborn, living and dying only once, and it is the task of the living to assist the spiritual component of the individual to separate from the physical world. At the time of death the spiritual component of the individual splits into three parts: the *totemic soul*, the *ancestral soul*, and a third aspect the Aborigines consider the *Trickster*.

The *totem soul* is that part of the spirit related to where the person was born, and the totemic animal and plant species at that birth location. The placenta was buried in that location at the time of birth by the mid-wife. The body of the deceased reciprocates for the gifts received from the animating forces that were sacrificed to sustain the life of humans. What is important is that "in this exchange, the spiritual development of the tribal person contributes to the deepening spiritual unfolding of the entirety of the natural world."[37]

The *ancestral soul* resonates with the Creative Ancestors of the Dreamtime. These Dreamtime Ancestors are metaphysical archetypes. This part of the soul travels to an area of the star constellations that resembles a particular animal and has an energy pattern that was painted in a geometric clan design on the abdomen at the person's first initiatic rite and again at death. The Aborigines believe, "The energy of the celestial field resonates with the geometry of the painted design and acts as a guide for the spirit in the journey to the heavens."[38]

The *Trickster* aspect can be defined as the ego soul. "It is the spiritual source that binds us to the finite...(and) works throughout life to plant the possibilities of a sort of earthly immortality."[39] The entire tribe moves and leaves the area where a death occurred to keep this part of the soul from trying to reattach to life in an avoidance of death and the journey to the stars.

The combination of the initiatic rites and the rites at death remind me of the vision quest (little death) and the actual physical death of the body. The regions of the sky to which the soul returns remind me of the concepts of astrology and the ideas centered around the celestial alignments of one's birth. From my Christian tradition, the soul has an immortality and ascends to heaven to a mansion in the sky. This relationship to the stars is also mentioned in the story of Christ's birth and the arrival of the Magi, who followed His star.

I had not contemplated the concept of ego not ascending. Ego and soul are so enmeshed in our thinking, or at least have been in mine. Nor, am I clear in my thinking about the scientific theories of particle and wave that have arisen out of quantum physics and how that effects these traditional beliefs in a *place*, rather than a *state*.

Australian Aborigines and Native Americans offer the same description of the ancestral realms:

> It is an unending, unchanging, version of the gathering-hunting life which we have lived on earth...except the game is more plentiful... These statements express the certainty that the afterlife cannot be anything but a reflection of the quality of consciousness and the state of being implicit in the life form each of us develop in our lives on earth.[40]

Rolling Thunder teaches Boyd that "We all live many lifetimes... We go through different lives; and sometimes we are able to put together the different lives... We go from one life to another and we should have no fear of death. It is just a transition."[41] Personally, I don't know what I believe about reincarnation. I do know from my own experience that there is something, an after-life, a transition. Then again, if we trust quantum physics, reincarnation is believable in the exchange of particle and wave.

We have now completed the eight directions of the Medicine Wheel, as I have come to practice it. A summary of the journey and its tools can be found in appendix D.

The second and third premises or proposals will be explored further in the next two chapters. Then in our final chapter, I will look at the first premise once more—the integration of the nature-based and Christian spirituality of my life's path that blends and transcends either path separately.

I would like to invite the reader now a little further into my world and talk about the healing of my inner shadow child that I call Liliput. This is a nickname that my mother-in-law gave me when I married. I was very small and weighed eighty-six pounds. My wedding dress was a size four, cut down to almost fit me. She derived the name from the book, *Gulliver's Travels*. So let us travel a little while through Liliput's life.

CHAPTER TEN

Life Comes "Full Circle," Story of Liliput

"If we are to survive and thrive as humans on planet Earth, we will need to dive deeply into the roots of the shamanic era and retrieve our intimacy with all forms of the Universe. Moreover, the current crisis of the planet is in the loins of the Earth; therefore, a nature-based community whose roots reach deep into these loins can provide a vessel to journey into and through the crisis."

The quote above by William Taegel taken from his book, *The Sacred Council of Your Wild Heart: Nature's Hope in Earth's Crisis,* is true for individuals, nations and the planet.[1] We change ourself from our roots to change the whole.

One of the stories from my vision quests and the support of a nature-based community and nature-based spirituality is the forward step toward healing of a trauma that affected the major part of my life with issues of security, trust (in self, others and Spirit) and self-esteem. I offer you this story to demonstrate how the "tools" I have learned in trauma mentoring effected this story and would be useful in mentoring others.

This is the story of the deep wound of a child. A child does not have the mental or emotional capability of comprehending life events, and those wounds remain buried, unless something or someone brings them to the surface. From the adult and witness perspective there is then the opportunity to heal them, no matter the context of the drama.

The first tool I choose to apply is Don Beck and Christopher Cowan's *Spiral Dynamics*.[2] The levels of the spiral taken from their book include what is called the first tier. This tier includes the "memes" (levels) labeled in the colors: beige, purple, red, blue, orange and green in that order of ascent. The second tier is labeled yellow and turquoise. I will discuss the application of these "Memes (levels of development influenced by life conditions) later in the appendix on "Tools for Mentoring."

Another of the tools used for healing trauma came from Hal and Sidra Stone's work "voice dialogue." Hal Stone and Sidra Stone in their book, *Embracing Our Selves,* write regarding the importance of learning about the sub-personalities that operate within us... "Without this understanding, we are in the powerless position of watching different sub-personalities drive our psychological car, while we sit in the back seat or, worse yet, hide in the trunk."[3]

My name is Lillie. This is my story, as true as I can remember it. It begins with a moment of trauma and how that moment impacted my life for nearly seven decades. The story is in third person so that the shadow of the inner child is clear. I will tell the story intermittently from Lillie's adult aware self and her inner vulnerable child. This story would require a shamanic pathway through a vision quest and psychological mentoring tools to grant the clear light of understanding and compassion within my soul. It would allow a small child to once again trust.

Little girl lost

I would like to introduce the reader to a little girl, not quite three and a half years old. I will call her "Liliput," like the small people in *Gulliver's Travels*.

174

Liliput had a little brother almost two. One day the little girl's mother took the two small children to a strange place, a private orphanage owned by a physician.

That night Liliput could not sleep. Where was she? Where were her parents, or her beloved grandmother? Night lights gleamed across the hardwood floors in long rays under the rows of cribs. The child thought she was too big to be in a crib and began to suck the two middle fingers on her left hand. Liliput was very afraid up in the corner of the crib, but she did not cry or scream.

The next morning, the little girl was served oatmeal for breakfast. Liliput did not like it and refused to eat. Over the next few days, it was decided that if Liliput would take the smaller toddlers to the bathroom in the night, she could have cornflakes, and so it was that the small child became a very responsible little caretaker.

Soon Liliput contracted chicken pox. The disease was so severe that she was tied to her crib to prevent her from scratching and scarring her body. Terrified from being tied, she became very quiet and sad.

Trying to find God

The little girl's grandmother had taught her that God loved her, so when she recovered, Liliput had an idea. One morning, she decided that she and her brother needed to go live with God. Liliput gave many glasses of water to her little brother and to herself, believing they would drown and go live with God. It did not work, of course, and the little girl turned inward losing hope.

Returning to the family and entering school

It would be thirteen months before Liliput's mother and father remarried and came back for the children. Liliput was past four and a half years old by then and in the fall went to school. She did not feel like she connected with the other children. They knew each other from the neighborhood.

The little girl did not like taking naps either, and that was required in kindergarten. The very first day of school, Liliput was in big trouble. The little girl stepped on her glasses getting up from her sleeping pad. They were broken. Liliput was so scared she ran away from school. It took her a long time to find the apartment building in the strange new neighborhood. (Years later, Lillie would attend therapy only a block from that apartment building.) The school immediately called Liliput's mother, who found the little kindergartener sitting on the front step. Liliput was spanked and sent to bed without supper for running away.

Lost again

That winter, three weeks after Liliput's fifth birthday, Pearl Harbor occurred. In the spring, her father left for boot camp. Once again, she was uprooted and afraid. There were many changes: new towns, new faces and new schools. Liliput chewed her fingernails, walked in her sleep, began stuttering and had many bad dreams. She began to think, "I am all alone. No one likes me. No one loves me. Everyone leaves me." The little girl no longer trusted her angry, distant mother. Liliput was too young to understand her mother's problems and stress.

Over the next few years, Liliput tried to be a good student (her parents valued education immensely), make friends and be liked by her teachers. She tried to be very grown up and responsible. The inner truth was Liliput felt very alone. As she tried to go to sleep at night, she began to comfort herself by counting in skip addition: *1, 2, 3...4, 5, 6...7, 8, 9...1, 2, 3...* This is a habit, or immature meditation, Lillie continues under stress even today.

Growing up only to lose the roots of family again

When her father returned from World War II, Liliput was almost ten years old. The years continued with school, adolescence and dating, first jobs. Then Lillie married a man her father approved of in 1955. One day, Lillie discovered that she and her husband were walking different paths. She was divorced in 1986 after thirty-one years of marriage and retreated deep within herself, unable to speak above a whisper. Her parish priest sent her to a therapist. When it became time for group therapy, Lillie would find herself a safe corner of the room in which to sit. Was her inner Liliput retreating to the corner of her crib? There was no awareness of this possibility at the time. Lillie just did not feel safe. Group therapy was not effective for Lillie, but her encounter with the Earthtribe was.

Finding an alternative family

As the next few years went by in the 1980s, Lillie went to many sweatlodge events. One day, two different people at an event said something that hurt her feelings. She did not want anyone to see her cry, nor did she know how to confront or express her pain and confusion. Lillie walked a long distance around a very large ranch to the front gate, obtained her car and drove an hour and a half back to her home. She was so upset and crying that she went straight to bed. Unconsciously, Lillie's inner vulnerable child, Liliput, had surfaced.

The inner Liliput vowed never to go back. During that week, she struggled with her powerful feelings. Lillie had a deep commitment to psychological work and decided even though she might be embarrassed or wounded again, she would return to therapy. In the process of working through the episode with her mentor, Lillie made a commitment to herself and to her therapist to face her shadows and never again to physically run away.

In his book, *Integral Spirituality*, Ken Wilber states, "Especially in the early stages of I formation—this phenomenological history of the damaged I (especially during the first few years of life)—is part of the entire movement to understand the shadow, to understand the disowned self..."[4] Lillie did not know that she had not found a shadow she would later name "Liliput." Over the next few years, Lillie began to believe she had done her psychological work, was fairly happy and well-adjusted. In many ways she was, and her therapy had ended. However, Lillie was not aware that just beneath the surface of her life, still deeply wounded and unable to trust, unable to believe she was loveable, was a little girl named Liliput.

Now, Lillie and Liliput had a deep love for the nature-based path and the community called the Earthtribe that had developed over a period of more than twenty years. They deeply cared for Lillie's mentor and Pipe trainer. Lillie had decided to vision quest in the spring to honor her 70th birthday the coming fall. As was customary, Lillie's mentor and guide would prepare her for a year in advance of the quest. During that year, Lillie's teacher wanted her to begin to learn the art of detachment.

A vision quest journey into the world of Liliput

One morning, the day after Christmas, Lillie's mentor spoke to her of a Buddhist leader that considered himself "not enlightened," because the leader cared too much about what people thought and said. Suddenly, without warning, her teacher turned from walking in front of her on the path and said, "Lillie, I could care less what you think or feel." There was no time for awareness or connection to the earlier lesson.

In his book, *Waking the Tiger*, Peter Levine explains that symptoms can return without warning, triggered by an incident, that have remained dormant for many years. For Lillie it had taken seven decades for the buried wound to erupt. Levine states:

> Common occurrences can produce traumatic after-effects that are just as debilitating as those experienced by veterans of combat or survivors of childhood abuse (or abandonment). Traumatic effects are not always apparent immediately following the incidents that caused them.[5]

Liliput grabbed the steering wheel of Lillie's psychological car. This was the lifetime message for Liliput from the time she had arrived at the orphanage years before.

William Taegel in *Natural Mystics* also explains some of what Lillie experienced, and how it opened the door for healing. Taegel believes that time away from our daily world (ordinary culture) is needed to accomplish the work of reducing the domination of a sub-self, like the wounded child. "As you become practiced in calling for the inner voices without judgement and embracing them with awareness, then the way is paved for the calling forth of the soul from the background."[6] When we discover these damaged parts of the self, they assist in directing us deeper into the implicate order.[7] This work/growth was not visible to Lillie at the time, but let us continue with the story.

The inner child Liliput believed the relationship with her mentor was ended. Lillie found herself standing near a barbwire fence off the path and some distance from where the comment was made. Lillie did not know how she had arrived there, only becoming suddenly aware that she was about to put her hand upon the barbs. She was determined not to cry. Lillie desperately wanted to turn and run. Yet, she had promised herself years before never to run away and to face her challenges.

Lost again

Lillie could not remember anything else spoken that day, or how she arrived back home. All she could think was, "I can never return. I'll never go back. Everyone I ever care about leaves me." The grief was unbearable and overwhelming.

A few days later, on New Year's Day, Lillie went out to sit in the swing for her meditation time. She observed the oaks and birds, the sun in the leaves. Then for several hours the pain came in depth. Lillie entered the direction of the West on the Medicine Wheel. William Taegel describes this direction on the Medicine Wheel:

> In the West is the direction of endings, shadows,
> death, and gratitude in the Earthtribe tradition. The
> energy of the West aids us in the journey into the
> darkest and lightest areas of our lives—places we
> are afraid to go. Yet, go we must if we are to gain
> strong hints of our inner identity.[8]

This journey would become the most profound teaching of all the years of Pipe training and mentoring instruction Lillie had experienced.

In Lillie's inner world, Liliput was a very small child sitting on a rock in the middle of a roaring river. There was no light, no hope. Liliput rose out of the depths of Lillie's heart and soul, a "no-thing," abandoned, lost, unlovable, totally rejected. Lillie and Liliput tried to ignore and hide these feelings, but deep within struggled with the grief for months, actually for nearly two years.

William Taegel explains, "These troublesome emotions in our personality capture us, so we tend to move away from and disown them. Yet, if we move into them, listen to them, bring their point of view into our awareness, we have the possibility of transcending them."[9] He then notes the following about the experience of encountering the wound:

Such wounds separate you from the Ground of your existence. If you persist, you will eventually discover that aspect of your soul, your hidden identity, that knows how to connect deep with the Source of Life. In a Shamanic paradigm this movement from the edge of the circle that is dominated by fixation/compulsions to the center core of Spirit might be called *soul-retrieval*.[10]

Turning point of trust

The vision quest year in 2006 was the turning point for healing. Lillie's mentor had given her a challenge that was most likely one of the most meaningful Christmas gifts she would ever receive. Peter Levine states, "Fortunately, the same immense energies that create the symptoms of trauma, when properly engaged and mobilized, can transform the trauma and propel us into new heights of healing, mastery, and even wisdom. Trauma resolved is a great gift, returning us to the natural world of ebb and flow, harmony, love, and compassion."[11]

This is how Lillie perceives the gift. This is Lillie's truth of what came to her on her quest in 2006. Lillie encountered the "living breath of Spirit" and was filled with the knowledge that she was loved, safe and could trust someone fully. Liliput did not have to die to live with God. Spirit was as near as her breath. Lillie and Liliput were at peace.

Bill Plotkin in his book, *Soulcraft,* speaks of experiences like Lillie's encounter on her quest that would give her strength. "Yet, this strange image gives you faith to risk extending yourself into the world, to go out on a limb, to be radical and wild, to live for something greater than your individual life, to go forward in the world and live for something greater."[12] He explains a little deeper:

An encounter with soul on a vision quest might come as a dream, a waking image, or through a

sensory encounter with a being in nature. The image
or perception may be visual, kinesthetic, or auditory,
or some synesthetic blending of modalities... A soul
image is experienced as a violation, a ravishment by
the sacred that trounces all your prior beliefs about
who you are and why you are here.[13]

The next day, as Lillie told her elders of her experience, she
was looking at her mentor. Lillie realized that she would always
trust him to hold the Pipe stem steady when the Pipe bowl of
prayer is heated up. Peter Levine speaks of this issue of trust in
Waking the Tiger, "We need support from friends and relatives, as
well as from nature. With this support and connection, we can
begin to trust and honor the natural process that will bring us to
completion and wholeness and eventually peace."[14]

Bear Heart would carry this teaching even further and
say, "Love and forgiveness are synonymous. There's hardly any
division at all. God likes to forgive—when we say 'God is love,'
we can also say 'God is forgiveness'."[15] Lillie had no awareness
at the time of the spiritual task she was given of forgiveness and
love. What was overwhelmingly clear was the trust, which I,
Lillie, the author, also believe is synonymous.

It took a good while for Lillie to integrate this experience
for herself and her inner child Liliput, but there was a certainty
to it. Lillie had steadfastly continued with her therapy in years
past and with her Pipe training and academic studies in the
present. Taegel asserts, "Healings always happen where awareness, compassion and persistence abound. Healing refers to the
deeper search for reconnection with the true identity of the individual with the One."[16]

The elders named Lillie, "Beauty's Breath" (Beauty being
a word for Spirit). Later when Lillie was more aware and ready
to hear it, her mentor explained that she would not have been
open to this experience with Spirit without the journey into the

West, the encounter of experiencing being a "no-thing" (this encounter with the "dark night of the soul").

As William Taegel explains in *Natural Mystics*:

Entering the Spirit world—the domain of awareness, power, perspective, and compassion—requires a jolting inner experience that connects with the transcendence of all Creation. This vision comes from beyond and within. You have to be born of the Spirit to make the journey, insists the prophet/shaman Jesus. This birth experience is the bedrock of inner wisdom, the beginning of the wheel, the East. You cannot, Jesus thunders, enter the Kingdom (his term for the upper world and the implicate order) unless you are born anew (John 3). No exceptions. So we in the Earthtribe use shaman and Nature mystic interchangeably.[17]

Full circle

My life had come full circle from Lillie to Liliput to the adult Lillie, or in more explicit terms it had moved through the Medicine Wheel, rising in its spiral.

I received a tremendous gift from Spirit on the vision quest of 2006, fasting, meditating and supported by Earth and Sky. Not only did I find trust in my mentor, I found trust in Spirit. Nature-based spirituality brought me out of basic survival. This inner child, too young to have guidance from Christianity, could respond to the sensory.

How then do we show gratitude for the unmerited gifts we receive?

Expressing gratitude

My thoughts turn now to the planetary crisis of global warming, destruction of our oceans, other dangerous practices and the need to extend reciprocity to Grandmother Earth for all the gifts we receive from her bounty; not only physically in food and sustenance for our needs, but psychologically, emotionally and spiritually, as we evolve as a species.

We as a species, like small children, take and receive with joy, but without maturity of giving back and protection. This is true for our culture with our elders, as well. It is not meant cruelly; it is just not considered in our awareness. We can accomplish small changes as individuals. However, we have greater impact with nature-based community.

CHAPTER ELEVEN

Grandmother Earth and Reciprocity

In the beginning chapters, I promised to discuss the direction of Grandmother Earth again as a spiritual issue. As I read the news, many issues come to the forefront about the planetary crisis we are facing. There is the practical physical issue of survival of the species, but more important is the spiritual component that begs to be addressed.

Don Miguel Ruiz in *The Four Agreements* speaks of the earth much as Lawlor's discussion of the Aboriginal Dreamtime. Ruiz speaks of all of life as we know it as dreamed for us by our ancestors, including such things as laws, religions, rules, governments, holidays:

> We are born with the capacity to learn how to dream, and the humans who live before us teach us how to dream the way society dreams... (We) hook the child's attention and introduce these rules into his or her mind... Attention is the ability we have to discriminate and to focus only that which we want to perceive... We learned a whole reality, a whole dream.[1]

Ruiz's comments raise the question in my mind, "What is our dream for our planetary home?" There are so many parts of the dream that have become a nightmare. We have a plethora of crises that include population, environmental hazards (air, land

and water) and extinction of species. Let us explore the crises and then address some personal and political responses. These issues regarding the planetary crises are truly a spiritual quandary for our souls, whether it is recognized or not.

Population

A projection was made that on October 31, 2011, "the world will welcome its seven billionth person."[2] We could be facetious and say, "Trick or treat," but things are really serious. The news raises deep questions in my mind. How are we going to feed and shelter all of these people on this planet that we essentially are ravaging? How are we as a species going to impact this planet to a further degree? Are we even considering these issues? Should we even consider these issues?

Ed McGaa answers these last two questions in this manner, "Regardless of philosophical, religious or theological persuasion, we must begin immediately to meet on some common ground to slow down and eventually halt the polluting and unbalancing causes (on our) Mother—Mother Earth."[3] What type of birth control can humanity undertake that all will consider? Would couples be willing to have only one child? If so, it would not take many generations to lower population substantially.

Consumerism and petroleum products

It appears to me that in our culture we tend to sacrifice the individual and the good to expediency, money and oil. There are great corporations that appear to exploit others. We are sacrificing our young men to wars in order to control oil producing nations around the globe. This is a strong red and orange combination of memes.[4] Even beyond the issue of fuel, if we don't become more caring and honest, we can destroy the world of our children and grandchildren. We, individually and collectively, are destroying our clean water, space and air. The ozone layer is being diminished. Do we utterly refuse to go within ourselves and reflect long enough to make good choices from our souls?

Once in a while a voice speaks up like President Obama pushing for cooperation and the good of each individual. He is working diligently for good health care for all and the end of racism in this country. (It remains to be seen if the work is effective or just becomes political rhetoric.) This Presidential platform is a green meme attitude of community and good for all. This call to unified compassion leads us closer as a culture to Sacred Spirit and awareness. Is it possible for this unified compassion to extend beyond the human species to all species and the environment?

Lame Deer thinks the "ghost dance" has been misunderstood and sets forth a desire to bring back the dance, interpreted in a new way, as a metaphor and aid:

> (After) eighty years I believe that more and more
> people are sensing what we meant when we prayed
> for a new earth and that now not only Indians but
> everybody has become an "endangered species." So
> let the Indians help you bring on a new earth
> without pollution or war.[5]

William Taegel invites us to go back to our indigenous roots, our *Wild Heart*, to heal ourselves and the planet.[6] The call to conscious awareness is arising for many thinkers; yet, it is not always heard.

Global warming and its effects

Long ago in 1975, an article appeared in the U.S. journal *Science* that was ignored. Its title asks "Are We on the Brink of a Pronounced Global Warming?" The article was prophetic. Yet, the resistance to this knowledge is very strong. In the article, Hanley reports:

187

> The desire to disbelieve deepens as the scale of the threat grows, concludes economist-ethicist Clive Hamilton...and others who track what they call "denialism" find that its nature is changing in America, last redoubt of climate naysayers. It has taken on more of a partisan, ideological tone. Polls find a widening Republican-Democratic gap on climate.[7]

Due to these warnings, in 1989, U.S. Oil and coal interests formed the Global Climate Coalition trying to prevent the economy from invading their profits. It was later discovered that oil giant Exxon disbursed millions per year to encourage doubt about global warming from fossil fuel consumption and carbon dioxide emissions. Years later, a "document emerged showing that the industry coalitions' own scientific team had quietly advised it that the basic science of global warming was indisputable."[8]

Just this August this study reported that "hundreds of species are retreating toward the poles, egrets showing up in southern England, American robins in Eskimo villages. Some, such as polar bears, have nowhere to go. Eventual large-scale extinctions are feared."[9] The weakened trees are attacked by beetles and food crops like wheat, corn and rice are failing.

In Texas, the extreme drought, worse than any in recorded history, has dried the rivers and depleted the lakes. Castro reports in the *Huffington Post* that Texas rice farmers are very concerned about the possibility of the Colorado River Authority cutting off water to the southern coastal plains to maintain supplies for the cities. Most farmers can survive one bad year like this past one, but two years without water brought on by halting the river's surface supply for irrigation would devastate crops and bankrupt them.[10]

Hanley quotes Wally Broecker in an interview. From his big-windowed office overlooking the wooded campus of the

Lamont-Doherty Earth Observatory in Palisades, New York, Wally Broecker, Columbia University geophysicist, observed the deepening of the desire to disbelieve has become more polarized with the Republicans oppositional and the Democrats pushing for action. Broecker also noted, "Eventually it'll become damned clear that the Earth is warming and the warming is beyond anything we have experienced in millions of years, and people will have to admit..." He stopped and laughed. "Well, I suppose they could say God is burning us up."[11]

Drought and fire

It certainly seemed that way in Texas in September. Fire and possible evacuation warnings were everywhere.

The first week of September 2011, I returned to my home about 6:00 p.m with a friend from a shopping expedition for something I needed for a wedding and a brief dinner out. My friend said to me, "Lillie, come look at the moon. It is weird." Crossing the lawn in order to see what she was exclaiming about, I said, "That is not the moon. That is the sun." The sun was an extremely large deep red ball surrounded by dark grey. It looked like some sort of eclipse.

Going inside the house, I checked my e-mails. Another friend was asking what the smoke was. There had been a fire earlier in the week that I could see from the northern ridge spread more than a mile wide across the southern ridge of Wimberley Valley near the home I lived in last year. It was visible from another Earthtriber's second story windows. It took two and a half days for the fire fighters to put it out with trucks and helicopters. I e-mailed my acquaintance back and told her, "No, the Saddleridge fire to the south is out. The smoke is west of me toward you."

My dinner friend and I decided to go reenter my car and drive to what is called "Devil's Backbone" on the southern side of the valley. There is an overlook there of the west to east flow of the valley. There were no visible fires in the valley, but there was smoke to the south and west, the northwest and the east. We were nearly surrounded by large fires.

Canyon Lake to the southwest was extinguished first. The Spicewood fire was captured at the Pedernales River (which is nearly bone dry from the drought) and would take nearly a week to extinguish. The Bastrop fire blazed on for weeks and burned more than fifteen hundred homes and many thousands of acres that included forestland that won't grow back in my lifetime. Wimberley, where I live, was literally surrounded by fires in the four directions. From Skyline Ridge Overlook, one could see the Bastrop fire a good thirty miles away for days. If one went outside, the air was filled with the smell of smoke.

A hurricane had moved through from the Gulf to our east. On the west side the thirty mile an hour plus winds blowing north to south on the west side of the storm and the extremely low humidity of the drought had created a disaster beyond man's control. In the case of the Bastrop fire, the winds had toppled a dead tree onto power lines and sparked the inferno. When they burn, the dying pines and juniper are instant torches.

Stone reported in the International Business Times, "Nearly 190 wildfires erupted in Texas over the last week."[12] In the Bastrop fire alone over 35,000 acres burned and four people died. Meanwhile, a fire near Houston burned more than 20,000 acres. Texas has been declared a disaster area, and there will be federal aid for the victims. However, on the news, Congress is fighting between the Republicans and the Democrats how to pay for the needs of the people.

The other side of the argument presents itself that we have endured immense droughts in the past prior to any global warming caused by humankind. Cook, et al,. wrote about mega-droughts in North America that occurred in the previous millennium:

- (Perhaps) the most famous example is the "Great Drouth" (sic) of AD 1276-1299 described by A. E. Douglass (1929, 1935).

- This 24-year drought was eclipsed by the 38-year drought that was found by Weakley (1965) to have occurred in Nebraska from AD 1276 to 1313, which may have been a more prolonged northerly extension of the Great Drouth.

- Two extraordinary droughts discovered by Stine (1994) in California lasted more than two centuries before AD 1112 and more than 140 years before AD 1350. These megadroughts occurred in the so-called "Medieval Warm Period." (All of this happened prior to the strong greenhouse gas warming that began with the Industrial Revolution.[13]

Texas is taking measures to preserve water during the drought. In my small town, we are on what is called "stage three" water rationing. I am allowed to water on Monday and Thursday either before 7:00 a.m. or after 7:00 p.m., and this is done by hand-held hose only for the flower beds, not lawns (Grass has not grown this summer. There is only bare earth.). There is not enough water to protect the trees. A person would not be able to water long enough and deep enough to aid them, so many of the trees are dead or dying. The creeks and river beds are dry. One could drive on them like a road.

Kennedy reported on the extreme drought that began in October 2010 and spread over twelve percent of the United States from Arizona to Florida. This area experienced the warmest July on record in 2011 with temperatures two to six degrees Fahrenheit above normal monthly averages. Kennedy noted:

Texas and Oklahoma have been particularly hard hit... Farmers and ranchers throughout the region rely upon rain and green pastures for producing crops and raising livestock. Texas has never experienced so little rain prior to and during the primary growing season.[14]

An article came out from *24/7 Wall St.* discussing the rapidly growing low water supply for human use. The article stated:

Worse still, the problem has no ready solution—and probably has no solution at all... China's wheat crop failed last year because of drought. The southeastern U.S. has become close to a dust bowl. The portions of north Africa and impoverished central Africa are in the midst of water shortages that almost certainly will not improve.[15]

In his book, *Earth in the Balance, Ecology and the Human Spirit*, Al Gore, deeply troubled by what he could perceive as the crisis of our planet, visited and reported about different areas of the world to determine the extent of the devastation. He visited the Aral Sea, which was once the fourth largest inland sea in the world, comparable to our Great Lakes. It is now a desert of sand.

The fishing boats, some large enough to process fifty tons of fish, sit on the sand still moored at their docks. The shoreline has retreated more than forty kilometers away. The small town of Muynak still cans fish, but the fish are brought through Siberia from the Pacific Ocean more than a thousand miles away. The draining of the immense sea was caused by an ill-conceived irrigation plan. The devastation took less than ten years. The fishermen in desperation tried to dig a deep canal for miles, but it is just a deep trench in the sand.[16]

Air pollution

In 1988, Gore visited the Trans-Antarctic Mountains, where a scientist showed him in the layers of annual ice the change that occurred in the amount of pollution trapped in the ice following the passing of the Clean Air Act. That small reduction had an impact in the remotest, least accessible place on the earth.[17]

Ocean pollution, destruction of ocean habitats, and overfishing

The oceans that comprise three quarters of the earth's surface are a major concern, as well. For instance, "This year The United Nations General Assembly, for the first time ever, will conduct an open review of regional and national actions to protect deep-sea species and ecosystems on the high seas from the harmful impacts of fishing."[18]

Scientists are calling for an end to industrial deep-sea fishing. The ocean is similar to a watery desert with areas like oases that contain fish and coral reefs. The harvesting of these fish, however, is more detrimental than closer to shore, because it takes much longer for the areas to replenish. The trawlers fish from what was originally a depth of about five hundred feet in the 1950s to a depth closer to seventeen hundred feet currently. Deep coral reefs are being destroyed as the areas are depleted before the trawlers move on to another area. The fishermen are working in the deep sea because the areas near shore have been exhausted.[19] The president of the Marine Conservation Institute, Elliott Norse said in a news article in The Washington Post, "The world has turned to deep sea fishing 'out of desperation'... We're now fishing in the worst places to fish... These things don't come back."[20]

An internationally formed group of marine scientists would like an end to government subsidies that support deep-sea fishing, because the fisheries are unsustainable. The large metal plates scrape the ocean floor. Deep ocean fish mature very slowly. For example, the orange roughy prized by the wealthy as a delicacy do not sexually mature for thirty years and live about one hundred and twenty five years. Corals that are destroyed live for four thousand years and are extremely slow growing.[21]

Christian in a *Huffington Post* news article reports Ray Hilborn, professor of aquatic and fishery sciences at the University of Washington, as stating, "The study was correct that deep-sea fishing is not managed... They're basically saying we shouldn't do it without saying what we should do... Long-lived species can be sustainably managed. They can be managed if they are harvested at a low rate and have a science program set up that regulates their abundance."[22] My question is how this might be enforced. Perhaps, the United Nations will arrive at an answer acceptable to the good of the planet.

Changes in sea life due to warming of oceans

Other things are occurring in the oceans. Giant King Crabs nearly a meter in width have developed in the warming ocean and are invading and colonizing in the Palmer Deep, the "Antarctic Abyss," that is four thousand three hundred feet deep, where the environment was once too cold for them. The number of species in the areas colonized by the crabs is one quarter of that in areas that escaped the invasion.[23]

Last month, a study published in the journal *Science* showed that climate change is driving animals to the poles in search of their more normal natural habitats. *The Guardian* called it "one of the clearest examples of climate change in action." In fact, the leader of the research, Chris Thomas, professor of conservation biology, told *The Guardian* that for the past 40 years, animals and plants have been "shifting 20 cm per hour, for every hour of the day, for every day of the year."[24]

Scientific reports: warming changes in oceans

Other changes are developing in the warming oceans. Tuesday evening, September 13, 2011, prior to a two day conference in

Brussels, a two hundred page report was released on approximately one hundred projects funded by a collaboration of seventeen European marine institutes. It was called Project CLAIMER. These are the results:

- Rising temperature of ocean water is causing a proliferation of the Vibrio genus of bacteria, which can cause food poisoning, serious gastroenteritis, septicemia and cholera.

- Millions of euros in health costs may result from human consumption of contaminated seafood, ingestion of water borne pathogens, and to a lesser degree, through direct occupational or recreational exposure to marine disease... Climatic conditions are playing an important role in the transmission of these diseases.

- The paper also describes a host of other effects of ocean warming, both documented and forecast, including melting ice, rising sea levels, coastal erosion, increased storm intensity and frequency, along with chemical changes in the sea itself, including acidification and deoxygenation...

- It is not only the range of changes that has scientists concerned, but the speed of them.[25]

Contamination of rivers and fertilizers

Along the Gulf of Mexico from New Orleans south to well below Matagorda Bay, this deoxygenation has already occurred and created a dead zone of six thousand, seven hundred and sixty-five miles. Nitrogen from the farmers fertilizers and urban run-off wastes have flowed down the Mississippi River. These nutrients feed large algal blooms that then die and sink, decomposing and depleting the oxygen in the water. Those fish that can swim away leave. Other creatures in the ecosystem just die.

This destruction of the ecosystem ruins "some of the most productive fisheries in the world."[26]

Garbage pollution and gyres

Another issue is what is called the "Great Pacific Garbage Patch." This is a vortex or gyre of marine litter in the central North Pacific Ocean that extends over an immense area. Estimates vary according to the plastic particulate, chemical sludge and debris found in the area, but it is thought to encompass approximately two hundred seventy thousand square miles.

There are five major gyres. The North Atlantic gyre is also filled with garbage. The ocean currents sweep by the northwestern United States and carry this debris for about six years until it settles into the central vortex of the gyre. The currents also sweep past Japan and carry debris for about a year into the gyre.

The plastic degenerates into small particles that concentrate and deplete the availability of oxygen. Some of the plastic gives off toxic gasses as it degenerates. Some debris is visible, but the greatest majority is not. It hangs suspended in the water as miniscule pollutants. Ship pollutants are of some concern, as a cruise ship of three thousand passengers produces over eight tons of solid waste weekly. Most of this waste is organic. However, this source is not the main pollutant.[27] The main source is polymers, and the report gives a scientific explanation of the pollutants effect:

> The polymers of plastic become extremely small...,
> long-lasting, ...and end up in the stomachs of marine birds and animals, and their young... The floating debris can absorb organic pollutants...PCBs, DDT, and PAHs...mistaken by the endocrine system as estradiol, causing hormone disruption. Consumed by humans resulting in their ingestion of toxic chemicals,...(and) marine plastic also facilitates the spread of invasive species that attach to

floating plastic...drift(ing) long distances to colon-
ize other ecosystems.[28]

No one country has claimed responsibility for the gyre's
pollution and clean-up, although it has been noted that two
hundred sixty-seven species have been contaminated world
wide, but efforts are being made through individual groups like
the one formed in April 2008 by Richard Sundance Owen, a
building contractor and scuba dive instructor. The Great Pacific
Garbage Patch Treaty was written in order to attract different
entities willing to sign and become responsible for an effort to
clean the gyre. Leaders of United Nations' states may also sign
this treaty and assist with the responsibility.[29] Hopefully, with
new interest, change and clean-up efforts will occur.

Oil pollution

The seas are also being polluted with oil. British Petroleum's
Deepwater Horizon oil rig exploded on April 20, 2010. It killed
eleven workers and was nearly impossible to stop. It became
the worst oil spill in United States history, worse than the Exxon
Valdez tanker in 1989. The Gulf of Mexico was filled with two
hundred and five million gallons of oil. It destroyed marine life,
coastal habitats and fishermen's livelihoods. It would take until
September 19, 2010 before the spill and leak were halted.[30]
There is now a lawsuit against British Petroleum (BP), because
they were over budget and did not heed the danger of shallow
gas, nor was the drilling cement adequate and dry enough.[31]

Mendleson reported in the *Huffington Post* regarding
Clayton Thomas-Muller and the oil sands protest. This is another oil pipeline issue currently causing hundreds to protest and
be arrested in Canada. TransCanada Corporation wants to develop the Alberta oil sands. Clayton Thomas-Muller of the Indigenous Environmental Network believes the protest movement

is gaining strength stating, "This is one of those sea-change moments, not just for First Nations, but for everybody who is concerned about the psychotic energy policy of Canada, and their attempts to market dirty tar sands to the world."[32]

Nuclear pollution and earthquakes

Another major issue for the protection of the earth developed with the recent earthquakes. The earthquake and tsunami in Japan on March 11, 2011 damaged their nuclear plant, and it was leaking radioactivity into the water and air for days. The Nuclear Regulatory Commission in the United States made public a staff report that requests an immediate check of the one hundred and four nuclear reactors in the U.S. The urgency to assess the risks of earthquake and flooding damage was intensified again with the recent Virginia earthquake, which was more shaking than a nuclear plant was built to withstand. Safety recommendations will take up to two years to complete. Daly of the *Huffpost Green* spoke with Tony Pietrangelo, senior vice president and chief nuclear officer for the Nuclear Energy Institute, who said, "'The August 23, 2011 quake, coming so soon after the Japan crisis, does heighten attention to seismic (risk), no question about it, but the lack of serious damage shows there's a lot of margin built into these plants.' He hoped regulators would not try to force changes too quickly. 'We don't want to do it twice. We want to do it once and get it right'."[33]

Political efforts toward change

George Dvorsky recently wrote for the Institute for Ethics and Emerging Technologies five reasons he believed the Copenhagen Climate Conference failed to achieve a binding agreement to address the climate crisis. He believes that the present social and political structures are not equipped to cope with the pending catastrophe.

The five reasons Dvorsky lists that caused the talks to fail are as follows:

1. Nation states are far too self-serving.

2. Democracies are too ill-equipped and irresolute to deal with pending crises.

3. Isolationist and avaricious China.

4. The powerful corporatist megastructure.

5. Weak consensus on the reason for global warming.

Dvorsky states that rather than *ad hoc* conferences:

I'd like to see the United Nations assemble an international and permanent emergency session that is parliamentary in nature, debating and acting on the problem of anthropogenic climate change. The decisions of this governing board would be binding and impact on all the nations of the world.[34]

It is reported in a news article by Gelineau that there have been several climate control conferences in Kyoto, Copenhagen, Brazil and Mexico. Gelineau reports on the statements made at the summit in Sydney, Australia, "United Nations Secretary-General Ban Ki-moon said Thursday (September 1, 2011) that urgent action was needed on climate change, pointing to the famine in the Horn of Africa and devastating floods in northern Australia as examples of the suffering caused by global warming."[35] Lashing out at skeptics of climate change during a speech he made at the University of Sydney, Ban argued that science has proven climate change is real. "He is in Australia for a series of meetings following his attendance at an annual forum of South Pacific island leaders in New Zealand earlier this week. He also made stops in the Solomon islands and Kirbati, low-lying South Pacific island nations threatened by sea levels."[36] As Ban stood on the shore of Kirbati and watched the ocean, he spoke, "High tide shows it's high time to act... We are running out of time."[37]

Zeller reports in *Huffpost Green* that Al Gore is said to be facing an "uphill battle." In the 1990s, seventy-one percent of the American public responding to a Gallup poll favored the environment over the economy. The economic downturn we have been facing as a country has reversed that trend. As the economy continues to "down spiral," economic interests are prioritized high above environmental issues. Environmental stewardship, a sensible climate policy and clean energy advocates are struggling to find a voice. Republicans in Congress and on the campaign trail are identifying the Environmental Protection Agency as the source of the economy woes. Many, despite the overwhelming evidence, argue that climate change is still a matter of debate only among the planet's preeminent scientists. They ignore the voices of more than a thousand Americans and their supporters, who are willing to be arrested to protect the Alberta tar sands from a pipeline development.[38] Bill McKibben, the activist, has called these tar sands "the continents biggest carbon bomb."[39]

In the news, it is considered a scandal that a half billion dollars went to finance a solar technology company under the Obama administration. In spite of all this conflict Al Gore believes that if more people open their minds and hearts and question that change will take place. He states:

> The greatest opportunity for change lies in the
> hearts of those who have rejected the science but
> who are right now asking themselves a question.
> Have they been fooled by the oil companies and the
> coal companies? Have they been taken for a ride by
> the large polluters who have been putting out mis-
> information?[40]

When speaking with Climate Reality Projects' Alex Bogusky, Al Gore asserted that even the words "climate change" have become politically incorrect. Gore contends that:

> Powerful polluters...see it as a useful strategy to try
> to convince the public that the scientists are liars
> and that they're greedy and they're making stuff up.
> All in the service of their overarching strategy of
> creating enough doubt to persuade people that there
> shouldn't be any sense of emergency about address-
> ing this crisis.[41]

Personal response to crises

As an individual, I agree that something is going on with the earth and its overall climate and health. As an individual in a small town in Texas, it is difficult to know how to address these issues. They are in my awareness, and I have made some small changes. Even in a house I lease, I have put in a small orchard and two planting beds for vegetables.

I purchased a car in 2008 that operates on about thirty miles to the gallon, as opposed to the twelve miles to the gallon on my previous automobile. I make a distinctive effort to make one loop for my errands to post office, druggist, grocery store, etc. That one small effort enables my car to run on one tank of gas per month. If each of us make what small changes we can in our footprints on this planet, even those small changes added together would be immense.

Earlier, I wrote about downsizing my home. It derived from an emergency. However, as I spoke of the changes I was making, many of my friends said they needed to do the same thing. There is really no sacrifice in my change of life style. Actually, there is a greater sense of peace and well-being in the adjustment. We are a consumer society that has reached its limits.

It is time to be aware of our behaviors. They are not only a practical issue, they are a spiritual issue.

One day a young man came to one of the sweatlodges I attend. He had on a faded t-shirt that read *save our species*. It was a reminder to awaken to the fact Will Taegel expressed:

> *We are an aspect of Nature. We are the cells of Mother Earth. We are Her awareness reflecting on the meaning of our recklessly prodigal ways. We are her aspects reading beyond denial to the hope of new practices and habits.*[42]

Communal and collective response to the crises

Al Gore addresses the new choices we are making on the planet since what Gore calls the "Great Transformation" that began in 2009, when a new direction was established with solar, wind, and geothermal generators for electricity and conversion to electric cars. Nations became creative and began to compete and develop new technologies. Gore makes the following affirming statements:

- The most important change that made this transformation possible is something that is hard to describe in words. Our way of thinking changed.

- The earth itself began to occupy our thoughts. Somehow, it became no longer acceptable to participate in activities that harmed the integrity of the global environment.

- Young people throughout the world led the way in this change in our thinking. Businesses that lagged behind lost customers and employees and then they, too, began to change.

- The ability we gained in 2010 to see Earth from space all the time also played a role in subtly but powerfully raising our constant awareness that we all share the same home. Once the argument about whether the crisis was real was over, we shifted into high gear, and the change became unstoppable.

- Once again, we should have remembered we were capable of such changes in consciousness.[43]

When we think of changes as a community, we can develop solar power, alternative fuels, water collection systems, wind-driven power farms, means of cleaning our oceans and water supplies, organic farming techniques. The list can be endless with our creativity. Dave Abram states in *The Spell of the Sensuous* that "it is only at the scale of our direct, sensory interactions with the land around us that we can appropriately notice and respond to the immediate needs of the living world..."[44] "A human community that lives in a naturally beneficial relationship with the surrounding earth (and air) is a community, we might say that lives in truth... They are in accord with a right relation between...people and their world."[45]

Vision Quest 1998: A teaching from Mother Nature

When it seems overwhelming and scary, I remember a vision quest in 1998. We were in Montana on Dr. Taegel's cousin Ned, Braided River's, ranch. We were to go out and sit for twelve hours.

I went out after the two o'clock morning Pipe. I did not think to ask anyone to be a supporter, so I started off down the road alone. I walked into the woods, not realizing how dark it would become. I could barely see the road and noticed a big flat white rock on my right. I decided since I could not see the edges and the way of the land I had better stop where I was. I wound up putting my prayer ties in the road knowing we were all on a private ranch.

Sitting down on my towel, I realized fairly quickly that the ground was permafrost. I was freezing my behind side. The mosquitoes began to attack. They are huge. I tried to light some sage hoping to drive them off and have the illusion of some warmth. The matches were too wet, so I crawled under my rain gear. We had been told to take a whistle with us, but I didn't own one.

The Father loves the flowers on the vine

Suddenly, I heard something. Frightened, I jumped up. It was a small mouse. Feeling foolish, I began to walk around my circle to try to warm up. I spoke to God, "I came out here for a prayer of gratitude for my new grandson. Instead, I am cold, the mosquitoes are 'eating me up.' I have an attitude." Gradually, I began to see little flowers along the edge of the road. As the dawn began to lighten different colors would show up. Intrigued by their beauty, I began to sing. Dave Abram states that what occurs in a vicinity creates the power or tells the event in its expressive potency. "The songs proper to a specific site will share common style, a rhythm that matches the pulse of the place, attuned to the way things happen there."[46] This is my song entitled *The Father Loves the Flowers on the Vine*:

> The Father loves the flowers on the vine.
> The little brown mouse, the owl flying high.
> The tallest tree, and the farthest star,
> The smallest ant, and the deepest sea.
>
> The Father loves the flowers on the vine.
> The Father loves the flowers on the vine.
> The Father loves the flowers on the vine...
> All I made is mine," says He.
>
> The Father loves the flowers on the vine.
> The Father loves all mankind.
> With eyes of brown and blue and green.
> The Father loves you and me.

The Father loves the flowers on the vine.
The Father loves the flowers on the vine.
The Father loves the flowers on the vine...
"All I made I love," says He.

The Father loves the flowers on the vine.
The Father loves variety...
All the colors of the Medicine Wheel.
"All I made is good," says He.

The Father loves the flowers on the vine,
The Father loves the flowers on the vine.
The Father loves the flowers on the vine...
"All I made I love," says He. (Author, 1998)

The day dawned with sunshine, and I sat down in my circle again. About midday, a little chipmunk hopped up on the large boulder. It watched me for a while. Then it ran over to the edge of my prayer ties. I thought it might come near me, but it retreated back to the rock and chattered in a fussy manner. It did this two or three times. It would never step over the little string of ties. Finally, it decided to run around the circle and disappeared into the woods. I thought, "That's how we so often react. All we need to do is take one tiny step, but we think the barrier is too big."

Later in the afternoon, Ned's big dog Lucy, a Border collie, came along. She grabbed my prayer ties and started to run. I yelled, "Drop that." The dog dropped the ties and left. I decided that was my signal to return to camp. No one saw me come back, and I took a shower. People told me the catering truck came barreling down the road around the sharp turn right after I left. People were frightened, because they thought I was still sitting in the road.

That evening I was gifted the name, *Tiger Lily*.

Like the lesson of the chipmunk in the vision quest when I feel doubtful and overwhelmed about what one person might can do regarding the current crises, I think each of us can over-come our frustrations and hesitations and take that small, seem-ingly insurmountable step to help the planet. We can become "ti-gers" in our efforts. I have never been politically active, but per-haps I need to look at my reserve. We can be aware of the gifts of the planet, each a small flower of creation and protect them. These issues are bigger than a mouse, but they are approachable.

Spiritual aspects, justice and responsibility

I happened to read an article by Rabbi Edward Bernstein that speaks to the spiritual aspect of reciprocity. Rabbi Bernstein moved from Ohio to Florida and noticed that Ohio's weather was hotter than Florida this summer. He also discovered that the traditional rain every afternoon in Florida had become er-ratic and sporadic.[47]

Bernstein speaks of the Sh'ma, Deuteronomy 11:13-21. He notes that for the ancient Israelites and their agrarian economy, God's reward and punishment was best explained and ex-pressed in terms of weather. "Follow God's ways and receive abundant rain in its season to yield plentiful harvests; stray from God's ways and risk drought and starvation."[48] Rabbi Bernstein then asks that question that always puzzles us and speaks to the issue of justice:

> Is that the way the world works? Time and again we witness the righteous suffer and the wicked prosper. How can the prominence of the second paragraph of the Sh'ma in Jewish liturgy be reconciled with hu-man experience? It is no longer primitive to believe that human behavior affects the natural order. On the contrary, we are now aware that we have the power to destroy or to preserve our environment.

> When a whole society does the right thing, behaves in the right way, learns to love God and love their neighbors, the overall quality of life for everybody

gets better. If everybody lived such a life, we would all feel the reward in our day, environmental stewardship and society's virtuous behavior are intertwined with each other. My hope is that humanity will heed the call of this ancient Scripture to clean up our planet and restore justice to the world.[49,50]

In my mind, this justice would extend to all of creation, and the world would, as the Native Americans say, "Walk in balance." Bear Heart gives the Native American point of view, as follows: "Everything is part of the Sacred Hoop and everything is related. Our existence is so intertwined that our survival depends upon maintaining a balanced relationship with everything within the Sacred Hoop."[51] Rolling Thunder speaks of this era of the end of the Mayan calendar and our planetary crises as a "day of purification... The traditional Indian does not await some kind of ecological doomsday. Instead, he awaits the moment of climax with hopeful anticipation... (Mother Earth will perform a) physiological adjustment."[52]

The Christian Church and others are making headway with organizations like the National Religious Partnership for the Environment formed in 1993. The change needs to be even more profound as Christianity considers loosening the entrenched concept of Plotinus and Aquinas' Great-Chain-of-Being that placed all creation below mankind.[53]

My hope and prayer is that all people and faiths will come to the realization that our home, "Mother Earth," is a living beautiful part of the enormous creation of Spirit. She needs to be loved and respected, not exploited and harmed. Prayerfully, we as aspects of Mother Earth will make an adjustment in our life styles and consciousness.

Only yesterday, I observed a male cardinal, a bluejay, a yellow bird with facial markings in black like the cardinal, and what I took to be two wrens with yellow breasts and grey wings come to the birdbath in my back yard all at the same time. It was incredible to see so many bright colors on a January day. What a great loss it would be if they were to become extinct from pesticides and contaminates, lack of food or water.

May we pray for the change of awareness.

Let us turn now to the apex of my journey and the conclusion in my mind that set the intention of my first proposal that "Christianity and Nature-based Spirituality impacts my life path and spiritual belief system, yet transcends and includes both traditions."

CHAPTER TWELVE

Include and Transcend:
The Apex of My Journey

In this chapter, I explore the inclusion of Christianity and Nature-based Spirituality, and how I believe these two religious processes have merged and transcended into a belief system greater than the whole in my soul's journey.

Christianity challenged and tested

It was the year 1968, a few days before Easter, when our son John Karl died. A beautiful baby with auburn hair and brown eyes that seemed to glow with candles, he was only five days away from being six months old. My brother's birthday would be that Friday, which was Good Friday. I refused to bury my son on my brother's birthday, and we buried him on Maundy Thursday, the day the altar is stripped and the light removed from the sanctuary.

Easter was a devastating day as I dressed my little girl for church services in a dress I had made to match mine. We sat numbly through the services that were supposed to be filled with joy and then went to my parents' home. I have photographs, and my father looks as devastated as I was. My father bought a beautiful marker for the gravesite with an angel carved in the concrete, and a statue of Christ holding a child on His lap is very nearby in Forest Park Babyland Cemetery. I went there a few times, but I knew Karl's spirit was not there. When our baby died, John and I were in the process of John Karl's final adoption proceedings. It never occurred to us to ask, and we buried him in our name. The judge ruled that would close the adoption.

That summer, the last week of July, our caseworker from the adoption agency came to visit us. We were unaware that our second son had just been born on July 28th. I was still so deep in grief the adoption agency decided to wait. Our caseworker told me later that it was decided it would be best if our new baby weighed more than John Karl.

December 10, 1968, Faith Home placed Charles David in our arms. The next spring, we went to court for the final proceedings. Charles David was walking along the courtroom pew holding on to stabilize himself. Paula Kathleen, our four-year-old daughter, was sitting beside him. Judge Solito called her up before his high bench. She marched bravely up and said, "Yes sir?" Judge Solito leaned over and said, "I know what your parents want, but do you want Charles David to be your brother?" Paula cried out, "Yes sir," ran to the pew, grabbed the diaper bag and started to run out the courtroom doors. John leaped up from his seat and captured her hand. Judge Solito laughed, ruled "case closed," and we took our new family home.

Hope renewed; Easter comes again

Twenty-nine years and one day after John Karl's burial, Palm Sunday, April 5, 1997 (my brother's birthday), Charles David's wife gave birth to my first grandchild, Charlie (Charles David, Jr.). In our eyes, he was totally beautiful with light blonde hair and brown eyes. I called my brother just as the dawn showed pink and gold in the eastern sky. "You have a nephew. He is named Charles, like you." My brother said, "Now I can celebrate my birthday again." I had not known he had grieved John

Karl as deeply as I did. Easter had come for my family, for it
had been lost in our grief.

An Episcopal priest that was a personal friend christened
Charlie on the third day of his life, and we all took him to my
son's home. My son placed the new baby on my lap, so he
could go help his wife from the car up the stairs to their second
floor apartment. The baby's eyes lit up, and he threw his small
arms up toward me. My son and I were totally surprised, and I
was obviously delighted.

From the time Charlie was about three weeks old, I would
go and pick him up to go to church with me. Then my cousin
Mary and I would take him with us to lunch before returning
him home. This gave my son and his wife a break from responsibility and an opportunity for extra rest. It gave me joy. That
Christmas Eve little Charlie was wide-eyed at the candles and
music for the evening service as I carried him up the aisle for
Eucharist. My friends at church enjoyed his infant awe as much
as Grandmother Lillie did. I held him even closer as the priest
blessed him.

Acceptance and responsibility of the Pipe; my nature-based pathway

In late 1999, as previously mentioned, I was informed that I was
being offered a Pipe at the coming vision quest in May of 2000,
and I was to be thinking of my vows to Spirit. It was to be a
"grandmother Pipe." I decided to visit a reservation north of
Santa Fe, and I asked to speak with a grandmother of the tribe. I
was directed to a house. The grandmother was sitting on the
front steps. I stood at the edge of the property and waited for
her to acknowledge my presence. In a while, she motioned to
me. I walked a little closer and asked permission to speak with
her. She granted it, and I told her I would be receiving a Pipe
and would she be kind enough to tell me what she believed my

responsibilities should be. She pointed to a young man about fourteen years of age, who was standing at the edge of the yard. The grandmother told me, "You teach him the way."

My spiritual world was to take a profound turn, as I entered the eight years of traditional Pipe training.

I would like to pause here and speak of the legend of the Pipe, and how important it is to the indigenous plains people's religion from which I have a heritage. This is the legend of some of the White Buffalo Calf (Cow) woman's words and actions that brought the Pipe to "the people," as Joseph Brown translates for Black Elk in *The Sacred Pipe*:

> With this Sacred Pipe you will walk upon the Earth; for the Earth is your Grandmother and Mother, and She is sacred... Every step that is taken upon Her should be as a prayer... All the things of the universe are joined to you who smoke the Pipe—all send their voices to *Wakan Tanka*, the Great Spirit. When you pray with this Pipe, you pray for and with everything... *Wakan Tanka* has given you this Sacred Pipe, so that through it you may have knowledge.[1]

Carrying the Pipe challenged and tested

About six weeks before Mother's Day that spring of 2000, my mother's hip broke out from under her as she stood, and she fell. I stayed with her through her surgery, and she appeared to be healing well. The evening before Mother's Day, I went shopping for a gift for her. Upon returning to the house, I received a telephone call from my brother. My mother was dying.

We spent hours at the hospital that night before the physicians told us that her only hope was life support. The physicians were reluctant to act on that procedure, but my step-father insisted. The doctors told us they would perform the procedure if only one of us signed the papers to be the authority to turn the equipment off. It was decided that my brother, as a minister, would make that decision.

Mother's Day, my mother rallied, and I was able to speak with her for the last time. She asked for my brother. I went and called him. When I returned, evidently she no longer knew who I was and yelled at me twice, "Get out!" Stunned, I left. My brother told me later she said the same to him. That is why I have decided she was no longer cognizant. She went into a coma that afternoon from which she never returned.

The doctors told us not to visit or wait at the hospital. If she was to survive, Mother needed nothing that would take any of her energy. My brother and I both knew she most likely would not. My brother returned to New Orleans to finish a job for Boeing and NASA. My mother had been very pleased that I was to receive a Pipe. My step-father told me to go on and leave for the vision quest. One of my supporters was riding with me to the event. Nearly to the White Shaman Cave area, which was the vision quest site, I called home to check with my step-father, as I was doing daily. My step-father told me my brother was flying back. The doctors wanted to disconnect the life support system.

Vision Quest 2000: Acceptance of the test

Arriving at the campsite, I informed the leader and my supporters what was occurring, but did not speak of it to the other participants. We had a sweatlodge, and I was taken in the late evening to my site. It was located on a beautiful ledge overlooking a canyon with a broken arch and the desert, which stretched out into the distant view of Mexico. One of my supporters washed my feet. It was a beautiful and tender ceremony. Then they left me.

I was sitting in a chair with my back to the sun. In front of me rose two fronds of the ocatillo cactus. They shone tall and golden against the darkening deep blue eastern sky. I thought to myself that they looked like Jacob's ladder to heaven.

Something buzzed in my right ear. Automatically, I raised my hand to brush it away. It was not a horse fly like I first thought; it was a growling hummingbird that flew off toward the east through the cactus "ladder." Distracted from my meditative state and grieving for my mother, I went into my tent and lay down. It was so hot (It had been at least one hundred degrees that day.) that I changed into a light nightgown. Emotionally exhausted, I fell asleep.

In the middle of the night, I was awakened by a severe late spring storm that dropped the temperature into the forties. I pulled on some clothes and climbed into my sleeping bag. As I lay there thinking, I remembered that my mother's favorite bird was the hummingbird. I had given her many hand-blown glass images and a stained glass panel for her front window that were hummingbirds. I thought suddenly, "My mother told me 'good bye.' She has gone to a 'new beginning' with Spirit. That is what the hummingbird meant." I cried, but I was comforted.

The next day was cold with a foggy rain that was intermittent. I was out on the quest for three days and was ready to return to the encampment. To occupy myself that last morning, I packed my things and gathered my prayer ties. I walked to the edge of the canyon where I had been told not to go, but I felt the need to stand at the edge. Rather than cry, I began to sing. I sang for my mother. In my pathway, I have discovered that we each must find a way to express and make sense of our grief.

At the naming ceremony, I was given the name "Grandmother Song." My first reaction was very negative. I did not want that name. It took a while for me to realize I did not want my mother to give up the place of "grandmother" in my primary family. To accept the name was to let her go.

After the naming ceremony, I was gifted with the Pipe and began my eight year apprenticeship with my Pipe trainer. He was astonishingly patient with me, as I completed my grief work through my first year with the Pipe, which was considered "in the East." The training is dedicated to each of the eight directions in their order.

We left the campsite the next afternoon after a difficult climbing journey to the White Shaman Cave, where the leader, who quested until we arrived, was gifted with his name of "Clear Light." I was so tired and distracted with so many events that my supporter was driving. As we turned onto Interstate-10 to go back to Houston that Sunday, I called my brother. He told me that mother had been pronounced officially dead that morning.

My brother had chosen the casket, blue with white panels on all four corners. On each pearl-like panel were painted eagles. It fit with scripture, "I bore you up on Eagle's wings and brought you to myself" and Native American tradition that the eagle flies so high it connects with and represents Spirit (Exodus 19:4).[2] My brother asked me to choose the music. I chose "I Come to the Garden Alone," which had been sung at her mother's funeral, and "The Rose," the romantic song my parents had enjoyed together.

Tuesday was the funeral. Several of the Earthtribers came to support me. My grandson Charlie was sitting by his great-grandfather. A minister from Bethany Methodist Church, where my mother and step-father held membership, gave the service. At the end of the service, my little grandson looked up at the minister and solemnly said, "Thanks be to God." The minister looked a little surprised, but Charlie knew the ending response of the congregation when a service ends. Charlie leaned forward to see me at the other end of the pew and gave me a seri-

215

ous nod. Then he came to me as we rose to leave. I carried my three-year-old little Christian in my arms.

Fred Gustafson wrote an extremely profound statement about breath and death in his book, *Dancing Between Two Worlds: Jung and the Native American Soul*:

> An indigenous understanding of life requires an acceptance that life inhales and exhales our existence...with full expectation that the entire individuation of one's being will be a 'giveaway' to the generations before us and to those that will follow. It is a letting go to a wisdom greater than ours, to an unfolding of human consciousness of which we are only a small part but are required to engage as certainly as a midwife for the birth of a child.[3]

He further notes that "beauty based in the total life process that speaks of meanings greater than itself, that carries the images of both life and death, of creation's struggles, attainments and losses...holds the awareness of a wisdom not immediately given to words but to which the soul responds with a deep inner knowing."[4] My little grandson seemed to understand this even better than I.

Fulfilling the grandmother's teaching

In December before mother died, my daughter had a son. That Easter before Mother's Day, Justin Trahan Manuel had been christened at my church, where my daughter grew up. At the Eucharist, little Charlie, as he knelt by my side at the altar rail, had looked up from his knees at the priest and raised his cupped hands. The priest looked at Charlie's serious, comprehending face and gave him his first communion.

Later, as he grew, I would take Charlie to an Earthdance, and he danced the direction of the Sky with me. He entered his first sweatlodge. He learned about the Pipe. When he was about ten years old, he went with me to Cloudcroft to hear his spiritual grandfather speak.

At that meeting, I was asked to lead a children's lodge. Charlie helped me teach the meaning of the Pipe and the directions. I was fulfilling the teaching of the grandmother. Teach the children the pathway to Spirit. I have taught my grandson both pathways and combined them for him. Soon, Spirit willing, he will have an opportunity to "place his stake in the ground." He will have an opportunity for a spiritual rite of passage with a vision quest prior to becoming a man and having to fulfill our culture's military rite of passage.

I have not had the privilege of spending as much time with Justin, but we have a loving bond. My hope is that when I give him a copy of this book, he will find his grandmother's heart and spirit present and will seek the knowledge of his bloodlines. Not only am I part Lakota Blackfoot, his grandfather John was one quarter Cherokee.

Journey with the Pipe and Christ

The Pipe has led me into many directions I had no way of knowing I would go. I have performed a Nature-based and Christian funeral for a woman who was Nez Perce. There were approximately one hundred people present—family members and friends, including the woman's newborn granddaughter Sage. Recently, I performed a wedding in both traditions. There were about two hundred people there. A couple asked me to do a Nature-based ceremony to honor their twenty-fifth wedding anniversary. There were over one hundred and fifty people present. I was also invited to officiate a wedding in San Antonio, utilizing the Sacred Pipe, with approximately five hundred guests. I officiated another wedding for a couple from Iceland and an outdoor funeral, both with a Christian service and the Pipe combined.

217

For me, the combination of the two religions gives a larger "frame" in which to perform the ceremonies of life. It broadens my own spiritual base to include the natural world of which I am a part.

Teachings of my ancestors, two roads joined

When I was to celebrate my twenty-first birthday, my paternal grandfather gave me a copy of Yellow Knife's prayer written in my grandfather's hand:

> Oh, Great Spirit, whose voice I hear in the wind,
> Whose breath gives life to all the world.
> Hear me; I need your strength and wisdom.
>
> Let me walk in beauty, and make my eyes ever behold the red and purple sunset. Make my hands respect the things you have made and my ears sharp to hear your voice.
>
> Make me wise so that I may understand the things to be taught. Help me to remain calm and strong in the face of all that comes towards me.
>
> Let me learn the lessons you have hidden in every leaf and rock. Help me seek pure thoughts and act with the intention of helping others. Help me find compassion without empathy overwhelming me.
>
> I seek strength, not to be greater than my brother, but to fight my greatest enemy—Myself.
>
> Make me always ready to come to you with clean hands and straight eyes. So when life fades, as the fading sunset, my spirit may come to you without shame.
>
> —Yellow Knife, Chief of the Lakota-Sioux (1887)

It was my paternal grandfather's desire that I use it as a guide to live my life.

Equally profound in my formation, my maternal grand-father had decided when it was time for me to learn to read that I was to learn by reading the Bible. He told me that "if I was going to read, I should read something worthwhile." All of my visits with my maternal grandfather involved long walks, wherein he would take my hand in his large farmer's hand and name the plants we saw and tell me about God, as he perceived Him.

My paternal grandmother would take me to her farm near Slaton, Texas and wake me early to help her in the garden. She taught me her deep love of the earth. Her features revealed her Native American heritage, but she rarely spoke of it.

These three grandparents led me early in my formative years. Their teachings were lost to me in memory for many years but came back into my consciousness with my divorce, the appearance of the iridescent beetle and the flyer about Bear Heart's visit.

Like the double meaning of the eagles on my mother's casket, my spirituality includes my indigenous heritage and my Christian traditional background. Rolling Thunder in Boyd's book taught the following:

> It begins with respect for the Great Spirit, and the Great Spirit is the life that is in all things—all the creatures and the plants and even the rocks and the minerals. All things—and I mean all things have their own will, and their own way, and their own purpose; this is what is to be respected.

Such respect is not a feeling or an attitude only. It's a way of life, a way of *being* in the world.[5]

These teachings have been instilled in me from my grand-parents and my Pipe trainer. Bear Heart would say, "Our lives become more meaningful when we remember those that went before us."[6] These two "religions" and teachings intertwine into a fuller pathway in which I live and pray.

Wind Blow

This is my mother's death song I sang, standing at the edge, to carry her along the Milky Way to Spirit:

Wind blow on the canyon walls.
Wind blow on the desert floor.
Wind blow on our troubled souls.
Wind blow. North wind blow.

Rain fall on the canyon walls.
Rain fall on the desert floor.
Rain fall and bring new life.
Rain fall. Rain fall.

Birds sing from the canyon walls.
Birds sing from the desert floor.
Birds sing to teach us joy.
Birds sing. Birds sing.

Spirit in the canyon walls.
Spirit on the desert floor.
Spirit in the sky above.
Bless our souls. Bless our souls.
(Author, 2000)

One's path is a choice

Though some of the events of my life and vision quests that I have discussed may seem strange to the reader, Doug Boyd wrote something regarding Rolling Thunder that has meaning for me: "Though the unenlightened student might feel the need for evidence and reason, for immediate conclusions, the supreme teacher is above the need to prove his point or even to be understood."[7] My mentors opened wide vistas for me to enter or not.

Fred Gustafson wrote of the possibility of a Spirit Dance, "such a 'Dance' of heart and soul will call out for the return of our own indigenous nature, which has long been banished in the name of cultural and technological advancement, so that this nature will once again be respected and heard in both the personal and the collective realms."[8]

Living my vision for others

In October of 2011, I attended the Earthdance at Deer Dancer Ranch. Judith and I led the dance to the East. In this dance, the participants (tribe) took on the roles of all living things in my six vision quests. We reenacted for the benefit of all the gifts I had received from Spirit. Judith played me as the quester, and I was the narrator. I said later that I felt so whole, so complete.

Then I read the following: "The continuous dancing in the circle of wholeness to bring peace and renewal to the earth, plus re-imagining the Jesus mythos along indigenous lines, might indeed be helpful to all of us regardless of our cultural or religious orientation."[9] Black Elk also addressed the issue of dancing a vision. He said, "I think I have told you, but if I have not, you must have understood, that a man (woman) who has a vision is not able to use the power of that vision until after he (or she) has performed the vision on earth for the people to see."[10]

May it be so.

Perceptions and tensions defining and challenging my spiritual world

William Stolzman in his book, *The Pipe and Christ,* that compares the Lakota (nature-based) religion and Christianity made two statements that accurately depict how I perceive my spiritual world. The first statement was "Comparative study and involvement help point out deficiencies and weaknesses in religions. Thus, both religions together provide a stronger ladder with which to ascend toward the Sacred."[11] The second statement important for me was, "The differences established the uniqueness of each religion (Lakota and Christian). It was from the differences that each religion was able to contribute to a fuller life for each individual and people."[12]

My nature-based approach to spirituality grounds me in my body and connects me with the *numinous*, and my Christianity draws me forward to eternity. I personally need both perspectives—the sensory, concrete here and now of Spirit and the hope of the after-life I approached a few years ago—the Spirit without and the Spirit within.

"The Pipe and Christ are the central intercessory elements in the Lakota and Christian religions, respectively."[13] Together, they form my chosen pathway to the *numinous*, my deepest longing.

Though the path that I have chosen over the past twenty-six plus years has been difficult for some of my family and some traditional church members I encountered, it has proven its validity in my mind. Bron Taylor in *Dark Green Religion* speaks to this counter-tension: "Those engaged in salvation-oriented religions have also considered the forms of nature spirituality expressed by these figures (Thoreau, Burroughs and Muir) to be a spiritual path to nowhere or worse. So for some, dark green religions cause real harm and danger."[14]

Taylor is not concerned with what he thinks about dark green religion, but considers what matters is that people encounter their own meaning and spirituality and express that in the way they live in the biosphere. He states the following as part of his coda:

> What I have been looking for is a *sensible* religion, one that is rationally defensible as well as socially powerful enough to save us from our least sensible selves. If there is a sensible post-Darwinian religion, then there must be a *sensory* post-Darwinian religion. For this, dark-green religion is a reasonable candidate. [15]

222

Personally, this book helps me to understand the struggles surrounding traditional religious groups and nature-based religion. For me, it appears that some may call awe of nature religion and not yet discern what their spirituality truly is. It is an honest struggle, and each individual must decide for themselves where they are in their beliefs. I liked Taylor's statement: "What I have been looking for is a *sensible* religion, one that is rationally defensible as well as socially powerful enough to save us from our least-sensible selves," for he is true to the rationalism of this era.[16] However, he seems to be highly suspicious of intuitive mysticism. In my own spirituality, mysticism has an equal voice with my rationality. Also, I do not believe one needs to dispense with one's theism and still embrace nature-based spirituality.

In my mind, it requires wisdom to discern and integrate what is available and abundant to the soul. One does not have to throw away one's theism and choose animism or pantheism. Panentheism may partially speak towards the path I have chosen. William Taegel explains this concept which is also the conundrum of the mystic we spoke of in the chapter on the Ancestors:

> The conundrum of the mystic is that everything is within the Divine. The Sacred Mystery is more than the sum of all things, yet all things are within the Sacred Mystery. In theological circles, such a position is known as panentheism. Pantheism is that all is God. PanENtheism is all is within God, but God is more than all.[17]

I differ with Stolzman in that I do not think one must follow nature-based spirituality in one setting and Christianity in another. I truly believe they can blend. All the pathways have much to offer. Black Elk speaks of the different spiritual pathways one may take in life in the following manner:

> While not indifferent to their choices, he (Black Elk)
> still could bestow his blessing on those who sin-
> cerely embraced the religious forms. Besides sym-
> bolizing the cross, the image of a flowering tree also
> served as a visionary metaphor showing that "the
> Christian life" can have many branches that bear
> fruit, regardless of what name they bear.[18]

Huston Smith and Reuben Snake's book, *One Nation Under God,* describes the rituals of the Native American Church and the persecutions perpetrated on the people due to the use of peyote. Peyote has finally been tested enough and ruled a hallucinogen, rather than a narcotic. It is not even actually fully a hallucinogen and has many healing properties, especially with substance abuse, which seems ironic. The church, due to President Clinton signing Public Law 103-344 in 1993, may now freely use peyote in its church services.[19]

If you ban the use of sacraments in one church, you run the obvious risk of having all churches challenged regarding for instance the port wine that was regularly used in the Episcopal services I attend. I also carried this wine as a Lay Eucharistic Minister as part of the sacraments to shut-ins and hospitalized communicants. Persecution of this type endangers spiritual practices in all religions. Another important point Smith and Snake made was that the correlation of Christianity and Native American (nature-based) spirituality are mutually collaborative.[20]

My spiritual stance

To end my thoughts, I would like to express one more moment of my soul's journey with a poem I wrote that was once published by my rector in the Episcopal church's newspaper. Hopefully, one can discern the path I have chosen of nature-based spirituality and Christianity that form the "cup" that contains my spiritual life. Many paths lead to the "One." The quest for beauty, truth and goodness has been blessed with unmerited Grace.

Another way of considering this position was offered by William Taegel:

> Sojourners who grew up in cultural Christianity will...have to move outside that culture for a time and wrestle with ancestors from other traditions to see which of these teachers of the wheel belong in their inner council/wheel. Once you leave your religion of origin, you obtain freedom to return to the point of origin with maturity and transcendent neutrality.[21]

This moving out as I did in the beginning with questioning if there was a problem with my church or within myself made room to explore what I believed. This exploration offered a profound possibility to discover my *owned faith*, not just something I had been taught I should believe.

Like many, I have stumbled along to find my way. Some days it is clearer than others on the path; however, through that Grace it is a journey that has astounded me and is ever before me. As I mentioned in the first paragraph of this book, I once even thought it would be easier to just not be, to "just pack it in." What I have derived out of my journey is that these are powerful thoughts and feelings at that moment in time. However, they are not all that I/we are. We are infinitely more than the awareness of our thoughts and feelings at a particular moment. My prayer is that you dear reader will find your pathway clearer with awareness and compassion and that my words might be helpful. I gift you now with the path of my soul:

Poured to Fill Eternity

We climb the mountain of thought
And view the awakened peace,

Together stand frozen, caught,
Silent awe at holy place.

A place caught in early dawns
By the light of rising grace,
Surprising our hearts, like fawns,
Ready to flee—our pulses race.

Frantic default behind rocks,
Sharp rocks of questioning fears,
Defenses against fate's harsh knocks –
Forgetting God heals with tears.

When bitter cup is empty,
The wine of love is given:
Poured to fill eternity –
The Word of God is spoken.

With steps untried – though guided –
Dare depart the hidden place.
When the journey has ended,
God's love will reveal His face.

(Author, August 11, 1983)

Mitakuye o'yasin,
Puha,
Amen.

Waves, Stages, Levels of the Human Story: Evolution Toward Greater Complexity in Trauma Mentoring

First Tier

Beige (individualistic) – in the bush

- Requires subsistence needs to be met in order to remain alive.

- Thinking is automatic, process is survivalist.

- Person is enmeshed in Nature, not able to stand background.

- Conditions likely in Climate Warming events like Katrina.

- Research indicates we currently enter "The Long Emergency."

- Traumas occur at the survival level with primitive responses.

- Will I live or die? Is there water? Is there food?

- Who knows what to do in these conditions? Trauma mentors?

Purple (Communal) – Communal/Tribal – Enchanted Forest

- Life conditions of beige trauma subside enough for magic of life.

- Structures are tribal, processes are circular.

- In a good organization my people feel safe; our folk ways and rituals are honored.

- A mature person seeks to be safe within cohesive family.

- He follows the tribal leader.

- Individual is vulnerable to traumatic abuse of leader.

- Magical expectation that someone/thing out there will heal me.

- Altered States are valued as transformers of trauma.

- Sacred plants are often ingested to achieve the altered state.

- In the "Long Emergency" instant cures like drugs, religion.

- One with Nature without data to correct perceptions.

Red (Individualistic) – Exploitive/Egocentric – Jungle/battlefield

- People need to be dominated by strong leadership that gives rewards.

- Thinking is egocentric, structures are empires. The process exploitative.

- Healthy red thrives on honor, courage, and safety through strength.

- A mature person seeks to be macho, powerful and in control because *strength* and *respect* matter most. If healthy, assertive. If not, abusive.

- Might makes right ethic means trauma abounds through rape and pillage.

- Feelings are expendable.
- Hit back hard when injured. Eye for an eye. 9/11 mentality.
- Ignore trauma and get back in the field.
- Vulnerability is for the sissy.
- What doesn't kill me makes me stronger. Survival of the fittest.
- Nature is to be conquered and/or part of battlefield.

Blue (Communal) Moralistic/Prescriptive – use forest for Cathedral

- Build on Natural power spots, e.g. Chartres.
- People work the best when they are told how to do things the right way.
- *Order* and *stability* through *structure* and *enforced principles* of righteous living that ties to something larger than self. Trauma solved through obeying literal myth.
- Doing duty and being punished when failing to do so gives meaning to life. Trauma is result of disobedience.
- Thinking is absolutistic, structures are pyramidal, the process authoritarian.
- A mature person seeks to be purposeful and disciplined as directed by rightful higher authority.
- Myths are taken literally.
- Trauma is given firm structure like hospital, 12 steps, literal Bible.
- Dominion over Nature of Steward of Natural resources (stage of society in present).

Orange (Individualistic) – Rational/Economic – Forest for profit

- People are motivated by the achievement of autonomy, independence and material rewards. I want to achieve, win and get somewhere in my life. Competition. Win/lose if unhealthy. Win/win if healthy.

- Nature is a resource for profit.

- Nature is viewed as separate from humans and seen through technology.

- A mature person seeks to be successful, independent, innovative.

- Competitive winners unconstrained by structure, rules or principles.

- Objective studies and views of trauma. PTSD identified.

- Traumas are handled with insight, biofeedback, medication, and formal therapy.

- In its unhealthy form trauma is seen as opportunity for profit or an inhibitor of profit.

- Questioning of authority uncovers abuses and traumas of previous levels.

Green (Communal) – Social/Communitarian – Commune Back to Forest

- People want to get along and feel accepted by their peers.

- Cultural Creatives gain attention of researchers.

- Sharing and participating are better than competing.

- Thinking is relativistic, structures are egalitarian, processes are consensual. Win for me. Win for you. Emerging win for planet.

- In a good organization the people and our feelings come first as we join in a warm supportive community of equals that cares for its own.

- A mature person seeks to be warm and supportive so that all can grow and be fulfilled. Explore the inner beings of self and others.

- Traumas are handled with psychodrama, other experiential therapies, meditation, initiation into warriorhood, guided imagery (Voice Dialogue).

- Green descends and forms alliance with Purple. Rites such as the soul's journey, purification and cleansing, storytelling are retrieved and used to transform trauma.

- Nature is viewed as being in crisis through the Sierra Club and various environmental groups. Nature is in trauma.

- Eco-spirituality groups like the Earthtribe arise along the Nature-based psychotherapy directed to trauma.

- Tends to trust "state" experiences and ignore stages (rigor of practices).

Quantum Leap to the 2nd Tier

Yellow (Individualistic) – Natural Habitats valued and explored

- People enjoy doing things that fit who they are naturally without causing harm to others or excesses of self-interest.

- Accept the inevitability of nature's flows and forms.

- Mentors need free access to information and materials.

- Thinking is systemic, structures are interactive, processes are integrative.

- A mature person seeks to be functional and flexible within his/her own personal principles.

- Be independent within reason; knowledgeable as much as possible; caring, but realistic.

- Individual vision quests, workshops, meditation, and experimenting with new forms of trauma transformation, mainly on one's own.

- Innovators/mavericks see new possibilities in working with trauma.

- Traditional therapies, medications, hospitalizations are transcended but their usefulness is included.

Turquoise (Communal) – Global Village – Emerging Wisdom Culture

- Material world is Nature, including wilds, humans, and freeways.

- Spiritual bonds pull people and organizations together.

- Work must be meaningful to the overall health of life.

- Thinking is holistic, the structures are global and the processes are flowing and ecological.

- Traumas are seen in the light of our role in the living system.

- Embraces sub-selves who have been traumatized without getting dominated.

- Sees patterns throughout the Universe.

- Places individual story inside the larger story of Nature.

- Transcends personal trauma to assist in facing Earth's trauma.

- Forms alliances with emerging evolutionary groups around the planet.

– Creates dialogue where the other has a sense of spaciousness, much room to be different.

– Locates "evil" within the process and therefore brings opposites together. Reduction of diatribes.

– Trauma seen as part of the process, met with balance and awareness.

– Moves easily up and down the spiral to find a variety of resources for trauma. Humans are Nature becoming aware of itself in a new way.

– Notices the different memes as they arise and can move into them to offer mentoring in emergencies.

– Has full awareness of the "long emergency" of our current planet without getting caught up in pseudo drama or overwhelming fear.

– Steers course through hopelessness and despair, yet faces pain and suffering.

– Basic joy but unfailingly authentic.

Appendix B

Eight Standing Waves:
Dr. William Taegel, May 2011

WAVE #1 – *(beige wave downloads)*

Graves and Beck: download something called vMemes – value of survival

Kegan: downloads Subject/object relationship: instinctual response

J. Houston: downloads evolving self: pre-individual, self not formed

C. Gilligan: downloads morals: selfish or egocentric

Fowler: – downloads spirituality: free access to Primordial

W & J: (Drs. Taegel & Yost): primordial people download cycles of wisdom; often advanced

WAVE #2 – *(purple wave downloads)*

Graves & Beck: v MEME – downloads value of shaman, magic – Nature mystic

Kegan: sojourner sees own reflexes or impulses. Misses the Nature mystic

Houston: doesn't find the shamanic self (early Jean Houston). Misses the Nature mystic

Gilligan: downloads the moral intuitive/nature voice

Fowler: locates primordial mostly in unconscious. Misses the Nature mystic

W & J: Primordial shaman envisions cycles and sees
our current era

WAVE #3 – (red wave downloads)

Graves & Beck: vMEME – value of warrior, take
what I want, fierce individual

Kegan: self is controlled by needs & desires, detests
control of group

Houston: doesn't see the warrior self as crucial

Gilligan: sees warrior archetype as selfish morally
Fowler: doesn't see the spirituality of the warrior

W & J: initiation into warrior necessary: discipline,
persistence

WAVE #4 – (blue wave downloads)

Graves & Beck: vMEME – value of literal myth/law,
monarchy

Kegan: self witnesses impulses/desires & seeks
imperial control

Houston self develops conventional consciousness

Gilligan: morals evolve to what is good for group,
not just self

Fowler spirituality is literal/mythic, my god is the
best (only one), conform

W & J: Structure, control, and authority are
important; Chartres; Medieval Mysticism;
lecture/preaching; book centered; guru; early
Universities

WAVE #5 – (orange wave downloads)

Graves & Beck: vMEME – value of
rational/science/capitalist

Kegan: oddly unable to find anything in this wave
Houston: self evolves rational consciousness that
governs life

Gilligan: morals extended beyond family to tribe,
even nation

Fowler: spirituality questions of foundations. Pursuit of truth. Dialogue

W & J: rational inquiry and psychological work are essential. Mainline universities.

WAVE #6 – (green wave downloads)

Graves & Beck: vMEME – value of sensitivity, consensus, justice, noviolence

Kegan: self is interpersonal and can observe own needs/desires

Houston: self is developed and is post conventional (cultural creative)

Gilligan: morals extend beyond nation to all humans and all the Earth

Fowler: spirituality sees reality behind myth, holds opposites, global faith

W & J: horizontal rights, everything is related, reciprocity, Tech community, self-righteous activist, confronts denial, pessimist/optimist extremes, inner pusher dominates, spirituality not traditional or modern meditation mainly Eastern: yoga, etc.

Leap to 2nd Tier (Big set of rapids and FEW have made the jump)

WAVE # 7 – (yellow wave downloads)

Graves & Beck: vMEME – value of solitary seeker, okay with chaos/complexity

Kegan: self has full identity, witnesses interpersonal conflict, equanimous

Houston: beyond individual to trans-rational, transpersonal consciousness

Gilligan: self able to integrate previous levels of morality to Universal

Fowler: Universal spirituality, fears reduced, sacred activist

W & J: person learns soul retrieval (descent into Earth); telluric energies inclusive inner council; courage to be different; authentic; visionary; transitory relationships and community; creative; competent; keeps agreements; inner meditations; not captured by previous waves. Intentions through aware-ego; effective but detached from outcomes; more individually oriented.

WAVE # 8 – (turquoise wave downloads)

Graves & Beck: vMEME – able to move up and down spiral, all related

Kegan: communal self, able to witness own beliefs and self process

Houston: no different than #7

Gilligan: no different than #7

Fowler: no different than #7

W & J: builds longitudinal community; sees issues with clarity; sees danger with little fear; room to be yourself in their presence; laughter; holds opposites easily; takes care of vulnerability; owns shadow; moves quickly through conflict; balance of experiential and rational; altered states anchored in Nature; group meditations deeply connected through five senses to natural world; colorful ceremony; breathing moves easily through chakras; electric connection to earth; accesses all previous waves easily; provisional answers; grounded in newer sciences; retrieves wisdom of cyclical cultures; fully civilized yet questioning of civilization's foundation; transcends but includes technology; relaxed and unhurried; timely; develops primal skills of sustainability; primarily tribal in practices.[1]

Appendix C

Earth Circle Formation and Practice

The purpose of the Earth Circle is nature-based spirituality. The following is a synopsis of the process of the group. A topic in nature is pre-chosen prior to the meeting and announced in the e-mail invitation.

The small group centers on an aspect of nature each month and meets to discuss how that particular aspect relates to our individual life stories. Then the question is given, "How does this reflect Spirit's action in your particular life journey?" The small circle is a microcosm of how even larger circles might form or disintegrate.

A typical Sunday (or whatever day your group chooses) proceeds in the following manner:

1. We plan to meet outside unless the weather is too extreme.

2. It is agreed in advance that everything that takes place in the group is kept confidential.

3. We gather and hold a stone or small object like a glass heart. Silently, we pass this object to one another praying for the good of the group and invoking Spirit's presence. When each person has had an opportunity to place their energy and intentions into the stone, it is placed in the center of the circle. (I find it best to always place seating areas in a circle so that all can see each other and feel equal in the group.)

4. The talking stick or object used for that purpose is passed from one person to the next Each states how the aspect of nature chosen for that meeting impacts their life without interruption.

5. The talking stick goes around the circle a second time with each individual stating how Spirit's action is reflected in the participant's original story. This repetition also gives the group an opportunity to remember and reflect on the individual stories.

6. The third time around the circle each person comments on their current feelings in relation to what has just been said, and what they may now think might have altered in their original thoughts and feelings of the incident.

7. Upon completion of the third round, the talking-stick is placed in the center of the circle, and the group may comment to one another about what they heard, how it relates to their story, or how it relates to the universal story.

8. The group then closes with a small ceremony. My group enjoys a star hug, where we stand in a circle and place our palms against each other's sending love and energy to the group.

Personally, I then serve refreshments, but that is not necessary. I find it helps ease the ending and gives time for further bonding of the group. (Author, 2006)

Appendix D

Summary of Mentoring Tools

T his appendix will offer two parts: the order of tools explored in the Medicine Wheel and overall tools that I found useful in mentoring. Of course, this is just a taste of what is available to the mentor.

Summary of tools in my journey through the Medicine Wheel

Let us take time now and summarize the events, mentoring tools, and spiritual growth that I have been discussing through the chapters on the directions of the Medicine Wheel before we continue further. I hope you can see through the Medicine Wheel how the premises of this book and my life events are evolving and connect with the proposals with which I began this book: First, the integration of Christianity and Nature-based Spirituality impacts my life path and spiritual belief system, yet transcends and includes both traditions. Second, this integration is relevant to a ministry for the spiritual, psychological, emotional, physical growth and healing of individuals and groups by utilizing my form of integrated Nature-based Spirituality, leadership skills and mentoring tools. Third, the expansion of ideas and beliefs address the practical and spiritual purposes of sustaining the earth in the current planetary crises.

In the East, I spoke of hope and healing and the impact of the eco-field and the songlines of the Australian Aborigine. I visited my first vision quest with Bear Heart and Winged Medicine that resulted from my approach and encounter with the nature-based spiritual pathway.

I then turned toward the direction of the South, the direction of vulnerability and creativity, a feminine direction. Here I noted my financial vulnerability brought about by critical illness leading to bankruptcy (an event effecting many United States citizens and foreign countries), and my introduction to the sacredness of money. I related the psychological impact of bonding patterns (Stone and Stone's *voice dialogue*). Also, I noted the mentor/shaman as a storyteller and ceremonialist, and the mentoring of a neo-shaman with the question, "What are you between in your life, Lillie?" I introduced Beck and Cowan's spiral dynamics and Taegel's "council of selves."

The West is the direction of darkness and the shadow side of humankind, letting go, and gratitude. Here I explored the purpose of a sweatlodge (place of prayer). As symbolic of the dark side of mankind, I addressed my turmoil and confusion surrounding terrorism and the spiritual aspects of *good* and *evil*. Garrison addresses these issues in his book, *Civilization and the Transformation of Power*. I encountered the concept of dreaming as a teacher and Rupert Sheldrake's *morphic resonance*. Then I looked at the value system of the terrorist through Beck and Cowan's work and searched for any spiritual light or love in terrorist activities. Christian spirituality and nature-based spirituality both find the dark and light aspects of God, the One.

In the direction of the North, which is the young masculine or warrior, as well as the wind of healing, I looked at war and its impact on my life path through my personal experiences and the generations before and after me. I connected with Larry Winter's and Ed Tick's memories and reflections on Viet Nam.

The concept of spiritual warrior arose through my life experiences in Germany, and I began a broader context within my prayer life as I observed the television news surrounding the Gulf War and Desert Storm and my fears for my son. Three of the mentoring tools explored in this chapter were James and Jongeward's work in *transactional analysis*, Beck and Cowan's value level of the *purple meme*, and Gustafson's discussion of the "bond of violence."

Grandmother Earth is our next direction. Here I looked at the shaman/storyteller in four events: a teaching event as a supporter at a vision quest encampment, a stay in the hospital for medical tests (where I faced fear and was connected with my nature-based spirituality and Christian beliefs through media and music through Christian hymns), the nature-based mentoring of a client for trauma, and a recent vision quest in 2011, wherein I confronted my inner loneliness (a spiritual wound). The environment on my quest resulted in my contemplation of the environmental crises we are all facing on the planet. I looked at the following mentoring tools: Stone and Stone – sub-personalities and aware ego, *awareness* and the *witness state*, Taegel's "council of selves," Naparstek's use of imagery, and other tools like meditation, music, art, poetry, song and Lawlor's dreams, collective memories, and imaginings.

In the direction of Grandfather Sky, I explored the concept of *transcendence*. As tools, we explored Beck and Cowan's *spiral dynamics*, Ken Wilber's *four lenses* and Taegel and Yost's *stages of development and developmental perspectives*. I reflected on stories of a sweatlodge and an Earthdance. We were asked by our spiritual mentor, "How does trauma fit with love?" Then we investigated our own birth process. I explored a series of e-mails with my mentor in which I was developing a deeper and broader sense of what God *Is*. I looked at the use of myth in *The Golden Compass* and story as tools. I investigated myth from the viewpoint of

Beck and Cowan's spiral, and the use of guided meditation and ceremony ("The Ceremony of Remembering, *Lake Medicine*").

The direction of Relations led me to look at the responsibility of sacred leadership, the building of community (Earth Circle and Earthtribe), and collaborative leadership. I also explored a nature-based spiritual event at Enchanted Rock

In this chapter on the Ancestors, I explored the topic of death and the mentoring tool of the vision quest, but more importantly to me, I spent time with the melding of my Christian and Nature-based spirituality. They have become an integrated whole for me on this journey.

Other comments on mentoring tools

Many tools have been mentioned throughout the book. I would like to add a small summary and one or two others that may prove helpful. These are all wonderful tools, and there are many others. The greatest tool of all I have found is the reciprocal love from one's mentors and one's community.

As I thought about the experiences of my life I realized they fit into certain needs or prayers, and I wrote about them in the direction I thought they most fit and resonated with a particular direction of the Medicine Wheel. I also noted in this process that each story/prayer event was also supported by the other directions of the Medicine Wheel. The Medicine Wheel is not static or rigid. It flows with life and Spirit energy. Although the issue seems to address a particular direction, one prays the entire event around the Medicine Wheel. The Medicine Wheel can be used as a tool for clarifying one's issues with intention (prayer) and meditation.

The neo-shaman is adept at remaining aware in the 2nd tier of Beck and Cowan's spiral dynamics and at the same time moving up and down the spiral to meet others where they are, aware of his/her own personal oscillations on the spiral, and combines nature-based spirituality in the purple meme with scientific theory of the modern age.[1]

Another tool for the neo-shaman is the vision quest, and nature-based experiences like the ones at Enchanted Rock. These events remove one from the ordinary events and stresses of modern life and allow reconnection to the sensory world and the soul. The tools of the new-shaman of the spiral, sweatlodges, vision quests, and earth dances also have held a part in the healing of Liliput's trauma. I have included vision quests in the book, because along with the Medicine Wheel, they have had such a powerful impact on my personal and spiritual growth. The neo-shaman will be facile in moving up and down the spiral to meet the mentee and will also be able to recognize the inner selves personally within themselves and the person being mentored.[2,3]

An extremely important tool in the process is understanding the council of selves within us and the process of awareness observed by the witness state that reveals the aware ego and permits objective choices.[4,5] I'll discuss this a little further later in the chapter. Hal and Sidra Stone in their 2005 book on "Voice Dialogue," also give us insight into the parts of our selves that tend to guide our thoughts and behaviors.[6] These are parts like the *pusher, pleaser, inner child, protector/controller*, etc. There are examples of these in chapters three and ten. The tools of Voice Dialogue by Hal and Sidra Stone were specific in work with the inner council (like Lillie's shadow self of the vulnerable child, Liliput).[7,8]

Don Beck and Christopher Cowan in their book *Spiral Dynamics* offer us insight into the levels of development regarding values.[9] It is exceptionally useful, although it only relates to human beings. The levels of the spiral are color-coded and given as memes in ascending, developmental order. The use of this tool is fairly dominant throughout the book.

It is a book based on Clare Graves work and has a linear developmental process that Beck and Cowan color coded to aid in noting the differences. The phases are entitled "memes" and can overlap, or have positive and negative manifestations. Although, the process builds one upon another, I believe that we move through these memes ascending and descending many times in any given day, depending on life experiences, and Beck and Cowan speak of this oscillation. It is important to note again that these developmental values are strictly for human beings and have little, if any, connection with nature. They are helpful however in discerning one's own values and the values of others.

These levels from Beck and Cowan, and Will Taegel's "Eight Standing Waves" (listed in appendix B) are especially relevant in that they combine Beck and Cowan's work with other developmental theorists and can be expanded for the trauma mentor. Working through the levels of the spiral from Beck and Cowan's work helped give perspective and healing to the incidents of my own life and opened doors for mentoring others who have suffered through trauma.

Another tool that was useful is a rope spiral placed on the ground and a ladder. One steps first on the rope to the feelings and issue, then another step to the vulnerability, then to the shadow self, then to the center of the soul's work. Stepping back out of the spiral (hurricane), one goes to a ladder and steps above the issue. The facilitator expresses what was heard. From the witness state the participant can observe the issue without emotion.This exercise develops an aware ego.[10]

A mentoring tool I use in my community is the Earth Circle women's group. I spoke of it in the chapter on Relations. It is a nature-based approach to Spirit and healing. (How to form an Earth Circle can be found in appendix C.) Other tools that I have applied to this story I mentioned in chapter seven are Ken Wilber's four lenses and the use of Will Taegel's rope spiral on the ground and ladder explained in the paragraph above to observe an incident from a witness state.[11,12]

Another tool I found especially effective is the dance between two opposites: stepping left into a tension, stepping right into its opposite tension, stepping back into a witness position, stepping forward to the middle again with an aware-ego, and from that position making a choice.[13] Lillie stood between the tensions of her hurt inner shadow and the desire to escape pain (leave), and earlier knowledge that flight does not solve an issue; it only prolongs it. She stepped back and looked at her choices and decided to continue with the quest and to work with her mentor from an aware position that growth would only come from persistence. I have to admit it was not a quick fix; growth takes time.

We took Lillie and Liliput into Muriel James transactional work of Parent, Adult, Child, as well.[14]

James and Jongeward further explain, "The Adult ego state can be used to reason, to evaluate stimuli, to gather technical information, and to store this information for future reference."[15] For an entire year, I worked with my mentors on *reality testing*, with James and Jongeward's work. This reality testing was also a major part of my Pipe training. To understand others, it is incumbent upon the Pipe carrier to understand one's own inner world.

In any ego state, that is who we think we are at the time.

Autonomy is the ultimate goal of transactional analysis. My Pipe trainer "pushed me hard" to develop autonomy. The autonomous person has spontaneity, awareness and intimacy (aware, open and authentic; mind and body responding in unison in and to the now).

I came to realize that James' paradigm was helpful in a cognitive sense of teaching me a map. However, it was the nature-based spirituality and the mentoring Pipe sessions that gave me an actual experience of channeling the wounded child through the aware ego space. I believe one of the strengths of nature-based spirituality, in contrast with psychological and Christian models, is this dimension of experiential learning. It embodies the learning and leads to healing and spiritual wholeness.

We also have the work of Peter Levine and Bill Plotkin to assist us in understanding the inner impact of trauma on child and adult.[16,17] Peter Levine's work, like *Waking the Tiger*, is a strong approach to recovering trauma stored within the body.[18] As a mentor these tools and the full experience of them in practice are now available for me as a trauma and spiritual mentor and offer the opportunity to practice them with clients like Sara.

Will Taegel in our May 2011 class at Wisdom University on "Exploring Earth Wisdom and the Primordial Mind" gave us a classroom handout on eight "Waves and Stages" (eco-fields that are past, present and future) from his research and dissertation. This information combines the thoughts of several theorists, including Beck and Cowan (Appendix A).

The mentor also has available the tools of ceremony and creative art. One day for a meditation, a group went to a small spring at Ralston and chose to "lay a burden down" by placing a rock symbol at the foot of the spring.

Two days later, as I reflected on this meaningful event, I wrote the following poem. It defines for me the task of a nature-based mentor, the neo-shaman, who has learned to work with compassion and awareness.

Our Souls Take Wing

Slowly winds the path around the mountain face,

Long stretches of dappled sun flicker between
redwood giants,

Broad arms cast deepening shadows toward the
gorge below,

A hush expectant fills the summer air.

Silent we come, wending our way,

Mountain spring, flowing swiftly in its small
waterfall,

Chanting a gentle healing song.

Across a small footbridge the forest stands,

Patient witness to all above and below.

One by one, we lift large stone or small,

Stones like the inner burdens of our lives and souls.

One by one, we place them on Mother Earth's breast.

Hard it is to lay them down, an inner grief, do they
not define who we are?

Are they not worn, familiar shoes in which we
stand?

Looking skyward, then earthward, we kneel then
rise

To a baptismal cleansing from the small spring's
clear heart.

A mentor with loving hands and eyes, strong
embrace,

Prays a gentle blessing for our souls.

How could such love and freedom be for a weary
one like me.

A span of dark wings, silent in the forest deep, four
owls rise then rest,

Witness to our journey there, Spirit watching from
their eyes,

Drawing closer with each winged approach,

Sun-wise, each direction counted in the circle of life.

Deep in awe we tremble there, tears and song fill our
hearts.

—*Our souls take wing.*

(Author, 2008)

Events in my life seem to have come full circle. Rolling
Thunder speaks on the importance of the circle, as follows:

> The circle is the Great Spirit's emblem... When we
> met in Oklahoma, we formed a huge circle of all nat-
> ive tribes and we smoked the peace Pipe to the sun,
> and it stayed lit around that huge circle. Then the
> Iroquois brought out the board with writing on it
> and interpreted it. They said, "Today our tribes are
> united again..." and that circle (of peace) will go
> around the world.[19]

The most important tools for change in the world are the
inner community of the council of selves and the outer community based on awareness, compassion, transparency, resilience and truth. That is my commitment and prayer.

We have examined the second proposal that states, "This
integration is relevant to a ministry for the spiritual, psychological, emotional, physical growth and healing of individuals
and groups by utilizing my form of integrated Nature-based
Spirituality, leadership skills and mentoring tools" throughout
the book and within the appendices. We have further investigated the third premise, "The expansion of ideas and beliefs address the practical and spiritual purposes of sustaining the
earth in the current planetary crises" mainly in chapter eleven.

NOTES

Chapter 1: An Introduction to One Soul's Quest

1. Bear Heart & Larkin, M. (1996). *The wind is my mother*. New York: Berkley Books, p. 16.

2. Bear Heart & Larkin, M. (1996). *The wind is my mother*. New York: Berkley Books, p. 16.

3.Bear Heart & Larkin, M. (1996). *The wind is my mother*. New York: Berkley Books, p.139.

4. Bear Heart & Larkin, M. (1996). *The wind is my mother*. New York: Berkley Books, pp. 137-138.

5. Bear Heart & Larkin, M. (1996). *The wind is my mother*. New York: Berkley Books, p. 220.

6. Bear Heart & Larkin, M. (1996). *The wind is my mother*. New York: Berkley Books, p. 219.

7. Boyd, D. (1974). *Rolling Thunder*. New York: Dell, p. 37.

8. Boyd, D. (1974). *Rolling Thunder*. New York: Dell, p. 81.

9. McGaa, E. (1990). *Mother earth spirituality: Native American paths to healing ourselves and our world*. New York: Harper/Collins, p. 100.

10. Lame Deer, J. & Erdoes, R. (1972). *Lame Deer seeker of visions*. New York: Washington Square Press, p. 239.

11. Sneve, V. (1977). *That they may have life: The Episcopal Church in South Dakota*. New York: The Seabury Press, p. 70.

12. Neihardt, J. (1959). *Black Elk speaks* (Rev. ed.). New York: Pocket Books.

Chapter 2: Direction of the East: A Healing Prayer

1. Brown, J. E. (Ed.). (1971). *The sacred pipe: Black Elk's account of the seven rites of the Oglala Sioux.* New York: Penguin Books.

2. Ruiz, M. (1997). *The four agreements.* San Rafael, CA: Amber-Allen, p. 27.

3. Brown, J. E. (Ed.). (1971). *The sacred pipe: Black Elk's account of the seven rites of the Oglala Sioux.* New York: Penguin Books, p. 32.

4. Brown, J. E. (Ed.). (1971). *The sacred pipe: Black Elk's account of the seven rites of the Oglala Sioux.* New York: Penguin Books, p. 23.

5. Brown, J. E. (Ed.). (1971). *The sacred pipe: Black Elk's account of the seven rites of the Oglala Sioux.* New York: Penguin Books, p. 7.

6. Neihardt, J. (1959). *Black Elk speaks* (Rev. ed.). New York: Pocket Books, p. 52.

7. Bear Heart & Larkin, M. (1996). *The wind is my mother.* New York: Berkley Books, p. 235-238.

8. Taegel, W. (2010). *The sacred council of your wild heart: Nature's hope in earth's crisis.* Wimberley, TX: 2nd Tier, p. 133.

9. Taegel, W. (2011, May). *Standing waves.* Wimberley, TX: classroom handout.

10. Lawlor, R. (1991). *Voices of the first day: Awakening in the aboriginal dreamtime.* Rochester, VT: Inner Traditions International, Ltd., p. 71.

11. Lawlor, R. (1991). *Voices of the first day: Awakening in the aboriginal dreamtime.* Rochester, VT: Inner Traditions International, Ltd., p. 71.

12. Lame Deer, J. & Erdoes, R. (1972). *Lame Deer seeker of visions.* New York: Washington Square Press, p. 266.

13. Boyd, D. (1974). *Rolling Thunder.* New York: Dell, p. 10.

14. Gibson, J. W. (2009). *A reenchanted world: The quest for a new kinship with nature.* New York: Metropolitan Books, Henry Holt, pp. 65, 89.

15. Gibson, J. W. (2009). *A reenchanted world: The quest for a new kinship with nature*. New York: Metropolitan Books, Henry Holt, p. 96.

16. Lawlor, R. (1991). *Voices of the first day: Awakening in the aboriginal dreamtime*. Rochester, VT: Inner Traditions International, Ltd., p. 1.

17. Lawlor, R. (1991). *Voices of the first day: Awakening in the aboriginal dreamtime*. Rochester, VT: Inner Traditions International, Ltd., p. 104-105.

18. Lawlor, R. (1991). *Voices of the first day: Awakening in the aboriginal dreamtime*. Rochester, VT: Inner Traditions International, Ltd., pp. 298-299, 379.

19. Taegel, W. (2010). *The sacred council of your wild heart: Nature's hope in earth's crisis*. Wimberley, TX: 2nd Tier, p. 59.

20. Lawlor, R. (1991). *Voices of the first day: Awakening in the aboriginal dreamtime*. Rochester, VT: Inner Traditions International, Ltd., pp. 48-49.

21. Lawlor, R. (1991). *Voices of the first day: Awakening in the aboriginal dreamtime*. Rochester, VT: Inner Traditions International, Ltd., p. 234.

22. Gibson, J. W. (2009). *A reenchanted world: The quest for a new kinship with nature*. New York: Metropolitan Books, Henry Holt, pp. 10-11.

23. Stolzman, W. (1995). *The pipe and Christ* (5th ed.). Chamberlain, SD: Tipi Press, p. 66.

24. Gibson, J. W. (2009). *A reenchanted world: The quest for a new kinship with nature*. New York: Metropolitan Books, Henry Holt, p. 196.

25. Gibson, J. W. (2009). *A reenchanted world: The quest for a new kinship with nature*. New York: Metropolitan Books, Henry Holt, p. 108.

26. Gibson, J. W. (2009). *A reenchanted world: The quest for a new kinship with nature*. New York: Metropolitan Books, Henry Holt.

27. Gibson, J. W. (2009). *A reenchanted world: The quest for a new kinship with nature.* New York: Metropolitan Books, Henry Holt, pp. 116-117.

28. Gibson, J. W. (2009). *A reenchanted world: The quest for a new kinship with nature.* New York: Metropolitan Books, Henry Holt, p. 117.

29. Lawlor, R. (1991). *Voices of the first day: Awakening in the aboriginal dreamtime.* Rochester, VT: Inner Traditions International, p. 8.

30. Taegel, W. (2010). *The sacred council of your wild heart: Nature's hope in earth's crisis.* Wimberley, TX: 2nd Tier, p. 21.

31. Taegel, W. (2010). *The sacred council of your wild heart: Nature's hope in earth's crisis.* Wimberley, TX: 2nd Tier, p 18.

32. Lawlor, R. (1991). *Voices of the first day: Awakening in the aboriginal dreamtime.* Rochester, VT: Inner Traditions International, p. 89.

33. Lame Deer, J. & Erdoes, R. (1972). *Lame Deer seeker of visions.* New York: Washington Square Press, p. 108.

34. Bear Heart & Larkin, M. (1996). *The wind is my mother.* New York: Berkley Books, p. 94.

Chapter 3: Direction of the South: Trauma of Economic Crisis: The Road to Bankruptcy

1. Brown, J. E. (Ed.). (1971). *The sacred pipe: Black Elk's account of the seven rites of the Oglala Sioux.* New York: Penguin Books, pp. 37, 31.

2. Ruiz, M. (1997). *The four agreements.* San Rafael, CA: Amber-Allen, p. 51.

3. Taegel, W. & Yost, J. (2009). *Shamanic wisdom: Eco-spiritual journey through trauma of the environmental and economic crisis.* Wimberley, TX: 2nd Tier, p. 5.

4. Taegel, W. & Yost, J. (2009). *Shamanic wisdom: Eco-spiritual journey through trauma of the environmental and economic crisis.* Wimberley, TX: 2nd Tier, p. 5.

5. Stone, H & Stone, S. (1989b). *Embracing our selves: The voice dialogue manual.* Novato, CA: New World Library.

6. Bacevich, A. (2008). *The limits of power: The end of American exceptionalism.* New York: Henry Holt, p. 16.

7. Bacevich, A. (2008). *The limits of power: The end of American exceptionalism.* New York: Henry Holt, p. 62.

8. Stone, H. & Stone, S. (1989c). *Embracing each other: How to make relationships work for you.* Albion, CA: Delos, p. 73.

9. Stone, H. & Stone, S. (1989c). *Embracing each other: How to make relationships work for you.* Albion, CA: Delos., pp. 78-79.

10. Stone, H. & Winkelman S. (1989a). *Embracing each other: Relationship as teacher, healer & guide.* San Rafael, CA: New World Library, p. 79.

11. Stone, H. & Winkelman S. (1989a). *Embracing each other: Relationship as teacher, healer & guide.* San Rafael, CA: New World Library, p. 58.

12. Wilson, E. O. (2002). *The future of life.* New York: Vintage Books, A Division of Random House, pp. 130-131.

13. Alden, W. (2011. Medical bills drive Americans into bankruptcy as many struggle to pay debt. Retrieved August 19, 2011, from *Huffington Post* Website: http://www.huffingtonpost.com/2011/08/19/medical-bills-bankruptcy_n_931297.html, p. 1

14. McIntosh, S. (2007). *Integral consciousness and the future of evolution.* St. Paul, MN: Paragon House, p. 1.

15. Taegel, W. (1990). *The many colored buffalo: Transformation through the council of voices.* Norwood, NJ: Ablex, pp. 116-117.

16. Eisenstein, C. (2011, September). Living in the gift: Why we need to restore a sense of the sacred to the economy, *Ode: For intelligent optimists,* 8(4), 44-49, p. 45.

17. Eisenstein, C. (2011, September). Living in the gift: Why we need to restore a sense of the sacred to the economy, *Ode: For intelligent optimists,* 8(4), 44-49, p. 45.

18. Eisenstein, C. (2011, September). Living in the gift: Why we need to restore a sense of the sacred to the economy, *Ode: For intelligent optimists, 8*(4), 44-49, p. 45.

19. Eisenstein, C. (2011, September). Living in the gift: Why we need to restore a sense of the sacred to the economy, *Ode: For intelligent optimists, 8*(4), 44-49, p. 46.

20. Eisenstein, C. (2011, September). Living in the gift: Why we need to restore a sense of the sacred to the economy, *Ode: For intelligent optimists, 8*(4), 44-49, p. 46.

21. Eisenstein, C. (2011, September). Living in the gift: Why we need to restore a sense of the sacred to the economy, *Ode: For intelligent optimists, 8*(4), 44-49, p. 46.

22. Eisenstein, C. (2011, September). Living in the gift: Why we need to restore a sense of the sacred to the economy, *Ode: For intelligent optimists, 8*(4), 44-49, p. 46.

23. Eisenstein, C. (2011, September). Living in the gift: Why we need to restore a sense of the sacred to the economy, *Ode: For intelligent optimists, 8*(4), 44-49, p. 46.

24. Eisenstein, C. (2011, September). Living in the gift: Why we need to restore a sense of the sacred to the economy, *Ode: For intelligent optimists, 8*(4), 44-49, pp. 46-47.

25. Eisenstein, C. (2011, September). Living in the gift: Why we need to restore a sense of he sacred to the economy, *Ode: For intelligent optimists, 8*(4), 44-49, p. 47.

26. Eisenstein, C. (2011, September). Living in the gift: Why we need to restore a sense of the sacred to the economy, *Ode: For intelligent optimists, 8*(4), 44-49, p. 48.

27. Eisenstein, C. (2011, September). Living in the gift: Why we need to restore a sense of the sacred to the economy, *Ode: For intelligent optimists, 8*(4), 44-49, p. 48.

28. Waters, F. (1977). *Book of the Hopi.* New York: Penguin Books.

Chapter 4: Direction of the West: Terrorism

1. Peers, E. A. (Ed.). (1959). *The dark night of the soul.* Garden City, New York: Image Press, a division of Doubleday.

2. Ruiz, M. (1997). *The four agreements*. San Rafael, CA: Amber-Allen, p. 67.

3. Gall, C. (2088). Bombing at hotel in Pakistan kills at least 40. Retrieved September 21, 2008 from *The New York Times*: Http://www.Nytimes.com/2008/09/21/world/asia/2 1islamabad.html.

4. Garrison, J. (2000). *Civilization and the transformation of power*. New York: Paraview Press, p. 104.

5. Garrison, J. (2000). *Civilization and the transformation of power*. New York: Paraview Press, p. 109.

6. Garrison, J. (2000). *Civilization and the transformation of power*. New York: Paraview Press, p. XXVIII.

7. Beck, D. & Cowan, C. (1996). *Spiral dynamics: Mastering values, leadership, and change*. Madison, MA: Blackwell.

8. Garrison, J. (2000). *Civilization and the transformation of power*. New York: Paraview Press, p. 125.

9. Durant, W. & Durant, A. (1968). *The lessons of history*. New York: MJF Books, p. 81.

10. Durant, W. & Durant, A. (1968). *The lessons of history*. New York: MJF Books, p. 82.

11. Hamilton, E. (1957). *The echo of Greece* (eight printings). New York: W. W. Norton.

12. Beck, D. & Cowan, C. (1996). *Spiral dynamics: Mastering values, leadership, and change*. Madison, MA: Blackwell.

13. Eliot, T. (1963). *Collected Poems*. Orlando, Fl: Harcourt Brace, p. 200.

14. Hamilton, E. (1957). *The echo of Greece* (eight printings). New York: W. W. Norton and Company, p. 12.

15. Garrison, J. (2000). *Civilization and the transformation of power*. New York: Paraview Press, p. 66.

16. Hadot, P. (1995). *Philosophy as a way of life*. Malden, MA: Blackwell Publishing.

17. Garrison, J. (2000). *Civilization and the transformation of power*. New York: Paraview Press, p. 259.

18. Garrison, J. (2000). *Civilization and the transformation of power*. New York: Paraview Press, p. 307.

19. Garrison, J. (2000). *Civilization and the transformation of power*. New York: Paraview Press, p. 307.

20. Hamilton, E. (1957). *The echo of Greece* (eight printings). New York: W. W. Norton and Company, p. 81.

21. Garrison, J. (2000). *Civilization and the transformation of power*. New York: Paraview Press, pp. XXVII, XXVIII.

Beck, D. & Cowan, C. (1996). *Spiral dynamics: Mastering values, leadership, and change*. Madison, MA: Blackwell.

23. *Gunmen aimed to kill 5000, official says*. (2008 November 28), from AOL News: http://news.aol.com/article/gumen-aimed-to-kill-5000-officialsays/261363! icid+200100397X1214373.

24. *US Jewish meditation groups' members die in India* (2008, November 28) Retrieved November 20, 2008, from *AOL news*: http://news.aol.com/article/Jewish-group-confirms-rabbi-wife-killed/262322.

25. *Gunmen aimed to kill 5000, official says*. (2008 November 28), from *AOL News*: http://news.aol.com/article/gumen-aimed-to-kill-5000-officialsays/261363/icid+200100397X 1214373.

26. *Indian forces battle militants in Mumbai*. (2008, November 28). Retrieved November 29, 2008, from *AOL news*: http://www.news.aol.com/article/Indian-forces-battle-militants-in-mumbai/261363?icid+200100307x121348.

27. Garrison, J. (2004). *America as empire: Global leader or rogue power*. San Francisco: Berrett-Koehler Publishers, p. 81.

28. Garrison, J. (2004). *America as empire: Global leader or rogue power*. San Francisco: Berrett-Koehler Publishers, p. 154.

29. Sheldrake, R., McKenna, T. & Abraham, R. (2001). *Chaos, creativity and cosmic consciousness*. Rochester, VT: Park Street Press.

30. Garrison, J. (2004). *America as empire: Global leader or rogue power*. San Francisco: Berrett-Koehler Publishers, p. 101.

31. Moseley, Ray (2011, July). Norway terror: At least 17 dead, including youths. Retrieved July 22, 2011, from *Al Arabiya News*: http://www.english.alarabiya.net/articles/2011/07/22/158841.html.

32. Garrison, J. (2004). *America as empire: Global leader or rogue power*. San Francisco: Berrett-Koehler Publishers, p. 99.

33. Beck, D. & Cowan, C. (1996). *Spiral dynamics: Mastering values, leadership, and change*. Madison, MA: Blackwell.

34. Garrison, J. (2004). *America as empire: Global leader or rogue power*. San Francisco: Berrett-Koehler Publishers, p. 162.

35. Garrison, J. (2004). *America as empire: Global leader or rogue power*. San Francisco: Berrett-Koehler Publishers, p. 164.

36. Garrison, J. (2004). *America as empire: Global leader or rogue power*.San Francisco: Berrett-Koehler Publishers.

37. Garrison, J. (2004). *America as empire: Global leader or rogue power*. San Francisco: Berrett-Koehler Publishers, p. 151.

38. Garrison, J. (2004). *America as empire: Global leader or rogue power*. San Francisco: Berrett-Koehler Publishers, p. 153.

39. Garrison, J. (2004). *America as empire: Global leader or rogue power*.San Francisco: Berrett-Koehler Publishers, p. 163.

40. Garrison, J. (2004). *America as empire: Global leader or rogue power*.San Francisco: Berrett-Koehler Publishers, p. 152.

41. Garrison, J. (2004). *America as empire: Global leader or rogue power*.San Francisco: Berrett-Koehler Publishers, p. 152.

42. Garrison, J. (2004). *America as empire: Global leader or rogue power*.San Francisco: Berrett-Koehler Publishers.

43. Moyers, B. (2008, September 26). Interview with Andrew Bacevich. Retrieved October 16, 2008, from *Bill Moyers Journal*: http://www.Pbs.org/moyers/journal/09262008/transcript1.html?

44. Bacon, F. & Gough, A. (1915). *New Atlantis*. London, England: Oxford, p. 21.

45. US elections: 08: Obama acceptance speech in full: A speech by the new president-elect of the United States of America. (2008, November 5). Retrieved November 5, 2008, from *World News*: http://www.Guardian.co.uk/commentisfree/2008/nov/05/uselections 2008-barackobama.

46. Garrison, J. (2004). *America as empire: Global leader or rogue power*.San Francisco: Berrett-Koehler Publishers, p. 183.

47. Garrison, J. (2004). *America as empire: Global leader or rogue power*.San Francisco: Berrett-Koehler Publishers, p. 83.

48. Garrison, J. (2004). *America as empire: Global leader or rogue power*.San Francisco: Berrett-Koehler Publishers, p. 157.

49. Garrison, J. (2004). *America as empire: Global leader or rogue power*.San Francisco: Berrett-Koehler Publishers.

50. Garrison, J. (2004). *America as empire: Global leader or rogue power*.San Francisco: Berrett-Koehler Publishers, pp. 162-163.

51. Rouse, W. (1970). *The complete texts of great dialogues of Plato*. New York: The New American Library, p. 575.

52. Garrison, J. (2004). *America as empire: Global leader or rogue power*.San Francisco: Berrett-Koehler Publishers, pp. 164-165.

53. Goldberg, E. (2001). 9/12: How forming nonprofits eased the grief for victim's families. Retrieved September 12, 2011, from *The Huffington Post*: http://www.huffingtonpost.com/2011/09/12/the-impact of 9/12-how-for_n_957419.html, p. 2.

54. Goldberg, E. (2001). 9/12: How forming nonprofits eased the grief for victim's families. Retrieved September 12, 2011, from *The Huffington Post*: http://www.huffingtonpost.com/2011/09/12/the-impact of 9/12-how-for_n_957419.html, p. 2.

55. Goldberg, E. (2001). 9/12: How forming nonprofits eased the grief for victim's families. Retrieved September 12, 2011, from *The Huffington Post*: http://www.huffingtonpost.com/2011/09/12/the-impact of 9/12-how-for_n_957419.html, p. 3.

56. Bear Heart & Larkin, M. (1996). *The wind is my mother*. New York: Berkley Books, p. 162.

57.Neihardt, J. (1959). *Black Elk speaks* (Rev. ed.). New York: Pocket p. 36.

Chapter 5: Direction of the North: War, Violence, and Spiritual Emergency

1. Brown, J. E. (Ed.). (1971). *The sacred pipe: Black Elk's account of the seven rites of the Oglala Sioux*. New York: Penguin Books, pp. 38-39.

2. Abram, D. (1996). *The spell of the sensuous*. New York: Vintage Books, p. 237.

3. Abram, D. (1996). *The spell of the sensuous*. New York: Vintage Books, p. 237.

4. Ruiz, M. (1997). *The four agreements*. San Rafael, CA: Amber-Allen, p. 81.

5. Winters, L. (2007). *The making and un-making of a marine: One man's struggle for forgiveness*. New Paltz, NY: Millrock Writers Collective, p. 292.

6. Winters, L. (2007). *The making and un-making of a marine: One man's struggle for forgiveness*. New Paltz, NY: Millrock Writers Collective, p. 292.

7. US and UK government international intervention since 1945: Jordan. (n.d.) Retrieved April 29, 2010, from http://www.us-uk-interventions.org/Jordan_fullchron.html.

8. Beck, D. & Cowan, C. (1996). *Spiral dynamics: Mastering values, leadership, and change*. Madison, MA: Blackwell, p. 216.

9. Faisal II, of Iraq. (n.d.). Retrieved April 29, 2010, from *Wikipedia, the free encyclopedia:* http://en.wikipedia.org/wiki/Faisal_II_of_Iraq, 2010.

10. Hussein of Jordan. (n.d.). Retrieved April 29, 2010, from Wikipedia, the free encyclopedia: http://www.en.wikipedia.org/wiki/Hussein_of_Jordan.

11. US and UK government international intervention since 1945: Lebanon. (n.d.). Retrieved April 29, 2010, from http://www.us-uk-interventions.org/Lebanon_ fullchron.html.

12. Tick, E. (2005). *War and the soul: Healing our nation's veterans from post-traumatic stress disorder.* Wheaton, IL: Quest Books, Theosophical Publishing House, p. 262.

13. Gustafson, F. R. ((1997). *Dancing between two worlds: Jung and the native american soul.* New York: Paulist Press, p. 27.

14. Tick, E. (2005). *War and the soul: Healing our nation's veterans from post-traumatic stress disorder.* Wheaton, IL: Quest Books, Theosophical Publishing House, p. 278.

15. Tick, E. (2005). *War and the soul: Healing our nation's veterans from post-traumatic stress disorder.* Wheaton, IL: Quest Books, Theosophical Publishing House, p. 282.

16. Bogart, B. (2007, December). *Unwarranted influence: Chronicling the rise of US government dependence on conflict, Instance of US forces abroad since World War II.* (Updated January 8, 2007 by Richard F. Grimmett) Retrieved April 29, 2010, Eugene: University of Oregon: http/www. Intelligent Future.org.

17. Tick, E. (2005). *War and the soul: Healing our nation's veterans from post-traumatic stress disorder.* Wheaton, IL: Quest Books, Theosophical Publishing House, p. 286.

18. Tick, E. (2005). *War and the soul: Healing our nation's veterans from post-traumatic stress disorder.* Wheaton, IL: Quest Books, Theosophical Publishing House, p. 285.

19. Stone, H. & Winkelman S. (1989a). *Embracing each other: Relationship as teacher, healer & guide.* San Rafael, CA: New World Library.

20. Lawlor, R. (1991). *Voices of the first day: Awakening in the aboriginal dreamtime.* Rochester, VT: Inner Traditions International, Ltd.

Chapter 6: Direction of Grandmother Earth: A Vision Quest, Nature's Blessings

1. Brown, J. E. (Ed.). (1971). *The sacred pipe: Black Elk's account of the seven rites of the Oglala Sioux.* New York: Penguin Books, pp. 33-34.

2. Stone, H & Stone, S. (1989b). *Embracing our selves: The voice dialogue manual.* Novato, CA: New World Library, p.19.

3. Stone, H & Stone, S. (1989b). *Embracing our selves: The voice dialogue manual.* Novato, CA: New World Library, p. 18.

4. Stone, H & Stone, S. (1989b). *Embracing our selves: The voice dialogue manual.* Novato, CA: New World Library, p. 19.

5. Stone, H & Stone, S. (1989b). *Embracing our selves: The voice dialogue manual.* Novato, CA: New World Library, p. 19.

6. Stone, H & Stone, S. (1989b). *Embracing our selves: The voice dialogue manual.* Novato, CA: New World Library, p. 21.

7. Stone, H & Stone, S. (1989b). *Embracing our selves: The voice dialogue manual.* Novato, CA: New World Library, pp. 21-22.

8. McFarland, E. (2008). *The sacred path beyond trauma: Reaching the divine through nature's healing symbols.* Berkeley, CA: North Atlantic Books, p. 10.

9. Taegel, W. (1990). *The many colored buffalo: Transformation through the council of voices.* Norwood, NJ: Ablex, p. 36.

10. Levine, P. (2005). *Healing trauma: A pioneering program for restoring the wisdom of your body.* Boulder, CO: Sounds True, p. 9.

11. Naparstek, B. (2006). *Invisible heroes: Survivors of trauma and how they heal.* New York: Bantam Dell p. 175.

12. Naparstek, B. (2006). *Invisible heroes: Survivors of trauma and how they heal.* New York: Bantam Dell, p. 175.

13. Taegel, W. (1990). *The many colored buffalo: Transformation through the council of voices.* Norwood, NJ: Ablex, p. 117.

14.Taegel, W. (2010). *The sacred council of your wild heart: Nature's hope in earth's crisis.* Wimberley, TX: 2nd Tier, p. xviii.

15. Lawlor, R. (1991). *Voices of the first day: Awakening in the aboriginal dreamtime*. Rochester, VT: Inner Traditions International, Ltd, p. 8.

16. Taegel, W. (2010). *The sacred council of your wild heart: Nature's hope in earth's crisis*. Wimberley, TX: 2nd Tier, xvi.

17. Taegel, W. (2010). *The sacred council of your wild heart: Nature's hope in earth's crisis*. Wimberley, TX: 2nd Tier, p. 21.

18. Taegel, W. (2010). *The sacred council of your wild heart: Nature''s hope in earth's crisis*. Wimberley, TX: 2nd Tier, p. 21.

19. Lawlor, R. (1991). *Voices of the first day: Awakening in the aboriginal dreamtime*. Rochester, VT: Inner Traditions International, Ltd, p. 327.

20. Lawlor, R. (1991). *Voices of the first day: Awakening in the aboriginal dreamtime*. Rochester, VT: Inner Traditions International, Ltd, p. 321.

21. Lawlor, R. (1991). *Voices of the first day: Awakening in the aboriginal dreamtime*. Rochester, VT: Inner Traditions International, Ltd, p. 327.

22. Lawlor, R. (1991). *Voices of the first day: Awakening in the aboriginal dreamtime*. Rochester, VT: Inner Traditions International, Ltd.

Chapter 7: Direction of Grandfather Sky: Quantum Leaps & Evolutionary Spirituality

1. Taegel, W. & Yost, J. (2008, April). *The evolution of perspectives (lenses)*. Wimberley, TX: classroom handout.

2. Beck, D. & Cowan, C. (1996). *Spiral dynamics: Mastering values, leadership, and change*. Madison, MA: Blackwell.

3. Taegel, W. (2007, September). *Nature spiritual mentoring: Quantum leaps in evolutionary spirituality: the pull/push toward the 2nd tier*. Wimberley, TX: Publication of the Nature-based School for Spiritual Mentoring, p. 4.

4. Sheldrake, R., McKenna, T. & Abraham, R. (2005). *The evolutionary mind* (Revised ed.). Rhinebeck, NY: Monkfish Book Publishing Company, p. 10.

5. Taegel, W. (2007, September). *Nature spiritual mentoring: Quantum leaps in evolutionary spirituality: the pull/push toward the 2nd tier.* Wimberley, TX: Publication of the Nature-based School for Spiritual Mentoring, p. 1.

6. Sheldrake, R., McKenna, T. & Abraham, R. (2001). *Chaos, creativity and cosmic consciousness.* Rochester, VT: Park Street Press, p. 129.

7. Taegel, W. (2007, September). *Nature spiritual mentoring: Quantum leaps in evolutionary spirituality: the pull/push toward the 2nd tier.* Wimberley, TX: Publication of the Nature-based School for Spiritual Mentoring, p. 7.

8. Taegel, W. & Yost, J. (2008, April). *The evolution of perspectives (lenses).* Wimberley, TX: classroom handout.

9. Beck, D. & Cowan, C. (1996). *Spiral dynamics: Mastering values, leadership, and change.* Madison, MA: Blackwell.

10. Pullman, P. (1995). *The golden compass.* New York: Laurel-Leaf a division of Random House.

11. Taegel, W. (2007, December). *Some highlights of a kosmic map for today.* Wimberley, TX: class handout for Nature-based School for Spiritual Mentoring, p. 4.

12. Wilber, K. (2006). *Integral Spirituality: A startling new role in the modern and postmodern world.* Boston: Integral Books: An imprint of Shambhala Publications.

13. Taegel, W. & Yost, J. (2007). *90 days with nature.* Wimberley, TX: Publication of the Nature-based School for Spiritual Mentoring, pp. 2-3.

14. May, H. & Metzger, B. (Eds.). (1977). *The new Oxford annotated bible with the apocrypha* (Rev. ed.). New York: Oxford University Press, p. 883.

15. Wilber, K. (2006). *Integral Spirituality: A startling new role in the modern and postmodern world.* Boston: Integral Books: An imprint of Shambhala Publications.

16. Beck, D. & Cowan, C. (1996). *Spiral dynamics: Mastering values, leadership, and change.* Madison, MA: Blackwell.

17. Taegel, W. & Yost, J. (2008, April). *The evolution of perspectives (lenses).* Wimberley, TX: classroom handout, p. 1.

18. Taegel, W. & Yost, J. (2008, April). *The evolution of perspectives (lenses).* Wimberley, TX: classroom handout, p. 3.

19. Taegel, W. & Yost, J. (2008, April). *The evolution of perspectives (lenses).*Wimberley, TX: classroom handout, p. 3.

20. Taegel, W. & Yost, J. (2008, April). *The evolution of perspectives (lenses).* Wimberley, TX: classroom handout, p. 3.

21. Taegel, W. & Yost, J. (2008, April). *The evolution of perspectives (lenses).* Wimberley, TX: classroom handout, p. 3.

22. Taegel, W. & Yost, J. (2008, April). *The evolution of perspectives (lenses).* Wimberley, TX: classroom handout, p. 4.

23.Taegel, W. & Yost, J. (2008, April). *The evolution of perspectives (lenses).* Wimberley, TX: classroom handout, p. 5.

24. Taegel, W. & Yost, J. (2008, April). *The evolution of perspectives (lenses).* Wimberley, TX: classroom handout, p. 6.

25. Taegel, W. & Yost, J. (2008, April). *The evolution of perspectives (lenses).* Wimberley, TX: classroom handout, p. 6.

26.Taegel, W. & Yost, J. (2008, April). *The evolution of perspectives (lenses).*Wimberley, TX: classroom handout, p. 7.

27. Wilber, K. (2006). *Integral Spirituality: A startling new role in the modern and postmodern world.* Boston: Integral Books: An imprint of Shambhala Publications.

28. Taegel, W. & Yost, J. (2008, May). *Lake medicine.* Wimberley, TX: Publication of the Nature-based School for Spiritual Mentoring, pp. 8-9.

Chapter 8: Direction of the Relations: Sacred Leadership: Building Resilient Community

1. Lame Deer, J. & Erdoes, R. (1972). *Lame Deer seeker of visions.* New York: Washington Square Press, pp. 102-103.

2. Wheatley, M. J. (1994). *Leadership and the new science: learning about organization from an orderly universe.* San Francisco: Berrett-Koehler, p. 65.

3. Wheatley, M. J. (2007). *Finding our way.* San Francisco: Berrett-Koehler, p. 16.

4. Beck, D. & Cowan, C. (1996). *Spiral dynamics: Mastering values, leadership, and change.* Madison, MA: Blackwell, p. 203.

5. Taegel, W. (2010). *The sacred council of your wild heart: Nature's hope in earth's crisis.* Wimberley, TX: 2nd Tier.

6. Taegel, W. (2010). *The sacred council of your wild heart: Nature's hope in earth's crisis.* Wimberley, TX: 2nd Tier, p. 80.

7. Beck, D. & Cowan, C. (1996). *Spiral dynamics: Mastering values, leadership, and change.* Madison, MA: Blackwell., p. 80.

8. Wheatley, M. J. (1994). *Leadership and the new science: learning about organization from an orderly universe.* San Francisco: Berrett-Koehler, p. 38.

9. James, M. & Jongeward, D. (1996). *Born to win: Transactional analysis with gestalt experiments* (25th anniversary edition). Cambridge, MA: Perseus.

10. Eliot, T. (1963). *Collected Poems.* Orlando, Fl: Harcourt Brace, p. 200.

11. Taegel, W. (2010). *The sacred council of your wild heart: Nature's hope in earth's crisis.* Wimberley, TX: 2nd Tier, p. 59.

12. Wheatley, M. J. (1994). *Leadership and the new science: learning about organization from an orderly universe.* San Francisco: Berrett-Koehler, pp. 66-68.

13. Walker, B. & Salt, D. (2006). *Resilience thinking.* Washington, DC: Island Press, Preface.

14. Walker, B. & Salt, D. (2006). *Resilience thinking.* Washington, DC: Island Press, Forward.

15. Mindell, A. (1992). *The leader as martial artist: techniques and strategies for resolving conflict and creating community.* Oakland, CA: Lao Tse Press, Words Distributing Company.

16. Beck, D. & Cowan, C. (1996). *Spiral dynamics: Mastering values, leadership, and change.* Madison, MA: Blackwell.

17. May, H. & Metzger, B. (Eds.). (1977). *The new Oxford annotated bible with the apocrypha* (Rev. ed.). New York: Oxford University Press, p. 146.

Chapter 9: Direction of the Ancestors: Who Me? A Mystic?!

1. Cox, M. (1983). *Mysticism: The direct experience of God.* Wellingborough, Northhamptonshire, UK: The Aquarian Press, p.19.

2. Taegel, W. (2010). *The sacred council of your wild heart: Nature's hope in earth's crisis.* Wimberley, TX: 2nd Tier, pp. 78-79.

3. Moody, R. (1975). *Life after life.* New York: HarperCollins, pp. xiii, xiv.

4. Moody, R. (1975). *Life after life.* New York: HarperCollins, p. xix.

5. Moody, R. (1975). *Life after life.* New York: HarperCollins.

6. Moody, R. (1975). *Life after life.* New York: HarperCollins, p. 71.

7. Rouse, W. (1970). *The complete texts of great dialogues of Plato.* New York: The New American Library.

8. Taegel, W. (1990). *The many colored buffalo: Transformation through the council of voices.* Norwood, NJ: Ablex, p. 120.

9. Peers, E. A. (Ed.). (1959). *The dark night of the soul.* Garden City, New York: Image Press, a division of Doubleday.

10. Peers, E. A. (Ed.). (1959). *The dark night of the soul.* Garden City, New York: Image Press, a division of Doubleday, pp. 62-63.

11. Peers, E. A. (Ed.). (1959). *The dark night of the soul*. Garden City, New York: Image Press, a division of Doubleday, p. 46.

12. Merton, T. (1969). *Contemplative Prayer*. New York: Herder and Herder, p.96.

13. Merton, T. (1969). *Contemplative Prayer*. New York: Herder and Herder, p. 96.

14. James, M. & Jongeward, D. (1996). *Born to win: Transactional analysis with gestalt experiments* (25th anniversary edition). Cambridge, MA: Perseus.

15. Taegel, W. (1990). *The many colored buffalo: Transformation through the council of voices*. Norwood, NJ: Ablex, p. 109.

16. Taegel, W. (1990). *The many colored buffalo: Transformation through the council of voices*. Norwood, NJ: Ablex, p. 109.

17. Taegel, W. (1990). *The many colored buffalo: Transformation through the council of voices*. Norwood, NJ: Ablex, p. 109.

18. Tuoti, F. (1995). *Why not be a mystic? - an irresistible invitation to experience the presence of God – here and now*. New York: Crossroad, p. 19.

19. Taegel, W. (1990). *The many colored buffalo: Transformation through the council of voices*. Norwood, NJ: Ablex, p. 89.

20. Bear Heart & Larkin, M. (1996). *The wind is my mother*. New York: Berkley Books, p. 183.

21. Johnston, W. (Ed.). (1973). *The cloud of unknowing: And the book of privy counseling*. Garden City, NY: Image Books, a division of Doubleday, p. 84.

22. Taegel, W. (1990). *The many colored buffalo: Transformation through the council of voices*. Norwood, NJ: Ablex, p. 117.

23. Taegel, W. (1990). *The many colored buffalo: Transformation through the council of voices*. Norwood, NJ: Ablex, p. 119.

24. Cox, M. (1983). *Mysticism: The direct experience of God*. Wellingborough, Northhamptonshire, UK: The Aquarian Press, p. 18.

25. Taegel, W. (2010). *The sacred council of your wild heart: Nature's hope in earth's crisis*. Wimberley, TX: 2nd Tier.

26. Taegel, W. (2010). *The sacred council of your wild heart: Nature's hope in earth's crisis*. Wimberley, TX: 2nd Tier, p. 80.

27. Cox, M. (1983). *Mysticism: The direct experience of God*. Wellingborough, Northhamptonshire, UK: The Aquarian Press.

28. Taegel, W. (1990). *The many colored buffalo*. Transformation through the council of voices. Norwood, NJ, p. 159.

29. Taegel, W. (1990). *The many colored buffalo*. Transformation through the council of voices. Norwood, NJ, pp. 168-169

30. Bear Heart & Larkin, M. (1996). *The wind is my mother*. New York: Berkley Books, p. 246-247.

31. Lame Deer, J. & Erdoes, R. (1972). *Lame Deer seeker of visions*. New York: Washington Square Press, p. 167.

32. Brown, J. E. (Ed.). (1971). *The sacred pipe: Black Elk's account of the seven rites of the Oglala Sioux*. New York: Penguin Books, p. 8.

33. Brown, J. E. (Ed.). (1971). *The sacred pipe: Black Elk's account of the seven rites of the Oglala Sioux*. New York: Penguin Books.

34. Lame Deer, J. & Erdoes, R. (1972). *Lame Deer seeker of visions*. New York: Washington Square Press, p. 178.

35. Waters, F. (1977). *Book of the Hopi*. New York: Penguin Books, p. 193.

36. Waters, F. (1977). *Book of the Hopi*. New York: Penguin Books.

37. Lawlor, R. (1991). *Voices of the first day: Awakening in the aboriginal dreamtime*. Rochester, VT: Inner Traditions International, Ltd., p. 344.

38. Lawlor, R. (1991). *Voices of the first day: Awakening in the aboriginal dreamtime*. Rochester, VT: Inner Traditions International, Ltd., pp. 344-345.

39. Lawlor, R. (1991). *Voices of the first day: Awakening in the aboriginal dreamtime*. Rochester, VT: Inner Traditions International, Ltd., p. 345.

40. Lawlor, R. (1991). *Voices of the first day: Awakening in the aboriginal dreamtime*. Rochester, VT: Inner Traditions International, Ltd., p. 350.

41. Boyd, D. (1974). *Rolling Thunder*. New York: Dell, p. 262.

Chapter 10: Life Comes Full Circle: Story of Liliput

1. Taegel, W. (2010). *The sacred council of your wild heart: Nature's hope in earth's crisis*. Wimberley, TX: 2nd Tier, p. 131.

2. Beck, D. & Cowan, C. (1996). *Spiral dynamics: Mastering values, leadership, and change*. Madison, MA: Blackwell.

3. Stone, H & Stone, S. (1989b). *Embracing our selves: The voice dialogue manual*. Novato, CA: New World Library, p. 16.

4. Wilber, K. (2006). *Integral Spirituality: A startling new role in the modern and postmodern world*. Boston: Integral Books: An imprint of Shambhala Publications, p. 125

5. Levine, P. & Frederick, A. (1997). *Waking the tiger: Healing trauma: The innate capacity to transcend overwhelming experiences*. Berkeley, CA: North Atlantic Books, p. 45.

6. Taegel, W. (2003). *Natural mystics: Journey to your true identity*. Austin, TX: Turnkey Press, p. 91.

7. Taegel, W. (2003). *Natural mystics: Journey to your true identity*. Austin, TX: Turnkey Press.

8. Taegel, W. (2003). *Natural mystics: Journey to your true identity*. Austin, TX: Turnkey Press, p. 76.

9. Taegel, W. (2003). *Natural mystics: Journey to your true identity*. Austin, TX: Turnkey Press, p. 128.

10. Taegel, W. (2003). *Natural mystics: Journey to your true identity*. Austin, TX: Turnkey Press, p. 127.

11. Plotkin, B. (2003). *Soulcraft: Crossing into the mysteries of nature and psyche*. Novato, CA: World Library, p. 213.

12. Levine, P. & Frederick, A. (1997). *Waking the tiger: Healing trauma: The innate capacity to transcend overwhelming experiences*. Berkeley, CA: North Atlantic Books, p. 21.

13. Plotkin, B. (2003). *Soulcraft: Crossing into the mysteries of nature and psyche*. Novato, CA: World Library, pp. 220, 313.

14. Levine, P. & Frederick, A. (1997). *Waking the tiger: Healing trauma: The innate capacity to transcend overwhelming experiences*. Berkeley, CA: North Atlantic Books, p. 36.

15. Bear Heart & Larkin, M. (1996). *The wind is my mother*. New York: Berkley Books, p. 107.

16. Taegel, W. (2003). *Natural mystics: Journey to your true identity*. Austin, TX: Turnkey Press, p. 66.

17. Taegel, W. (2003). *Natural mystics: Journey to your true identity*. Austin, TX: Turnkey Press, p. 45.

Chapter 11: Grandmother Earth and Reciprocity

1. Ruiz, M. (1997). *The four agreements*. San Rafael, CA: Amber-Allen, pp. 4-5.

2. Kelly, T. (2011b) World population expected to hit 7 billion on halloween. Retrieved September 25, 2011, from *The Huffington Post*: http: www. Huffingtonpost.com/2011/09/24/world-population-halloween-2011-7-billion-_n_979191.html, p. .

3. McGaa, E. (1990). *Mother earth spirituality: Native American paths to healing ourselves and our world*. New York: Harper/Collins, p. 43.

4. Beck, D. & Cowan, C. (1996). *Spiral dynamics: Mastering values, leadership, and change*. Madison, MA: Blackwell.

5. Lame Deer, J. & Erdoes, R. (1972). *Lame Deer seeker of visions*. New York: Washington Square Press, p. 224.

6. Taegel, W. (2010). *The sacred council of your wild heart: Nature's hope in earth's crisis*. Wimberley, TX: 2nd Tier.

7. Hanley, C. (2011). Global warming: Why Americans are in denial. Retrieved September 24, 2011, from *The Huffington Post*: http://www.huffingtonpost.com/2011/09/24/ global-warming-why-americans-deny_n_979177.html, pp. 1-2.

8. Hanley, C. (2011). Global warming: Why Americans are in denial. Retrieved September 24, 2011, from *The Huffington Post*: http://www.huffingtonpost.com/2011/09/24/ global-warming-why-americans-deny_n_979177.html, p. 3.

9. Hanley, C. (2011). Global warming: Why Americans are in denial. Retrieved September 24, 2011, from *The Huffington Post*: http://www.huffingtonpost.com/2011/09/24/ global-warming-why-americans-deny_n_979177.html, p. 3.

10. Castro, A. (2011). Texas rice industry could be devastated by colorado river change. Retrieved September 21, 2011, from *Huffpost Green*: http://www.huffingtonpost.com/2011/ 09/21/texas-rice_n_973560.html, p. 1.

11. Hanley, C. (2011). Global warming: Why Americans are in denial. Retrieved September 24, 2011, from The *Huffington Post*: http://www. huffingtonpost.com/2011/09/24/ global-warming-why-americans-deny_n_979177.html, p. 2.

12. Stone, M. (2011). Texas wildfires: 1,554 homes destroyed, 17 people missing. Retrieved September 14, 2011, from *International Business Times*: http://www.btimes.com/articles/ 21189720110911/texas-wildfires-201...houston- 1-554- homes-destroyed-17-people-missing-forest-service.html, p. 1.

13. Cook, E. R, Seager, R., Heim Jr., R. R., Vose, R. S., Herweijer, C. & Woodhouse, C. (2009). Climate change reconsidered: Of droughts and megadroughts in North America. Retrieved September 13, 2011, from the Website of the *Nongovernmental International Panel on Climate Change* (NIPCC): http://www.nipccreport. org/articles/ 2010/oct/27 oct2010a3.html, p. 3.

14. Kennedy, C. (2011). Drought baking the southern United States.Retrieved September 16, 2011, from *NOAA Climate Services*: http://www.climateresearch. noaa.gov/article/ 2011/drought-in-he-southern-united-states, pp. 1-2.

15. McIntrye, D. (2011). World running out of water. Retrieved November 1, 2011, from 24/7 Wall St.: http://247wallst. com/2011/10/28/world-running-out-of- water, p. 1.

16. Gore, A. (1992). *Earth in the balance: Ecology and the human spirit*. New York: Rodale.

17. Gore, A. (1992). *Earth in the balance: Ecology and the human spirit*. New York: Rodale.

18. Christian, B. (2011). Deep-sea-fishing: Marine scientists call for sustainable alternatives. Retrieved September 14, 2011, from *Huffpost Green*: http://huffingtonpost.com/ 2011/09/09/deep-sea-fishing-not-sustainable-marine-scientists-trawling_n_954508.html, p. 4.

19. Eilperin, J. (2011) Scientists call for end to deep sea fishing. Retrieved September 14, 2011, from the *Washington Post*: http://www.washingtonpost.com/national/ health-science/scientists-call-for-end-to-deep-sea-fishing/2011/08/30/glQaApPjc71_story.html.

20. Eilperin, J. (2011) Scientists call for end to deep sea fishing. Retrieved September 14, 2011, from the *Washington Post*: http://www.washingtonpost.com/national/ health-science/scientists-call-for-end-to-deep-sea-fishing/2011/08/30/glQaApPjc71_story.html, p. 2

21. Christian, B. (2011). Deep-sea fishing: Marine scientists call for sustainable alternatives. Retrieved September 14, 2011, from *Huffpost Green*: http://huffingtonpost. com/2011/09/09/deep-sea-fishing-not-sustainable-marine-scientists-trawling_n_954508. Html.

22. Christian, B. (2011). Deep-sea-fishing: Marine scientists call for sustainable alternatives. Retrieved September 14, 2011, from *Huffpost Green*: http://huffingtonpost.com/ 2011/09/09/deep-sea-fishing-not-sustainable-marine-scientists-trawling_n_954508.html, p. 2.

23. Kelly, T. (2011a). Giant red crabs take over. "Antarctic Abyss:" climate change blamed. Retrieved September 13, 2011, from *Huffpost Green*: http://www. Huffingtonpost.com/2011/9/12/giant-red-crab-invasion-climate-change_n_56290.html.

24. Kelly, T. (2011a). Giant red crabs take over. "Antarctic Abyss:" climate change blamed. Retrieved September 13, 2011, from *Huffpost Green*: http://www. Huffingtonpost.com/2011/9/12/giant-red-crab-invasion-climate-change_n_56290.html, p. 1.

25. Melvin, D. (2011). Bacteria spreading in warming oceans scientists find in new report. Retrieved September 13, 2011, from *Huffpost Green*: http://www. huffingtonpost.com/2011/09/13/bacteria-spreading-in-warming-oceans_n_960147.html, p. 1.

26. Edds, J. & Kline M. (2011). Happening now:Dead zone in the gulf. Retrieved September 16, 2011, from *OceanToday*:http://oceantoday. Noaa.gov/ happnowdeadzone/html, p. 1.

27. Great Pacific Garbage Patch. (n.d.) Retrieved September 13, 2011, from *Wikepedia, the free encyclopedia*: http:en.wikipedia.org/wiki/Great_Pacific_Garbage_ Patch, 2011.

28. Great Pacific Garbage Patch. (n.d.) Retrieved September 13, 2011, from *Wikepedia, the free encyclopedia*: http:en.wikipedia.org/wiki/Great_Pacific_Garbage_ Patch, 2011, p. 5.

29. Great Pacific Garbage Patch. (n.d.) Retrieved September 13, 2011, from *Wikepedia, the free encyclopedia*: http:en.wikipedia.org/wiki/Great_Pacific_Garbage_ Patch, 2011.

30. Louisiana oil spill 2010 photos: Gulf of Mexico disaster unfolds. (2010, April 30). Retrieved September 13, 2011, from *Huffpost Green*: http://www.huffingtonpost. com/2010_n-558287.html#s172644&title=Gulf_Oil_Spill.

31. Weber, H. R. & Cappiello, D. (2011). BP oil spill: New evidence cites more mistakes. Retrieved September 13, 2011, from *Huffpost Green*:http://www.huffingtonpost. com/2011/09/13/bp-oil-spill-new-evidence_n_ 961138.html.

32. Mendleson, R. (2011). Alberta oil sands: Protest planned in Ottawa, pipeline advocates hit back. Retrieved September 24, 2011, from *The Huffington Post*: http://www. huffingtonpost.ca/2011/09/23/alberta-oil-sands-protest_n_978603.html, p. 5.

33. Daly, M. (2011). NRC staff: Reassess earthquake risk at nuclear plants. Retrieved September 13, 2011, from *Huffpost Green*:http://www.huffingtonpost. com/ 2011/09/12nrc-staff-reassess-earthquake-nuclear-plant_n_958939.html, p. 3.

34. Dvorsky, G. (2011). *Five reasons the Copenhagen climate conference failed.* Retrieved September 13, 2011, from *Institute for Emerging Ethics and Technologies*: http://www.ieet.org/index.php/EET/more/dvorsky201 00110/html, pp. 1-2.

35. Gelineau, K. (2011). Ban Ki-Moon talks climate change in Australia. Retrieved September 8, 2011, from *The Huffpost Green*: http://www.huffingtonpost.com / 2011/09/08/ban-ki-moon-on-climate-_953554. html, p. 1.

36. Gelineau, K. (2011). Ban Ki-Moon talks climate change in Australia. Retrieved September 8, 2011, from *The Huffpost Green*: http://www.huffingtonpost.com / 2011/09/08/ban-ki-moon-on-climate-_953554. html, p. 1.

37. Gelineau, K. (2011). Ban Ki-Moon talks climate change in Australia. Retrieved September 8, 2011, from *The Huffpost Green*: http://www.huffingtonpost.com /2011/ 09/08/ban-ki-moon-on-climate-..._953554. html, p. 1.

38. Zeller, T. (2011). Al Gore's new climate campaign faces uphill battle. Retrieved September 15, 2011, from *Huffpost Green*: http://www.huffingtonpost.com/ 2011/09/15/al-gore-climate change-//1316101295&ocod+,aoing-grid7%7Cmain5%7 Cd127%7Csec1_link3%7C95994, p. 2.

39. Zeller, T. (2011). Al Gore's new climate campaign faces uphill battle. Retrieved September 15, 2011, from *Huffpost Green*: http://www.huffingtonpost.com/2011/09/15/al-gore-climate change-//1316101295&ocod+,aoing-grid7%7Cmain5%7Cd127%7Csec1_link3%7C95994.

40. Zeller, T. (2011). Al Gore's new climate campaign faces uphill battle. Retrieved September 15, 2011, from *Huffpost Green*: http://www.huffingtonpost.com/2011/09/15/al-gore-climate change-//1316101295&ocod+,aoing-grid7%7Cmain5%7Cd127%7Csec1_link3%7C95994, p. 3.

41. Al Gore on climate change deniers: It's crucial to "win the conversation." (2011, August 30). Retrieved August 31, 2011, from *Huffpost Green*: http:// www. huffingtonpost. Com/2011/08/30/gore-climate-change-deniers_n_940802.html, p. 2.

42. Taegel, W. (2010). *The sacred council of your wild heart: Nature's hope in earth's crisis*. Wimberley, TX: 2nd Tier, p. 25.

43. Gore, A. (2009). *Our choice: A plan to solve the climate crisis*. New York: Rodale, p. 401.

44. Abram, D. (1996). *The spell of the sensuous*. New York: Vintage Books, p. 268.

45. Abram, D. (1996). *The spell of the sensuous*. New York: Vintage Books, p. 264.

46. Abram, D. (1996). *The spell of the sensuous*. New York: Vintage Books, p. 182.

47. Bernstein, E. (2011). Recovering ancient scripture to face modern challenges. Retrieved August 23, 2011, from *Huff Post Religion*:http://www.huffingtonpost.com/rabbi-edward-bernstein/jewish-environmentalism-shema_b_929921.html.

48. Bernstein, E. (2011). Recovering ancient scripture to face modern challenges. Retrieved August 23, 2011, from *Huff Post Religion*:http://www.huffingtonpost.com/rabbi-edward-bernstein/jewish-environmentalism-shema_b_929921.html, p. 2.

49. Bernstein, E. (2011). Recovering ancient scripture to face modern challenges. Retrieved August 23, 2011, from *Huff Post Religion*:http://www.huffingtonpost.com/rabbi-edward-bernstein/jewish-environmentalism-shema_b_929921.html, p. 2.

50. Bernstein, E. (2011). Recovering ancient scripture to face modern challenges. Retrieved August 23, 2011, from *Huff Post Religion*:http://www.huffingtonpost.com/rabbi-edward-bernstein/jewish-environmentalism-shema_b_929921.html, p. 3.

51. Bear Heart & Larkin, M. (1996). *The wind is my mother*. New York: Berkley Books, p. 190.

52. Boyd, D. (1974). *Rolling Thunder*. New York: Dell, p. 51.

53. Gibson, J. W. (2009). *A reenchanted world: The quest for a new kinship with nature*. New York: Metropolitan Books, Henry Holt.

Chapter 12: Include and Transcend: The Apex of My Journey

1. Brown, J. E. (Ed.). (1971). *The sacred pipe: Black.Elk's account of the seven rites of the Oglala Sioux*. New York: Penguin books, pp. 5-8.

2. May, H. & Metzger, B. (Eds.). (1977). *The new Oxford annotated bible with the apocrypha* (Rev. ed.). New York: Oxford University Press, p. 91.

3. Gustafson, F. R. ((1997). *Dancing between two worlds: Jung and the native american soul*. New York: Paulist Press, p. 126.

4. Gustafson, F. R. ((1997). *Dancing between two worlds: Jung and the native american soul*. New York: Paulist Press, p. 131.

5. Boyd, D. (1974). *Rolling Thunder*. New York: Dell, p. 52.

6. Bear Heart & Larkin, M. (1996). *The wind is my mother*. New York: Berkley Books, p. 229.

7. Boyd, D. (1974). *Rolling Thunder*. New York: Dell, p. 73.

8. Gustafson, F. R. (1997). *Dancing between two worlds: Jung and the native american soul*. New York: Paulist Press, p. 29.

9. Gustafson, F. R. (1997). *Dancing between two worlds: Jung and the native american soul.* New York: Paulist Press, p. 29.

10. Neihardt, J. (1959). *Black Elk speaks* (Rev. ed.). New York: Pocket Books, p. 173.

11. Stolzman, W. (1995). *The pipe and Christ* (5th ed.). Chamberlain, SD: Tipi Press, p. 214.

12. Stolzman, W. (1995). *The pipe and Christ* (5th ed.). Chamberlain, SD: Tipi Press, p. 209.

13. Stolzman, W. (1995). *The pipe and Christ* (5th ed.). Chamberlain, SD: Tipi Press, p. 189.

14. Taylor, B. (2010). *Dark green religion: Nature, spirituality, and the planetary future.* Berkley: University of California Press, p. 70.

15. Taylor, B. (2010). *Dark green religion:Nature, spirituality, and the planetary future.* Berkley: University of California Press, pp. 220, 222.

16. Taylor, B. (2010). *Dark green religion:Nature, spirituality, and the planetary future.* Berkley: University of California Press, p. 322.

17. Taegel, W. (2003). *Natural mystics: Journey to our true identity.* Austin, TX: Turnkey Press, p. 163.

18. Steltenkamp, M. F. (2009). *Nicholas Black Elk: Medicine man, missionary, mystic.* Norman: University of Oklahoma, p. 123.

19. Smith, H. & Snake, R. (1996). *One nation under God.* Santa Fe, NM: Clear Light Publishers.

20. Smith, H. & Snake, R. (1996). *One nation under God.* Santa Fe, NM: Clear Light Publishers.

21. Taegel, W. (2003). *Natural mystics: Journey to our true identity.* Austin, TX: Turnkey Press, p. 68.

Appendix A: Waves, Stages, Levels of the Human Story

1. Taegel, W. & Yost, J. (2008, August) *Waves, stages, levels of the human story: Evolution toward greater complexity in trauma mentoring.* Wimberley, TX: classroom handout

Appendix B: Eight Standing Waves

1. Taegel, W. (2011, May). *Standing waves*. Wimberley, TX: classroom handout.

Appendix C: Earth Circle Formation and Practice

1. Rowden, L. (2006) "Earth Circle Formation and Practice." Wimberley, TX.

Appendix D: Tools for Mentoring

1. Beck, D. & Cowan, C. (1996). *Spiral dynamics: Mastering values, leadership, and change*. Madison, MA: Blackwell.

2. Beck, D. & Cowan, C. (1996). *Spiral dynamics: Mastering values, leadership, and change*. Madison, MA: Blackwell.

3. Stone, H. & Winkelman S. (1989a). *Embracing each other: Relationship as teacher, healer & guide*. San Rafael, CA: New World Library.

4. Taegel, W. (1990). *The many colored buffalo: Transformation through the council of voices*. Norwood, NJ: Ablex.

5. Taegel, W. (2010). *The sacred council of your wild heart: Nature's hope in earth's crisis*. Wimberley, TX: 2nd Tier.

6. Stone, H. & Stone, S. (2005). *An introduction to voice dialogue & the psychology of selves: For therapists, counselors and other healing arts professionals*. Albion CA: Delos.

7. Stone, H. & Winkelman S. (1989a). *Embracing each other: Relationship as teacher, healer & guide*. San Rafael, CA: New World Library.

8. Stone, H & Stone, S. (1989b). *Embracing our selves: The voice dialogue manual*. Novato, CA: New World Library.

9. Beck, D. & Cowan, C. (1996). *Spiral dynamics: Mastering values, leadership, and change*. Madison, MA: Blackwell.

10. Taegel, W. (2010). *The sacred council of your wild heart: Nature's hope in earth's crisis*. Wimberley, TX: 2nd Tier.

11. Wilber, K. (2006). *Integral Spirituality: A startling new role in the modern and postmodern world*. Boston: Integral Books: An imprint of Shambhala Publications.

12. Taegel, W. (2010). *The sacred council of your wild heart: Nature's hope in earth's crisis*. Wimberley, TX: 2nd Tier.

13. Taegel, W. (2010). *The sacred council of your wild heart: Nature's hope in earth's crisis*. Wimberley, TX: 2nd Tier.

14. James, M. & Jongeward, D. (1996). *Born to win: Transactional analysis with gestalt experiments* (25th anniversary edition). Cambridge, MA: Perseus.

15. James, M. & Jongeward, D. (1996). *Born to win: Transactional analysis with gestalt experiments* (25th anniversary edition). Cambridge, MA: Perseus, p. 224.

16. Levine, P. & Frederick, A. (1997). *Waking the tiger: Healing trauma: The innate capacity to transcend overwhelming experiences*. Berkeley, CA: North Atlantic Books.

17. Plotkin, B. (2003). *Soulcraft: Crossing into the mysteries of nature and psyche*. Novato, CA: World Library.

18. Levine, P. & Frederick, A. (1997). *Waking the tiger: Healing trauma: The innate capacity to transcend overwhelming experiences*. Berkeley, CA: North Atlantic Books.

19. Boyd, D. (1974). *Rolling Thunder*. New York: Dell.

Made in the USA
San Bernardino, CA
15 July 2013